Making Better Coffee

Making Better Coffee

*How Maya Farmers and Third Wave
Tastemakers Create Value*

Edward F. Fischer

UNIVERSITY OF CALIFORNIA PRESS

University of California Press
Oakland, California

© 2022 by Edward F. Fischer

Cataloging-in-Publication Data is on file at the Library
of Congress.

ISBN 978-0-520-38695-2 (cloth)
ISBN 978-0-520-38696-9 (pbk.)
ISBN 978-0-520-38697-6 (ebook)

31   30   29   28   27   26   25   24   23   22
10   9   8   7   6   5   4   3   2   1

CONTENTS

Conclusion
197

Figure 1. Elika Liftee at the 2020 United States Coffee Championships.

Introduction

One Saturday morning in mid-January 2020, Elika Liftee was getting ready to make a special cup of coffee. He was backstage, behind a row of blue trade-show curtains that had transformed a former factory in Nashville, Tennessee, into the site of a qualifying round for the United States Coffee Championships. Conversations were hushed as competitors consulted with their teams and rehearsed presentations. On the other side of the divide, audience members found their seats while technicians double-checked the equipment. This was one of two qualifying events held across the country that year, and the forty-one competitors in Nashville had claimed their spots by placing in one of dozens of regional feeder rounds. The winners would advance to the national championships.

Liftee's background is at once cosmopolitan and provincial. Born in Japan to an Air Force mother and a Hawaiian father, he grew up in Oklahoma. It was a typical Midwestern childhood, as he describes it, but with a kitchen stocked full of papaya, guava, and other tropical foods. He attended college for a few semesters, then worked several odd jobs before finally landing a position at Onyx Coffee Lab in Rogers, Arkansas. In a progression characteristic of many coffee professionals, he first visited Onyx as a customer—he was a regular in his college days—and when they brought him on as an employee, he started as a barista and moved up through the ranks before becoming a trainer. At one point he was promoted to café manager, but he found that he liked working with coffee more than handling people. At Onyx, his interest in coffee became an obsession: after soaking up as much as he could on the job, he would go home and watch YouTube coffee videos and read research reports from the UC Davis Coffee Center.

The Nashville event was Liftee's third attempt at the Brewer's Cup competition. Preparing, he explains, always starts with a story, and this time he decided to tell his own story.[1] For the coffee he chose a naturally processed Gesha—a prized varietal of the *Coffea arabica* species—grown on the La Palma y El Tucán farm in Colombia. Onyx paid US $212 a pound for the beans at a time when commodity coffee was trading for $1.04 per pound on the New York exchange, but Liftee was enchanted by its range of flavors, from pineapple nectar to plum and black tea. Natural processing, in which the fruit is allowed to partially rot off the beans, imparts a fruity acidity, and Liftee wanted to use those notes to reflect his heritage.

The Brewer's Cup is one of five tracks in the United States Coffee Championships; there are also competitions for baristas, roasters, tasters, and mixologists. Contestants train for months, sometimes years, to prepare, investing time and money to hire coaches, search out obscure coffees with unusual flavors, and practice their skills. With detailed protocols covering everything from water quality to grinder specifications, this is no casual contest. Entrants each have ten minutes to brew and present their coffee to a panel of three judges. The coffee will be tasted at three temperatures (70°C, 40°C, and 30°C) and rated on a scale from zero to ten in seven areas (aroma, flavor, aftertaste, acidity, body, balance, and overall taste). Points are added up, along with an evaluation of service and presentation, to produce an overall numerical score. Taste may seem particularly subjective, but the judges have been trained in sensory evaluation techniques, and there is surprisingly little variation in scores.

The organizers go to great lengths to make these competitions as objective as possible, but a lot still rests on the hard-to-quantify art of storytelling, the narrative brewers tell to situate their coffees and justify their choices. When he takes the stage, Liftee tells the story of La Palma and El Tucán while he heats the water and grinds the beans, talking about the couple who run the farm and their dedication to cultivating unusual varietals. He places ten grams of ground coffee in each of the three Kalita Wave ceramic drippers, explaining that the Japanese brand's unique design helps bring out subtle flavor notes. As he lifts the kettle, Liftee tells the audience that he will use an unconventional quick pour technique—forcing the hot water through the grounds in two minutes rather than the usual three-and-a-half to four—and that the coffee's floral and fruity flavor notes will become more prominent as it cools. With individual cups presented to them, the judges pull out their tasting spoons, dip into the brew, and slurp loudly, rolling the liquid around in their mouths before spitting it out and contemplating their scores. In the final tally, Liftee earns 162.83 out of a possible 200 points and claims the top spot. He went on to win the national championships the following month with the same coffee and presentation, and he would have been a strong contender in the world championships in Australia, but they were cancelled that year due to the COVID-19 pandemic.

.   .   .

From an anthropological perspective, such competitions can tell us a lot about underlying cultural values and power dynamics.[2] When I first started exploring the world of high-end coffees, it felt at once familiar and exotic. I considered myself a pretty serious coffee drinker, spent a lot of time in coffee shops, and was conversant with trends in artisanal foodstuffs. Still, I felt like an interloper at competitions and trade shows, out of my league among all the professionals and aficionados committed to the craft of coffee, with their own specialized language, customs, and opaque points of reference. Over time, I came to see how the high-end coffee world, as a cultural community, orients itself around certain values that transcend the beverage itself: a dedication to craft, a quest for quality, a veneration of authenticity, and a commitment to building social relationships through the commercial trade. There is certainly competition and discord, bad actors and better ones, contradictions between ideals and practice, but the most common refrain in my many conversations with coffee professionals was around the common project of finding and producing better coffee—better tasting and better for the farmers who grow it.

For a social scientist, this raises a number of questions: What makes a coffee "better"? What goes into a coffee like the La Palma y El Tucán Gesha to make it worth $212 a pound? At the coffee shop, we are asked to pay more for quality, but who decides what constitutes "quality"? For most customers, selection is akin to looking at a restaurant's list of unfamiliar wines: the price indicates quality rather than the other way around. Baristas and traders talk about quality as if it were an objective characteristic out there in the world—something to be discovered, ideally in exotic, out-of-the-way places. For many professionals and serious consumers, the quest for quality is a self-evidently virtuous pursuit—progressive, even liberating, in its rejection of lowest-common-denominator mass production.[3]

The irony is that in looking for quality, these same coffee professionals and enthusiasts are also defining what constitutes quality. Through conversations and competitions, they work out among themselves conventional understandings about which traits should be valued and which should be discounted, the flavors that are in and those that are out, what commands a price premium this season and what does not.[4] In this system, the real power derives from the ability to define what quality is—not in the celebrated labor of finding quality, but in determining what gets measured and what gets valued. Put another way, power in these markets comes not from control over the means of production but from the ability to channel symbolic sorts of worth. Many—perhaps most—Third Wave professionals and enthusiasts see themselves as involved in a larger project to liberate food systems from industrial-scale production, to promote artisanal excellence, and to embed supply chains in more equitable social relations. Yet cosmopolitan quests for authenticity and quality intersect with colonial histories of economic power and racial exclusion in morally complicated and politically fraught ways.[5]

Using the case study of specialty coffees grown in the highlands of Guatemala and sold by craft roasters in the United States, this book explores how economic gain is realized through translating different conceptions of worth across material, cultural, and political value worlds—and what this can tell us about the twenty-first century global political economy. The high-end coffee trade illustrates the importance of intangible and symbolic attributes in adding economic value; it also highlights how such commodity circuits operate within a neoliberal matrix of power linked to legacies of colonialism. I focus on Third Wave coffees: single-estate, artisanally roasted varietals that command high prices—$20 and up for a twelve-ounce bag of whole beans in the early 2020s. To justify these prices, great emphasis is placed on quality "in the cup": the way coffee tastes and the terroir, processing methods, and other material inputs that produce sought-after flavors. Beyond that, consumers are also paying for symbolic values—a narrative connection with the grower, the novelty of discovering new flavors, an appreciation of the craft.[6]

My research looks at how people create value. When we say "value" in the singular, we generally mean price, but when we say "values" in the plural, we mean moral and cultural and political and symbolic sorts of value. I am interested in how these different measures of worth are intertwined with one another, how they influence individuals' decisions, and how they become encoded in social conventions and institutions. Policy and public discourse tend to privilege economic and quantitative values over other kinds of worth—and increasingly so as cost/benefit analyses extend to more and more arenas of life. Certainly, market value has the appeal of being straightforward to calculate: with pounds and kilos, dollars and euros, there are solid metrics to go by, numbers that can be entered into spreadsheets to compare unlike things. But what about dignity or fairness or love? Such "imaginative values"—whose worth stems from a link to something transcendent, a desired but intangible ideal—resist quantification.[7] Instead, they rely on subjective measures of what is good or bad, better or worse; evaluation in these spheres requires judgment and not just calculation. The rub is that much of life is about balancing substantively different sorts of values, translating moral into economic values, or social into political values—something we all wrestle with every day in our personal and professional lives.

These personal struggles are not just a matter of moral character or free will but take place in particular social, political, and economic contexts that structure individual choices. Third Wave coffee production and consumption emerged from a particular history of liberal modernity and colonial social relations. It has flourished under the conditions of early twenty-first-century global capitalism,[8] including neoliberal deregulation and privatization; accelerated levels of connectivity through communication and transportation; post-Fordist forms of production,[9] with elaborate supply chains and flexible forms of accumulation; the rapid growth of investment in intangible versus material assets; the expansion of market logics into more and more areas of life; and the linking of identity to consumption patterns and marketing narratives.

Economics textbook and business reporters explain that supply and demand determine price, but that simple equation hides the complicated ways that demand emerges and how it is framed by market choices. For their part, consumers often rely on judgment devices to help determine the worth of an item; these are sometimes rational and rigorous (as with cost/benefit calculations) and at other times are vague and loose, based on imaginative values with no numerical equivalents.[10] At the rigorous end of the spectrum is standardization, a hallmark of Fordist mass production of commodities. The essence of a commodity is substitutability—one item within a class and grade is as good as another—made possible by standardization: in selling a gallon of Brent crude oil or a pound of Kenyan AA coffee on a commodity exchange, the specific producer does not matter, as any lot is assumed to be the same as any other. In contrast, high-end markets are marked by singularization, emphasizing the uniqueness of products, with the greatest gains realized by making an emotional connection with consumers based around shared values.[11] We see this in domain of origin designations: a Château La Tour St. Émilion Bordeaux, or a natural arabica varietal from the La Palma y El Tucán farm in Colombia, are valued for their distinctiveness. Selling products in these markets requires invoking narrative backstories that can become intertwined with a consumer's sense of identity, insinuated into people's lives through their views of themselves and their place in the world.[12]

Coffee is an ideal subject for a study of the interplay of material and symbolic values. Think of the different economic values that go into a cup of coffee—the price of cherry sold at the farm, the cost of beans bought by a roaster, what you pay at your coffee shop. That cup also likely has other values attached, perhaps paying a Fair Trade premium to support a moral cause, perhaps responding to a claim about the values of terroir or the biography of the grower. There may also be emotional attachments: a comforting morning ritual or the sociability of a shared moment with a friend. The coffee may invoke affective values, the smell and taste triggering memories and associations. Then think also of what the beans that went into that cup mean to those who pick them, how they link to their life projects and moral worlds.

At the heart of this book is a surprising story. For generations, Maya farmers in the highlands of Guatemala—forced off their ancestral lands in the late nineteenth and early twentieth centuries—were compelled to work under harsh conditions as seasonal migrant laborers on the Spanish- and German-owned coffee plantations that had taken their territory.[13] The 1990s and 2000s saw a dramatic shift in the international coffee market, part of a quality turn in high-end foods that gave rise to the proliferation of more distinct versions of formerly everyday products, from microbrew beers and artisanal olive oil to exotic salts and heirloom tomatoes. Coffee has played a significant role in this quality turn, and in a bit of poetic justice, the steep mountain slopes to which the Guatemala Maya had been displaced turned out to be ideal for producing the sorts of coffees the new market was seeking. This market shift created a boom in many Maya communities as former plantation workers began to grow and sell their own coffee. More recently, demand for even higher-quality Third Wave coffees has been the fastest growing sector of the coffee market. These coffees flourish in the high altitude and microclimates of Guatemala's western highlands, producing unusual and subtle flavors that command astonishingly high prices. Such prices are explicitly rooted in terroir distinctions, but just as important are the symbolic values—the stories and rarified language of the artisanal market—constructed around the beans.[14] The emphasis on narrative and symbolic aspects leaves Maya farmers at a disadvantage, as they lack the cultural and social capital needed to participate in the lucrative Third Wave market. Thus, the early quality turn disproportionately benefited Maya producers, but they have been largely left out of the Third Wave.

Third Wave coffee aficionados are earnestly pursuing a passion, trying to find new flavors and to make supply chains more just. For Maya farmers, coffee fits into traditional understandings of cosmological and agricultural cycles of regeneration—as well as providing income to pursue a better life. Connecting the dots, this book links the quest for quality among Third Wave enthusiasts in the United States to the lives and internet-fueled aspirations of Maya farmers who grow that coffee. In the specific contexts of coffee farms and coffee shops, and all the spaces in between, different sorts of values—material and economic as well as moral and social—come together to create the high-end coffee market. While success is often understood in terms of accumulating value, the real power is the ability to define what constitutes value[15]—in this case, constructing quality by translating the material qualities of the beans produced in places like Guatemala into narratives of authenticity, quality, and relationships.

GOING TO ORIGIN

Coffee buyers and roasters like to tell stories about the remote and exotic places they find particularly rare beans, and "going to origin" is considered a badge of honor. Anthropologists also like to tell stories of the distant sites of their fieldwork.

In 2014 Bart Victor and I traveled to western Guatemala with two students in search of what is considered some of the best coffee in the world. Early in the trip, after narrowly missing an oncoming bus barreling around a hairpin curve, we realized that our driver, César, was fearless. That turned out to be a good thing, as drug traffickers largely control this part of the country, which serves as a logistics hub for the bulk of Colombian cocaine heading to the United States. The narcos are better armed and better organized than the national police, and their justice tends to be swift and gruesome. Fearlessness is an attitude that commands respect around here, and César's swagger went a long way in justifying our presence. A group of gringos exploring back roads and asking questions about local farms could easily be misinterpreted. After several white-knuckle hours with César behind the wheel, we finally crested a hill to get a view of the Huehuetenango landscape, an expanse of green-blue mountains extending north to the Mexican border. Looking a little closer, we could make out coffee farms, large and small, in the canopies.

The helicopters and black tinted SUVs of the narcos contrast starkly with the grinding material poverty of the majority of the region's Maya inhabitants. On the side of the highway, women in traditional woven blouses, many with young children strapped to their backs, were selling five-gallon jugs of gas smuggled from Mexico. An unintentionally poignant sign pointed straight ahead to Guatemala and left toward La Democracia (figure 2)—this being a country with a long history of right-wing dictators and autocrats. Daily life hums along in places like these, but there is a palpable tension that the drug money and its violence bring. It occurred to us that a white van with "Tourism" stenciled

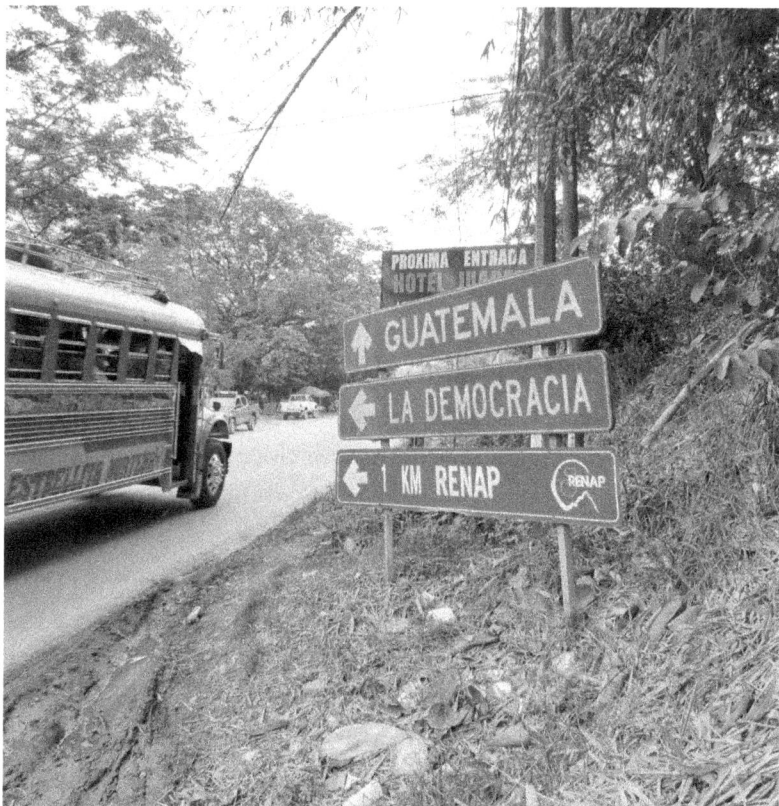

Figure 2. Left to La Democracia, Huehuetenango.

on the side might not have been the best choice of transportation, but César said not to worry, that he had us covered. The journey was vertiginous and bumpy. At one point we had to transfer to the back of a pickup truck to get over the last crest in the muddy, rutted road. The best coffee is grown high up, and coffee farms tend to be off the beaten path—even here, where the beaten path is off the beaten path.

Its unique geographic and climatic endowments make highland Guatemala ground zero for Third Wave coffee production. High-altitude coffees command significant premiums, and the terroirs of Guatemala's volcanic slopes produce a wide range of distinctive flavors. On that trip to Huehuetenango, we were looking for the Finca El Injerto, which had recently set a world record for the highest price received for unroasted coffee beans.[16] Its owner, Arturo Aguirre Sr., is the fourth-generation grower on these lands, and his son Arturo Jr. now helps run the operation. Their coffees routinely place prominently in cupping competitions and have won a number of awards. Arturo Sr., slightly stooped by age and with the wrinkled skin of someone who has spent long hours in the fields, told us that farming is not just a job for him, that it is in his blood, at the core of who he is. The Aguirres' land starts at about 1500 meters above sea level (masl), stretching up to around 3300 masl, and Arturo Sr. takes pride in pushing the coffee plants as high as they will go (some now grow at close to 2100 masl). Arturo Jr. shares his father's love of the land, but his real passion is building an internationally recognized brand for El Injerto. Arturo Jr. has cultivated relationships with trendsetting roasters in the United States, established the farm's online presence, and opened a few upscale coffee shops under the El Injerto name.

Arturo Sr. recounts that he made a conscious decision to keep a full range of coffee varietals and uphold standards of quality during the long periods when the market was down. "Everybody said I was crazy back then," he chuckles. "They were all going for volume without regard for quality and I was doing the opposite." It was not easy. As he tells it, they had to haul the coffee down the mountain by mule and would barely earn enough to cover their costs. But now his commitment to artisanal quality has paid off. In 2012 Korean buyers paid what was then a record-setting price of $500.50 a pound for a micro-lot of one of El Injerto's prized arabica varietals. This entire lot was only eight pounds, but the benchmark New York coffee futures price at the time was just over $170 per hundredweight, meaning that the El Injerto beans sold for about three hundred times the going rate. El Injerto sold that coffee through its own online auction, organized by Arturo Jr. as a way of cutting out the many layers of middlemen in the normal trade.

I did not try the coffee that cost $500 a pound, but even El Injerto's more reasonable (if still pricey) beans are exceptional. Their Bourbon varietal—if you like a rich, classic coffee taste—produces an almost perfectly balanced cup, with a deep chocolatey base and highlights of dark berries. Are their coffees worth the astonishing prices they command? Seemingly objective measures of taste and quality are called upon to justify price, but a significant part of the economic value comes from subjective and symbolic factors, such as the vicarious personal relationship with a producer, that play to a market shift among the global affluent toward artisanal and rare products.[17]

El Injerto is on the cutting edge of high-end coffee production, but there is also a whole commercial apparatus of roasting, marketing, and brewing that fuels Third Wave consumption. Roasters, baristas, and marketers—as well as the growing number of passionate amateurs and aficionados—play an active role in defining what quality is, how a *different* taste becomes a *more valued* taste. Third Wave enthusiasts are always chasing something new. One roaster I know recently marveled at a new find with a distinct cotton candy flavor. Such descriptions are far removed from how Maya farmers in Huehuetenango think about their coffee.

And there is the rub, for while sought-after coffees are now being produced in the Maya highlands of Guatemala, smallholding Indigenous farmers are largely excluded from the highest-value Third Wave trade. Producing exceptional coffees requires certain geographic conditions (soil, rainfall, altitude, and other elements of terroir), and Maya coffee farmers, like farmers around the world, highly value control over their land as a form of security in an unstable world. In its early days, the move toward quality coffee fueled an economic boom to which many smallholding producers in Guatemala attached aspirations for a better future for their families and communities. While the growing market affords many a degree of economic autonomy, farmers' sweat, toil, and devotion—of a sort less romantic than usually imagined in distant coffee shops—are but one part of the creation of value. The largest percentage of economic value extracted from the rarified prices of Third Wave coffees comes not from control of terroir but translating the material qualities of beans into the symbolic and imaginative narratives of affluent consumers. The Aguirres of El Injerto come from a different tradition than their Maya neighbors—their native language is Spanish and they embrace their European heritage. They comfortably straddle the realities of the farm and the desires of consumers in upscale coffee shops. This social position allows them to profitably translate different measures of worth across symbolic value worlds.

On neighboring lands, Indigenous smallholders produce equally good coffees, but they lack the social and cultural capital to tap into the highest-value segment of the market. Their investment in terroir seems to give them some degree of power, but the means of symbolic production are largely held by northern tastemakers. With affluent consumers valuing the unalienated fruits of labor, they often assume that paying high prices for coffee helps to counter the inequalities of the low-paid, unskilled agricultural economy.[18] Maya farmers may be blessed with the auspicious geographic and climatic endowments to grow high-end coffee, but market-setting power rests with those controlling the symbolic means of production. While apparently rewarding objective "quality," Third Wave trends structurally disadvantage smallholding Indigenous coffee farmers in Guatemala, who suffer from a dearth of the social and cultural capital that could help them convert their material endowments and technical expertise into economic rewards. This is a case where the consumer quest for artisanal excellence inadvertently reproduces inequalities, with the greatest gains in high-end coffee made not through control over the material means of production but through a capacity to define quality and translate its worth across value worlds.[19]

THREE WAVES

In April 2019 the Specialty Coffee Association (SCA) held its annual trade show at the Boston Convention Center. The cost of entry can top $1000 with all the extras, but this is a must-attend event in the high-end coffee world, bringing together growers, importers, roasters, baristas, equipment manufacturers, and scientists from across the globe. More than just a trade show, the Coffee Expo feels like both an academic conference and a fan convention. It is a place where those for whom coffee is a way of life as much as a business can get together and geek out over their shared passion. The main exhibition, held in a cavernous hall with seemingly endless rows of vendor booths, lasted four days, but the whole program stretched to a full week with pre- and post-expo options. Peter Giuliano, who had been recently named the SCA's scientific director, asked me to give a talk, and I readily accepted; the Coffee Expo is the sort of place that an anthropologist does fieldwork for a book like this. A working paper floating some of my ideas had been picked up by the coffee industry press, with one headline reading "A Marxist Takedown of High-End Coffee's Value Structure." While I draw on several of Marx's insights, a takedown had certainly not been my intent, and this forum was the ideal opportunity to set the record straight. In fact, I have great respect for coffee people like Giuliano, Liftee, Bob Bernstein (who runs Bongo Java in Nashville and helped start Cooperative Coffees), Aaron Duckworth (a master taster at Parisi Coffee in Kansas City), and the many others I met in the course of my research, all devoted in their own ways to the craft of coffee. Over the last years, I too have become a coffee nerd of sorts, relishing in the arcane minutiae and in-group feeling produced by shared sensory experiences.

All the same, as an anthropologist, I see this community and its rituals as cultural phenomena, and in that working paper I observed that the Third Wave's rarefied conventions of "quality" are social constructions linked to prestige hierarchies. The specialty coffee industry has built up elaborate scientific protocols to ground their definitions of quality in empirical terms, creating new metrics and standards for cupping and lexicons of taste. Coffee merchants, roasters, and tastemakers talk about "discovering" quality, as if it were independently out there in the world. There are certainly noticeable, objective differences in flavors between beans, some of them stark, but what those taste differences mean is learned, and what is considered quality changes over time. For example, the fruity acidity of naturally processed Ethiopian coffees, once seen as a defect, was celebrated at the 2019 Coffee Expo.

When I first started drinking it, good coffee was a fresh pot of Folgers, which came preground in foil packets, brewed in a stalwart commercial Bunn drip maker. It was the late 1980s and I was studying anthropology in college in Birmingham, Alabama, and waiting tables at a local steakhouse. I observed that more sophisticated customers, who also tended to be the best tippers, usually drank their coffee black. Likewise, the best waiters—the group of slightly older, somewhat world-weary full-time staff—also drank their coffee unadorned. These preferences carried an implicit moral disdain for adulterating quality: creamer in good coffee, or sauce on a fine cut of beef, was seen as hiding the very characteristics one was paying for. At the time I was deep into the works of sociologist Pierre Bourdieu, which led me to see the value judgments behind drinking coffee black and that such taste was a form of cultural capital, in this instance a mark of distinction shared between the most knowledgeable staff and the most cosmopolitan guests. Then and there, quality was denoted by the brand name label and the freshness of the brew.

That Folgers, which many restaurants still serve and you can find on your grocery store shelves, is emblematic of "First Wave" coffee: consistent if unexceptional blends mostly roasted by large firms and sold under familiar brand names that assure a standard level of quality. This First Wave of coffee consumption, which began in the early twentieth century, familiarized and normalized coffee, moving it from its exotic beginnings to an everyday staple. In its rise as a global commodity, coffee turned into a volume product, requiring huge economies of scale, and cheap labor, to produce significant returns. The plantation model of First Wave coffee was an agricultural variety of Fordism: capital intensive, regulated, and supplying a standardized and mass-produced commodity.[20]

Starting in the late 1960s and 1970s, but really taking off in the 1980s and 1990s, a new vanguard of U.S. coffee purveyors offered a Second Wave reaction to the bland uniformity of the major labels. Places such as Peet's in the San Francisco Bay Area and the Coffee Connection in Boston led the way, and by the late 1980s hundreds of local roasters and coffee shops in urban areas around the United States were acquainting consumers with higher-quality specialty coffees, espresso-based drinks, and added flavorings. This movement paved the way for Starbucks's mass-market version.[21]

The Second Wave was organized around post-Fordist strategies of decommodification: roasters set their offerings apart from the standardized uniformity of the commodity-grade trade by focusing on broad geographic origins (such as Kona and Blue Mountain) as well as emphasizing more just labor relations through fair trade. Molly Doane writes, "The profit that derived from enormous efficiencies of scale in the Fordist coffee market [was] replaced by profit derived from premiums assessed for quality and originality."[22] Second Wave buyers seek out higher-quality, and higher-altitude, beans and offer significantly higher prices for them. The Specialty Coffee Association, which held its first meeting in New Orleans in 1988, developed a one-hundred-point quality scale that serves as the industry standard. Coffees scoring above eighty are considered "specialty," and Second Wave coffees generally place in the mid-eighties. The Second Wave emerged alongside the demise of the International Coffee Agreement (ICA) quota system in 1989—a year that saw the fall of the Berlin Wall and peak employment at General Motors. The ICA had regulated supply and demand between producing and consuming countries, and its dissolution allowed for more competition in production, lowering barriers for new producers, and fed into the "quality turn" in affluent markets toward more distinctive products (in contrast to the homogeneity of Fordist mass production). The Second Wave shift in consumption fundamentally changed the face of Guatemalan coffee production in the 1990s and 2000s.

In no small part a realization of and reaction to the exploitative conditions of Fordist production in the First Wave, the Second Wave coffee market began to place a higher value on moral provenance, assuring customers that their coffee was bought at a fair price to compensate those whose labor produced it.[23] In her work on the value chain of New Guinea coffee, anthropologist Paige West documents how images of "poverty and primitivity" add value in marketing Second Wave coffee, playing with symbolic and affective qualities while eliding structural inequalities.[24]

In 1990, when I moved to New Orleans to start graduate school, there was a thriving Second Wave coffee scene in the city. Many associate New Orleans's coffee with a brew that includes chicory—as in the café au lait famously served with beignets at Café du Monde—but the city has a storied tradition of straight black coffee as well.[25] It has long been an important port for beans from Latin America, and it is where Folgers has been roasting on an industrial scale since the early 1960s. A natural addition to the city's vibrant food culture, one of the first specialty roasters was PJ's Coffee, founded in 1978. After moving to town, I became a fixture at the PJ's on Magazine Street, spending long hours on the back patio studying and writing. Like most Second Wave shops, PJ's offered whole beans from named regions (such as Antigua, Kona, and Blue Mountain) as well as different blends, roasting styles, and types of drinks, from espresso-based mixtures to cold brew. PJ's opened my eyes to a whole new way of experiencing coffee, although, conditioned from my time as a waiter, I avoided the flavored syrups that were also a Second Wave staple.

I was living in Nashville (birthplace of First Wave pioneer Maxwell House) when a new sort of coffee spot began to open up in the 2000s—small roasters that dealt in single-estate varietals that scored in the upper eighties and nineties on the SCA scale. This Third Wave emerged along with broader turn-of-the-millennium alternative food movements seeking to de-alienate food chains and stressing purity, authenticity, and artisanal, natural, and organic qualities.[26] By 2011 there were hundreds of artisanal roasters in urban areas across the country, including Crema and Barista Parlor in Nashville, and the Third Wave movement had its own national brands in Counter Culture Coffee, Intelligentsia, Stumptown Coffee Roasters, and Blue Bottle Coffee.

TABLE I

Three Waves of Coffee Quality

	SCA Score and Grade	Description
First Wave	75–79.99 Usual Good Quality (UGQ)	brand-name grocery-store blends that compete on consistency and price (e.g., Folgers, Maxwell House), mostly produced by large conglomerates
Second Wave	80–84.99 Very Good 85–89.99 Excellent	specialty coffees developed in reaction to the uniformity of First Wave blends starting in the late 1960s, and taking off in the 1990s and 2000s
Third Wave	85–89.99 Excellent 90–100 Outstanding	generally single-estate, micro-lot coffees distinguished by unique flavor profiles, unusual varietals, and craft roasting

The Third Wave dramatically accelerated the Second Wave's post-Fordist trends around quality and choice. In fact, the differences between the Second Wave and Third Wave are blurry. Confusingly, both are grouped into the overarching category of "specialty" coffee and are represented by the Specialty Coffee Association. Some argue that the distinction is one of degree rather than kind, but coffee professionals and connoisseurs (and, thus, the market) recognize the Third Wave as something distinct (see table 1).

Trish Rothgeb, then working as a barista and roaster in Oslo, coined the term "Third Wave" in 2002 to refer to the Nordic coffee scene's focus on unadorned quality—small operations committed to a sense of authenticity, roasting single-estate beans and trying to perfect cup profiles. The specialty coffee world quickly adopted Rothgeb's implied chronology of three waves, and I follow that convention in this book. Although the three waves of coffee were introduced sequentially, all three coexist as market segments, and, in urban areas at least, First, Second, and Third Wave coffees are readily available today.[27] Reflecting on what her turn of phrase came to mean in a 2019 *Los Angeles Times* interview, Rothgeb, who now co-owns Wrecking Ball Coffee Roasters in San Francisco, observed that the First Wave took place at home, the Second Wave took place in coffee shops, and the Third Wave is taking place "in the cup." We may see these waves as different spheres of valuation, each judging quality by their own moral and material metrics.

In the world of Third Wave coffee, terroir plays an important role in determining value. Coffee's complex flavor profile is especially sensitive to climate, moisture, and soil conditions; the highest-priced coffees are varietals sourced from single farms or sometimes even particular sections of a farm. Third Wave retailers routinely charge double or triple the prices of Starbucks, with small differences on the hundred-point scale resulting in huge differences in price. While using poetic descriptors ("notes ranging from dark berries and chocolate to citrus"), Third Wave purveyors emphatically focus on "quality in the cup," meaning the intrinsic properties of the beans and sensory perceptions of the brew.

This focus on what is in the cup also implies the ability to find and source a demanding level of quality, and so Third Wave roasters spend a lot of time building relationships with particular places and producers, like the Aguirres of El Injerto.[28] While coffee is almost never local, the Third Wave touts its model of "relationship coffee," a direct link between roaster and grower that can substitute virtual and vicarious connections for geographic proximity.[29] Relationship coffee also implies bypassing the certification regimes of the Second Wave (such as Fair Trade and Rainforest Alliance) to work directly with farmers—a neoliberal approach that seeks to reward individual farmer's abilities. In telling the stories of these connections, roasters have built up an elaborate symbolic edifice around the material qualities of fine coffee. To be clear, there is an objective reality to terroir distinctions: coffees grown in different places taste different, and one can fairly quickly learn to distinguish African from Latin American cup profiles. But equally important are the stories of provenance, an item's biography and the narrative link it provides with a producer. What is being sold in a cup of Third Wave brew is not just the material use value of the drug food but a whole set of symbolic values, including the imagined relationship with a farmer and his or her inspiring story. Third Wave coffees reflect a bourgeois consumer quest for excellence, artisanal authenticity, and a connection with the provenance of production propelled by roasters and aficionados resisting mass markets and Fordist homogeneity.[30] The physical and addictive properties of coffee are key to its appeal, certainly, but coffee also provides the foundation for imaginative narratives of quality and authenticity, and Third Wave consumers want something unique to reflect their values.

Walking around the 2019 Coffee Expo, with its live competitions for roasters and baristas, workshops on sensory science, and demonstrations of almost comically elaborate brewing devices, is both exciting and overwhelming. The terms of art and esoteric knowledge needed to navigate this world can be intimidating, and, like wine connoisseurs, coffee snobs can be tedious.[31] I overheard a heated debate about the differences in taste produced by using a flat-bottom versus a conical filter. There is definitely a look among the crowd—lots of aggressive facial hair and artful tattoos on the overwhelmingly white and largely male bodies.[32] Still, the coffee world is full of individuals more complicated than "coffee hipster" stereotypes. Coffee nerds, as they are apt to refer to themselves, pursue what they see as a virtuous dedication to the craft of the beverage. They seek out new and unusual flavors, heirloom varietals, and remote producers not just to make money, but also to pursue a sincere passion for coffee and a vision for a better future through transforming global agriculture supply chains. As Michaele Weissman shows in her book *God in a Cup*, Third Wave pioneers (such as Intelligentsia's Geoff Watts, Stumptown's Duane Sorenson, and Peter Giuliano, then of Counter Culture) have an obsessive zeal to uncover new coffees in the most remote places and a missionary fervor to spread the word about what they have found. It is hard not to admire their passion and determination.

GUATEMALA

In many ways, Guatemala is typical of coffee-producing countries. A former colony situated in the tropics with lots of high-altitude land, Guatemala has long depended on the export of a few key crops for its national economy. Dyestuffs such as indigo and cochineal were replaced in the nineteenth and twentieth centuries by coffee, bananas, and sugar, but the structure of producing primary goods with cheap labor for markets in the Global North persisted. Demetrio Cojtí argues that contemporary Guatemala functions as a neocolonial state, defined by the legacy of colonial systems of ethnic exclusion, modernist views of progress, and the concentration of political and economic power among a small elite.[33]

The overriding social fact about Guatemala, what informs and shapes all other aspects of its society, is the country's ethnic and economic inequality. The largest 3 percent of farms occupy about 65 percent of the country's arable lands, while the smallest 95 percent control 28 percent of the available land. Maya communities constitute the majority of inhabitants in most of Guatemala's coffee-growing regions—and poverty and malnutrition rates in those towns fluctuate with the going rate for coffee on the New York futures market. There are many impoverished non-Maya (*ladinos*), but Indigenous peoples suffer a double discrimination based on ethnicity as well as class.[34] About half the population are Indigenous, and by any measure—income, education, infant mortality, access to potable water—Maya communities suffer the most deprivation.

Ethnic tensions and economic inequalities built into Guatemalan plantation economies led to the emergence of several revolutionary groups in the western highlands in the 1970s and 1980s. The U.S.-backed military reacted with a genocidal campaign against Maya communities, a period known as *la violencia*. Although the war formally ended with peace accords in 1996, its legacy and lingering violence persist.[35] Gladys Tzul Tzul's work reveals a fundamental disconnect between

Maya communities and the Guatemalan state: from its neoliberal, neo-colonial position, the state wants to govern individual subjects, but Indigenous communities respond collectively. She argues that they are not just speaking different languages but are also coming from different ontologies of power.[36]

Depending on how one counts, as many as twenty-three different Mayan languages are spoken in this country the size of Tennessee (map 1). Maya ethnolinguistic groups are concentrated in the country's western highlands. Rural Maya households generally employ a variety of livelihood strategies to get by—maintaining subsistence plots of maize and beans, growing vegetables to sell in the market, and working as seasonal labor on a plantation.[37] Maya farmers tend to see value as ultimately derived from the earth, resulting in a strong cultural attachment to the land.[38] These ties are at once pragmatic and moral, linking agricultural cycles to cosmological principles of balance, reciprocity, and interconnectedness between human and nonhuman beings.

For virtually all of the twentieth century, coffee in Guatemala was grown on a small number of large, family-owned plantations (*fincas*) that depended on cheap seasonal labor, mostly coerced from Maya communities, to produce commodity-grade beans at relatively low altitudes. The coffee trade uses altitude of production, generally rendered in meters above sea level (masl), as a shorthand for overall quality. In Guatemala, coffee grown below 1350 masl is classified as Prime or Extra Prime (map 2); these are generally commodity-grade beans traded on global exchanges sight unseen. In contrast, coffee grown above 1350 masl earns a "Strictly Hard Bean" designation, indicating the quality of specialty-coffee grade beans. The shift in U.S. consumer tastes toward specialty coffees in the 1990s pushed the market toward higher-altitude coffees. This market shift has implications for Guatemala's highly unequal land distribution and ethnic relations. In Guatemala, production moved up the mountain slopes onto lands to which the region's majority Maya population had been relegated during colonization and subsequent land grabs. Since the 1990s, as many as fifty thousand Maya smallholding farmers in the highlands have begun growing coffee on their own small plots to supply the global Second Wave coffee market.

Farmers I have talked with are largely open to the free-market promise of hard work being justly rewarded; they say they would be happy to participate in a meritocracy, as they are used to playing with the cards stacked against them so severely as to crush hope.[39] Growing coffee is backbreaking work, and most Maya farmers live in very modest circumstances, with limited resources and opportunities. They are acutely aware of the perils of dependency on fickle global markets. Most would like something better, something more (*algo más*) for their children—maybe for them to open a store, or become a teacher—because they know how hard and precarious farming is. Coffee earnings and the spread of cell phones and the internet in rural Guatemala have fueled the growth of such aspirations. While few Maya farmers are getting rich, coffee has brought much-needed income to farming communities where a marginal improvement in material circumstances can mitigate the ever-present risk of catastrophic failure.[40] Controlling, even partially, the means of production allows farmers to access markets opportunistically and not just by obligation.[41] As they describe it, coffee represents an opportunity in a context of few opportunities, an imperfect but valued means to realize their desires for a better life; it is tied up with hopes, dreams, and desires that go beyond mere income to visions of the good life.[42] Hopes are often dashed in what Lauren Berlant terms "cruel optimism" and what Bart Victor calls "frustrated freedom."[43] Still, such dreams can tell us about the values that orient our interlocutors' engagement with the world, and this is true of Maya farmers and Guatemalan oligarchs as well as Third Wave roasters and hipster consumers.

Bill Hempstead, scion of one of Guatemala's coffee families and an insightful observer of the trade, first told me how the specialty coffee market was benefiting a large number of smallholding farmers at the expense of the traditional oligarchy, including his own family. He said that it was "the largest transfer of wealth in the history of the country," with smallholding farmers increasing their incomes and expanding

Map 1. Mayan languages in Guatemala.

their land holdings. Well aware that unequal access to land has fueled ethnic conflict and violent resistance in Guatemala over the centuries, I was surprised by his claims.

Having long studied Maya engagements with global markets, I felt compelled to dig deeper into this story. So, with my friend and colleague Bart Victor, I began researching the role of specialty coffee production among Maya farmers.[44] Over the course of a decade starting in

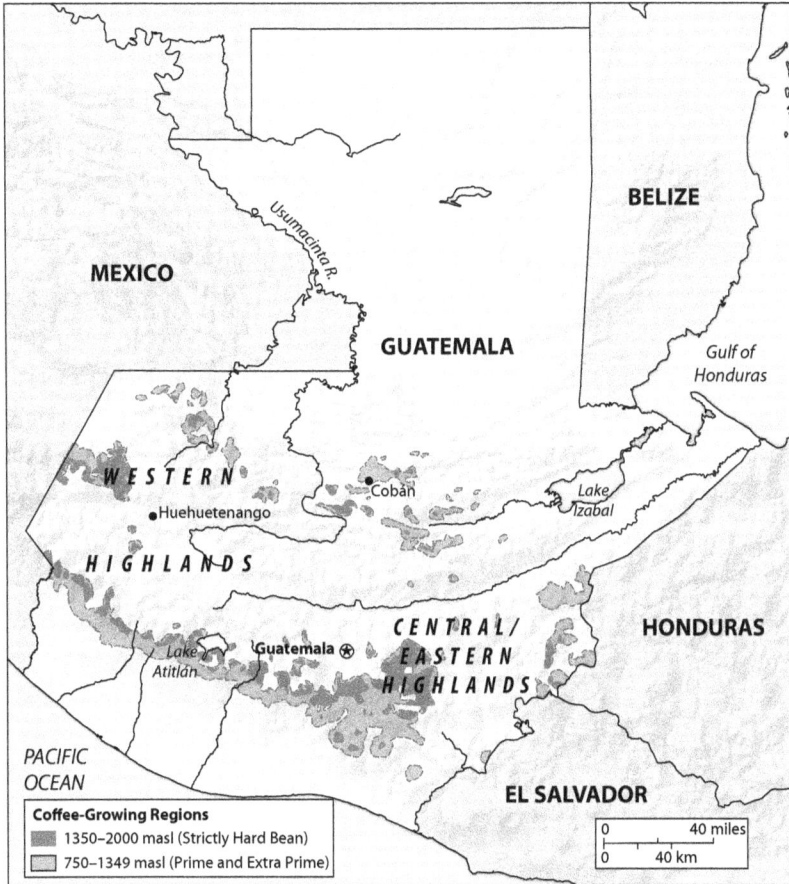

Map 2. Coffee-growing regions in Guatemala by altitude.

2010, we interviewed smallholding farmers and members of the coffee oligarchy in Guatemala. With Linda Asturias de Barrios, an anthropologist at the Universidad del Valle de Guatemala, and a team of her students, we conducted surveys and focus groups in fourteen coffee-growing communities. This book results from that research[45] and from my work with Third Wave roasters and coffee experts in the United States, focusing on how definitions of quality and determinations of taste are developed and promoted. The growing market for specialty coffee in the United States has in fact been a boon for many Indigenous smallholding farmers. Delving deeper, however, it turns out to be a story of risk as well as promise, of a political economy infused with moral and ideological as well as commercial values.

We found Maya farmers growing high-quality coffee as defined by conventional metrics but lacking the social and cultural capital to convert their endowments into the symbolic narratives so important for the high-end market. Consumer market shifts toward single-origin coffee create a tension between two models of economic risk and reward: cooperatives, with Fair Trade premiums that excel at minimizing risk, and "open" markets, with extraordinary rewards for those able to grow very high quality, single-estate coffees. Most Maya coffee farmers value cooperative organization and yet a growing number are defecting, pulled away by middlemen seeking the highest-quality beans before they get lost in an amalgamated blend of all cooperative members' harvests. This is a complicated moral as well as economic situation that farmers must navigate, one fraught with risks both financial and social, pitting individual gain against cooperative preferences.[46]

VALUE WORLDS AND COFFEE

At the two ends of the coffee commodity chain we find very different economic circumstances embedded in very different moral worlds but framed by the same neoliberal project: from smallholding farmers in places like Guatemala seeking some degree of economic security (that fits with their social world and cultural identity) to U.S. consumers hunting for ever more particular and unique sensory experiences (that fit with their social world and cultural identity).[47] This book explores the connections between these worlds, showing how social, political, and moral values get translated into economic worth through the trade in coffee. For Maya farmers, the coffee they grow carries particular cultural meanings that fit into local social and moral worlds—as well as an economic importance that reflects both the precarity of household finances and the enduring legacies of colonial relations of power. For their part, Third Wave coffee shops sell not only beans but the stories and values associated with them, translating narratives of authenticity and geographic origins into the argot of conscientious consumption— converting intangible values into financial gain. In this, symbolic and social aspects are not derivative of, or superfluous to, market value but constitutive of it.[48]

Capitalism depends on making incommensurate things commensurate, reducing complex particulars to the common denominator of market value. Anna Tsing calls capitalism a translation machine— translating natural resources, emotional attachments, cultural values, time, et cetera, ad infinitum, into commodities and, ultimately, into prices and profits.[49] This has taken on particular importance in late capitalist markets, such as that for Third Wave coffee, with symbolic values and intangible qualities invoked to distinguish goods and justify quality claims. Here I focus on how different sorts of values get translated across realms of valuation. The bulk of surplus economic value in high-end coffee is extracted not through the material trade but by arbitraging social and moral worth across distinct value worlds. These symbolic values can be artfully and profitably converted into higher prices. In this, power and profit come not from control over the material means of production but through differential access to the symbolic means of production and cultural capital. As a result, neocolonial inequalities are reproduced between the Global North and Global South, between oligarchs and farmers, between ladinos and Mayas.

Values are ideas and ideals about how the world should be and how one should act in it.[50] They anchor moral stances and help individuals judge the worth of things. Based on what is socially considered important and worthy, values are at once transcendent (their relevance extends beyond any particular circumstance or person) and highly variable across contexts. Values are often associated with an overarching notion of the good and virtue while they have also motivated and justified all sorts of injustices and atrocities, from colonial ventures to contemporary genocides. The values we celebrate tend to be "pro-social," meaning that they emphasize common purpose and the welfare of others over individual self-interest.[51] Yet not all values are pro-social: self-interest itself can be a value, and indeed it has been unflinchingly called upon by corporate executives and the editors of the *Wall Street Journal* not as a justification of last resort but as a virtue.[52]

Most values cannot be quantified or calculated in a precise manner, although those that can carry a weight of certitude. In both the public and commercial spheres, leaders have increasingly disavowed tough moral and political decisions onto algorithms and cost/benefit analyses that favor quantitative measures in an attempt to lessen decision-making biases.[53] This can be effective, but, as Marion Fourcade observes, even seemingly objective economic values rest on a whole range of cultural and ideological assumptions about the world and the scale and measure of "value."[54]

Values are internalized and adapted by individuals, but they are not just idiosyncratic desires. Their power comes from being recognized and sanctioned by others in a discourse community, transcending the desires of the moment or the person. The values people hold are most often vague, more like dispositions—a propensity to think in a certain way—than hard and fast mandates.[55] Not just strictures or rules, value positions provide a socio-cognitive basis for individual interpretation and improvisation.[56] People invoke different values in different circumstances to explain their actions and positions. Sometimes we try to live up to our values, and at other times we use values to justify our desires and behaviors. When applied, they are adapted in specific ways, depending on circumstances and competing ideals and desires. Aristotle observed that the art of living, the very nature of the human condition, rests with our capacity for judgment, the practical wisdom to balance the competing pulls of different values. The work of identity building involves constantly balancing and translating between substantively different, sometimes incommensurate, value worlds.[57]

Values cluster in certain domains—value worlds—with their own logics, truth conditions, and rubrics for judgment. Everyone participates in, and holds dear, many different value worlds, which can be large or small, parochial or cosmopolitan, localized or diffuse. They are fluid and porous constellations of ideals, with particular values creatively deployed, negotiated, and redefined in practice—and yet with a narrative consistency that provides (a sometimes contested) legitimacy.[58] For our purposes, the concept's loose boundaries and scalar promiscuity allow us to move back and forth across levels of analysis, between the global and the local, the structural and the personal, and to trace the varied threads that all intersect with the material object of coffee. Nietzsche observed that humans are evaluative creatures, always judging the world around us in terms of "good" or "bad," "better" or "worse"; value worlds provide the metrics for these judgments. In terming these systems "worlds," I call attention to the ontological implications—that they are not just different worldviews but different ways of creating the world.[59] As *worlds,* they are what David Graeber calls "imaginary totalities," frameworks of moral or material worth that are internally consistent, totalizing, and universalizing.[60]

Called on by individuals to evaluate words, deeds, and goods, value worlds share many features of Luc Boltanski and Laurent Thévenot's "orders of worth," Arjun Appadurai's "regimes of value," and Max Weber's "value-spheres."[61] Weber saw modern society as divided into five different spheres of value (economic, political, aesthetic, erotic, and intellectual), each with its own form of rational consistency, that sometimes conflict, forcing individuals to choose between "warring gods." Indeed, different spheres of value may compete for implementation, producing confusion and an interference whereby the logic of one world is used to misapprehend the meanings of another, what John Dewey called "trouble."[62] Joel Robbins identifies in such conflict a key source of cultural dynamism in his fluid and multiscalar approach to value-spheres.[63] Understandings of value often collide in moralized markets, where firms and individuals try to balance moral and economic ends.[64]

Boltanski and Thévenot look at how actions and ideas are justified by agents in indeterminate situations with multiple value systems. They outline six primary orders of worth (market, industrial, civic, domestic, spiritual, and social recognition), each an evaluative space with its own logic, and all ultimately linked back to a broad notion of the common good.[65]

It seems probable that, as Boltanski and Thévenot argue, all regimes of valuation are ultimately based in shared notions of a common good. Still, rather than delimiting a set of primary or primal value worlds, I find it useful to embrace their multiplicity, plasticity, and ambiguity.[66] Thus, what I present is less of a formal model and more of an analytic lens attuned to the artful practice of justifying and balancing different value worlds in market interactions and other domains of life. In this, I am following the lead of Victor Montejo, Gladys Tzul Tzul, and other Maya scholars who reject the stark divisions of Western epistemologies in favor of a more holistic understanding of how domains of life interact. Recognizing a broad plurality of values allows us to link the political-economic with the symbolic and moral, referring at once to values that orient conceptions of what is most important in life and to precise dollars-and-cents values of the material trade.[67] A focus on values also draws attention to the often hidden principles structuring economic activity in the context of neoliberal capitalism.[68]

Building on a long anthropological tradition of viewing economic activity as embedded in cultural contexts, this book documents that even in the hard-nosed business of international trade, coffee is about more than material transactions. For Maya farmers, coffee is meaningful in their lives in both cosmological and economic terms. Yet the object of coffee—the material thing—to which they assign values is also imbricated in other, distant value worlds through trade and consumption. Third Wave purveyors build their marketing on values produced by smallholding farmers, and yet those farmers are limited in their ability to set the terms of their engagement with the market.[69] The challenge, then, becomes understanding how worth is constituted in different value worlds and how nonmaterial enrichment occurs in translating between them.

WHAT FOLLOWS

"Follow the imbroglios," Bruno Latour enjoins, "wherever they may take us."[70] Such entanglements are not sidelines or distractions: they are the story. Thinking about how coffee moves around the world, the material and economic aspects may appear foremost. The coffee trade is, of course, about beans and dollars, but that is only part of the story. A material thing that satisfies a sensual desire and a physical craving, coffee has cascading effects that influence our mental states, social lives, and political systems. Since the Enlightenment, scientists and scholars have tried to create order out of the messy reality of the world, resulting in ever more narrowly defined fields of study and domains of life. Yet the world as it exists does not respect boundaries between the economic and the environmental, between the viral and the social, between the moral and the material. Lived experience seamlessly integrates these various domains, even if we prefer to separate them into the fields of anthropology, biology, chemistry, economics, philosophy, and so on.[71]

Here we have a lot to learn from Indigenous knowledge. Victor Montejo presents a Maya epistemology based on interconnectedness and interdependence—an ongoing back-and-forth between human and nonhuman actors that he terms a "Mayalogue," and Gladys Tzul Tzul writes about "webs of community and political forms," recognizing that nothing works in isolation but everything is intertwined in local, global, and international story lines.[72] In this way, fully understanding the coffee trade forces us to move beyond entrenched scholarly silos to uncover the dense web of relations that connects, for example, Maya farmers and Guatemalan oligarchs with artisanal roasters and conscientious consumers in the United States. Through this global circulatory system flows not just coffee beans but also political ideologies, cultural meanings, and individual hopes and fears.

While I was doing this research, it seemed that each question led to another, and another, and another—all substantively linked and all demanding answers. In the story as I tell it here, one thread starts at the molecular level, with the biochemical effect of caffeine awakening the senses, sharpening the mind, and focusing attention. Promoting these psychoactive properties, eighteenth- and nineteenth-century European coffeehouses provided an alternative to boozy taverns. Those places and their stimulant offerings stoked the rise of liberal and rational thought, including ideas of laissez-faire trade that folded back to provide the ideological grounding for the global commerce in commodities such as coffee, grown in places like Guatemala. Another strand of coffeehouse liberalism led to Austrian economics, a school of thought deeply skeptical of the state and committed to a fervent notion of market freedom that has been highly influential in economics and public policy across the world. These divergent threads—from the colonial coffee trade to neoliberal economic theory—come together again in the lives of Guatemala's coffee oligarchy. Their sprawling plantations were built upon forced labor and colonial legacies of racial exclusion, conjoining a European liberalism with Indigenous agricultural traditions and cosmologies. Coffee is part of a web of material, symbolic, and social relations that cross disciplinary and conceptual divides.[73]

The coffee trade may be seen as a dense network of connections that feed into one another. The farmer's economic activity concerns not only the market but also his or her family and social ties, religious and ideological beliefs, and relationship to nature and community. Likewise, a consumer's choice of a particular brew results not just from rational calculations of price and material utility; it is also embedded in a sense of identity and social position, economic and demographic status, and moral and emotional attachments. At every node along the trade circuit, similar strands of relations reverberate out from the material exchange, each reflecting different spheres of values. This book presents the coffee circuit as a series of conjunctures of different value worlds and shows how lucrative financial gains are made in artfully translating different sorts of values across domains of worth, from Guatemalan farms to Third Wave coffee shops. The implications extend beyond coffee. Integrating moral and symbolic with material and economic values into our models better represents the world as it actually is and better equips us to manage its problems.

The chapters that follow trace the many threads that emanate from the coffee trade, from the social worlds of Maya farmers to the ideological worlds of Guatemala's coffee elite to the symbolic worlds of Third Wave aficionados.[74] Following coffee as it travels around the world, intersecting with global capital and consumer markets, I take an ethnographic approach to focus on the people behind the commodity circuit—those who grow and harvest coffee, traders, roasters, consumers—and the culturally framed and often morally motivated choices they make. The commodity circuit of coffee is more than a string of commercial transactions; it is comprised of various value worlds intersecting. It turns out that what the market values is not always what people value, and I use the concept of "value worlds" to show how social, moral, and political values are balanced with the dollars and cents of market prices. In doing so, I make the case that high-end coffee can help us understand the ways symbolic values and intangible assets, as much as control over material resources, facilitate late capitalist accumulation.

Figure 3. Making a pour-over at Golden Sound by Barista Parlor in Nashville, Tennessee.

CHAPTER ONE

Creating Third Wave Values

Walking into Barista Parlor, a coffee shop in a rapidly gentrifying section of Nashville, Tennessee, one is struck by the dedication to craft and detail. Housed in a former transmission repair shop, the store projects a sense of simple, honest quality with a modern flair through its architecture and furnishings. Owner Andy Mumma credits his Mennonite upbringing with inspiring a commitment to handwork and artisanry; in word and deed, he appears driven by a pursuit of coffee excellence as much as making money—and he shows that the two need not be mutually exclusive. *Esquire* praises his store as "authentic," and, indeed, everything is local, from the reclaimed wood tables to the denim aprons and homemade Pop-Tarts. Everything, of course, except the coffee itself, even if it is roasted on site. But Barista's mission and branding create a warm glow around the carefully curated beans on the menu, extending the sense of an artisanal connection to farmers in faraway places, presumably likewise committed to the art of quality coffee.

The coffees on offer at Barista are all single-origin beans coming from named farms, set apart from one another by geography (not just Indonesia, Rwanda, or Guatemala, but particular regions within countries), altitude (many cognoscenti use "masl," meters above sea level, as a quick marker of overall quality), and descriptors that draw on an elaborate vocabulary of flavor analogies. For each of the six coffees on the menu, the farm of origin and varietal are noted along with tasting notes and a recommended brewing style. All of the coffees are pour-overs and take about four minutes to prepare; prices range from US $4 to $7.50 a cup, and there is no milk or sugar on the counter—one drinks this coffee straight.

As unique as it strives to be, Barista's space and aesthetic would be familiar to patrons of other Third Wave operations. These are generally small roasters with one or more cafes focused on a local market; they popped up in cities across the United States in the 2000s and 2010s. By 2021, Third Wave establishments were found in urban areas the world over, with the highest concentrations (by a significant margin) in the United States, Sweden, Norway, and Australia.[1] That year, Nashville, where I live, had six Third Wave roasters and twelve cafes selling Third Wave coffees. Before the COVID-19 pandemic, business was good: Third Wave was the fastest growing sector of the coffee business in the 2010s. It is still small compared to the $500 billion global coffee market, but its profit margins are high, demand continues to rise, and, within the industry, it has that ineffable quality of cool.[2] The Third Wave movement started with independent roasters, people like Mumma who wanted to indulge their passion as well as make a profit, and their operations give the impression of an almost obstinate dedication to craft combined with a scrappy zeal. From these beginnings, a few national chains emerged—including Stumptown, Intelligentsia, La Colombe, Counter Culture, and Blue Bottle—that attracted the interest of international capital. German investment firm JAB bought both Stumptown and Intelligentsia in 2015, while Nestlé purchased a majority stake in Blue Bottle in 2017.[3]

While there are a growing number of serious coffee aficionados, they still only constitute a fraction of a typical Third Wave shop's business. Thus, while retailers market exclusivity and access to a world of discerning aficionados, they also have to educate more casual consumers about what attributes are desirable and what constitutes quality worth paying a premium for.[4] This is a delicate balance. Menus can be opaque, using abbreviations and listing different plant varietals and processing methods, speaking the language of those in the know—and potentially intimidating those not conversant in the acronyms and lingo. At the same time, Third Wave shops are also places of community, where people with similar interests and tastes can congregate, even if that often means being alone together. In interviews, Third Wave professionals and enthusiasts alike repeatedly described coffee as a means of making social connections, between those drinking it together and between consumers and producers. They like to see themselves as part of a community, with shared values around craft, authenticity, and quality, and with their own language and customs that distinguish insiders from outsiders. They also like to point out that producing, roasting, and brewing specialty coffee calls on craft, science, and art—and working with coffee is a way of integrating these different ways of knowing the world into a coherent practice.

Third Wave retailers go to great lengths to justify their prices through objective quality as measured by tasting standards and conventions. Still, just as important are the symbolic and imaginative values at play: the relative positioning of conspicuous consumption; the imagined relationship with a producer; and, underwriting it all, the cultural and market shift among the global affluent toward less generic products. Their emphasis on nonmaterial values is characteristic of post-Fordist forms of production and consumption, in which intangible assets (from brands to algorithms) and symbolic attributes (appealing to emotion and identity) become just as important as material utility in distinguishing products—firms selling images and ideas as much as old-fashioned use value.

Operating in a type of "moralized market," Third Wave purveyors emphasize the social values that go into production, roasting, and brewing, promoting a sense of virtue in supporting craft and rewarding skill.[5] Their consumers are not only drinking a quality cup of coffee but are also buying into the values around quality, authenticity, and a connection to artisanal production. Paige West describes how specialty coffee importers and roasters invoke "an aura of social responsibility, political action, exotic locality, environmental sustainability, and social status" to distinguish their offerings.[6] Sarah Lyon refers to "lifestyle coffee," marketed around values that appeal to environmentally and socially conscientious consumers.[7] Such values resonate with how some consumers see themselves, becoming entwined with identities and moral stances in ways that extend far beyond the economic.

The current Third Wave coffee movement rides on a general growth in the global, high-end market for artisanally produced foodstuffs, from bourbons and chocolates to cheese and olive oil.[8] The language used to talk about Third Wave coffee borrows heavily from fine wine, invoking ideas of terroir and craft production, tapping into a bourgeoisie consumer pursuit of excellence and authenticity. This is a trend toward differentiation, with marketing narratives emphasizing distinctions between geographic origins, subtle flavor profiles, and relations with producers. Such stories act to de-commodify products, giving unique context and meaning to what might otherwise be just another undifferentiated commodity. This form of enrichment relies on different calculative devices,[9] such as, in the case of coffee, cupping protocols, flavor wheels, and numerical metrics for sensory perceptions.

This chapter describes the world of Third Wave coffee, what makes the product distinctive as well as the cultural values that animate roasters, baristas, and aficionados.[10] I show how the Specialty Coffee Association has worked with its member businesses and with several universities to create a small constellation of coffee research institutes and initiatives to develop new understandings and measures of quality. Much of this work seeks to quantify quality in the most objective ways possible, with tasting certifications, multijudge panels, and empirical metrics. Such rigorous processes can obfuscate the underlying truth that "quality" itself is socially constructed. This chapter examines some of the methods used to identify and evaluate flavors, showing how social conventions around quality emerge, linked to symbolic and imaginative values. This ethnographic work reveals how coffee-as-craft commands extraordinary prices.

THE COFFEE

The Third Wave focus on craft and provenance builds on Second Wave trends. In the business, Second and Third Wave roasters and retailers, large and small, are lumped together as "specialty coffee" and are both represented by the SCA. Still, the Third Wave is distinct from the Second not only in quality scores but in constituting a cultural community oriented around a set of common values. Third Wave coffees score in the high eighties and above ninety on the SCA's one-hundred-point scale, and they are usually grown at high altitudes (from 1400 masl up to around 2000 masl—the higher the better) to produce denser beans and sweeter, more intense flavors. Virtually all Third Wave coffees are "micro-lots," usually a few hundred pounds or less, from single farms. Sourcing and logistics are more much more expensive than with commodity coffee, which normally ships in container loads of forty thousand pounds.

Such coffees retail for about $4 a cup in Nashville in 2021, although I have paid as much as $15 for very special offerings. Whole beans sell for $18 and up for twelve ounces (down from the standard pound that many of us grew up with). While the baseline New York futures price for standard-grade washed arabicas averaged $1.11 per pound in 2020, exclusive micro-lots of Third Wave–quality green beans routinely wholesaled for more than $20 per pound.[11] A growing number of exclusive lots of green coffee have sold for more than $100 a pound, a ceiling first broken in 2007 by a storied Gesha varietal from Hacienda La Esmeralda in Panama. In 2012, the El Injerto Mocha (an heirloom varietal originally from Yemen) sold for a record $500.50 a pound.

A wide range of variables contribute to the taste of brewed coffee, including growing conditions, freshness (after roasting), grind size, water quality, and temperature at consumption. Unlike wine, for example, the material properties of coffee are significantly transformed at both ends of the supply chain: through agricultural techniques and processing at the farm and through roasting and brewing on the consumption side.

Such processing significantly affects flavor and quality—the roast is as important as the terroir in producing a particular cup profile—and these moments of material transformation provide the opportunity to incorporate intangible values into pricing. For our purposes, I will focus on a few key factors that contribute to material determinations of Third Wave quality.

Varietals and Terroir

Second Wave coffees are virtually all arabicas (of the species *Coffea arabica,* not Robusta, *Coffea canephora*), a sign of general quality. Third Wave coffees are also overwhelming arabicas, but they are further differentiated by subspecies varietal (such as Gesha, Bourbon, or SL-28), each with its own flavor characteristics and stories of origin. Third Wave coffees place great emphasis on geographic origins and the tastes imparted by terroir, which, when combined with a particular varietal can produce a range of unique flavor combinations. Such particulars set these small lots of coffee apart from not just the bulk commodity market, but also the large Second Wave market for specialty-grade coffee. Making coffees more unique and singular pushes up prices for the most sought-after lots.

Processing Method

Washed arabicas have long been the standard-bearer for quality, with the coffee fruit de-pulped and washed immediately following harvest. In contrast, "natural" processing—in which the cherries decompose on the beans—was historically associated with low-end bulk coffee from Brazil and East Africa. Yet Third Wave roasters and consumers have rediscovered the virtues of natural processing, which imparts a surprisingly fruity acidity to the cup. Now, the most sophisticated farmers are experimenting with new processing methods to produce particularly vivid flavors. These include variations of "honey" processing, a method in which cherries decompose for varying lengths of times before washing. The coffee that won Brazil's 2017 Cup of Excellence competition (and sold for $130.20 per pound) underwent a thirty-six-hour anaerobic fermentation process before pulping and drying. The judges gave it a score of 92.3.

Roasting

Green coffee beans, no matter the varietal or processing method, have a vegetative taste. Roasting is required to produce the flavors associated with coffee, and its practice is a mix of technology and art. Heating the beans induces a number of chemical reactions that produce gases, which build up pressure contained by an especially strong cell wall structure.[12] Maillard reactions start around 140°C, as sugars interact with amino acids to produce the flavor and aroma compounds we associate with roasted coffee. At about 175°C begins the "first crack," which is what it sounds like: the bean cracking open. At around 188°C, sucrose starts melting and then caramelizing. As the beans roast, acidity levels drop and bitterness increases. By adjusting temperatures and duration, roasters emphasize certain flavors and mute others. The quality of Third Wave coffees depends a lot on the artful balance of acidity and bitterness, which can enhance natural sweetness, and most are roasted on the lighter end of the spectrum to highlight the fruity and floral notes. The most common roast level for Third Wave coffee is a medium-light "city roast" (at about 218°C), which pulls out the widest range of traits associated with particular beans. Dark roasting can overwhelm subtle flavors—one starts to taste the roast more than the coffee—and is strategically used by large roasters, such as Starbucks, to impose consistency on beans.

Brewing Method (or Extraction Technique)

Particular coffees are often paired with recommended brewing methods, most a version of the simple pour-over (which is what it sounds like: slowly pouring 93°C water over ground coffee in a filter). Variations on the pour-over are identified by device brand names, including Chemex, V60, and the Kalita Wave, each producing slightly different flavor profiles that are calibrated with grind size and pour speed. Usually there is an initial quick pour, after which the grinds are allowed to "bloom" (releasing carbon dioxide) for about thirty seconds, followed by two more pours over about three minutes. While these low-tech methods are assumed to produce the cleanest cup, there is also increasing experimentation with automated systems that mimic a hand pour.

THIRD WAVE VALUES

The demographics of Third Wave professionals skew male and white, although increasingly there are exceptions. Most of the roasters and baristas I interviewed attended at least some college, but the field notably attracts a lot of autodidacts and those who take nontraditional career paths to pursue interests inside and outside of work. Even in the lower paid, hourly positions, many Third Wave workers spend at least some spare time reading about new market trends and findings in coffee research, even getting together at conventions and competitions to discuss and debate the finer points of fine coffee. For many, this a life project as much as a business. I find their passion and commitment compelling. "You have to know *why* you are doing things, or it is meaningless." I was listening to Nick Scott, a roaster at Parisi Coffee in Kansas City, explain why coffee was more than a job: "If you can't say *why* you are doing what you are doing, then your work is meaningless. I want to turn people on to those crazy flavors I'm discovering. I want to share what good coffee can be. That's why I do what I do."

The ethos of the Third Wave coffee world is explicitly oriented around "quality." It is seen not just as a competitive advantage but also as a moral touchstone, widely accepted as a virtuous end, an intrinsic good. Sarah Besky shows how pursuit of quality can be seen as "a way of liberating select consumers, conscientious retailers, and even some laborers from the entrenched systems of provision in which they find themselves."[13] One roaster told me, "We are all seeking quality," a phrase I heard again and again and one that seeks to reframe the competitive market as a common project, uniting diverse efforts. To some extent this is posturing, but for many this is a deeply held and felt "commitment to the fidelity of an Idea," as Alain Badiou phrases it: a sustained engagement with an ideal that gives meaning to individual lives and becomes intertwined with identities in ways that extend beyond market relations.[14] In coffee, we find such fidelity in the craft of roasters and aficionados searching out the highest-quality coffees and spreading the word about the virtues of drinking good coffee. Theirs is a project reflecting an interrelated set of values: dedication to craft and quality, regard for authenticity and distinctiveness, and commitment to relationships and community.

I do not mean to paint too rosy a picture of the Third Wave coffee business—it can be as cutthroat as any, and it is imbricated in structures of deep inequality. At the same time, for many on the roasting and consumer side, this aspirational rhetoric goes beyond just virtue signaling. Over and over, Third Wave professionals I talked to described theirs as a larger project of "making coffee better" by producing higher quality in the cup and improving equity in trade relations. Michaele Weissman describes early Third Wave pioneers as a small group who developed a passion for artisanal coffees before it was clear that there was money to be made, and became renowned for their singular focus on quality, brutal travel schedules, and ability to find the most exotic beans.[15] They talk about coffee with a passion and zeal that goes deeper than financial gain, driven by a devotion to quality and a commitment to growers. Some made small fortunes as the market boomed.

Outsiders might find it easy to be cynical about the high margins, rarefied language, and hipster styles of the Third Wave movement. Nick, for example, looks the part, his worn jeans and flannel shirt overshadowed by an impressive beard and artful tattoos. And he loves coffee. His is the almost missionary zeal of many who work in specialty coffee, showing commitment to a project that goes beyond just making a living. While this chapter critically examines the ways quality conventions in coffee are socially constructed, that should not denigrate the sincerity of the actors or the values they pursue. Shaping quality conventions involves a back and forth between enthusiasts and entrepreneurs, artisans and traders, most of whom see themselves as involved in a virtuous pursuit of excellence by promoting a quality product.[16] Like the artisanal cheesemaking Heather Paxson describes, the craft of coffee—perhaps the essence of all craft—is in artfully resolving tensions between conceptual ideals and material realities.[17] For many coffee professionals, this is a moral as well as an economic practice. Those like Nick want to make a positive contribution to the world of coffee, and to the world. They are aficionados earnestly trying to learn about and experiment with coffee, to share their sensory discoveries with others, and to promote quality over quantity while supporting more direct and just value chains. And to make some money if they can.

In chasing novelty and exotic flavors, Third Wave roasters seek to establish direct relationships with remote producers. Both Second and Third Wave marketing promotes a romanticized view of provenance, often including farmers' names and details about their lives. Third Wave coffees are usually "direct sourced," an intentionally vague term that implies a relationship between roaster and grower, although these are often mediated by exporters, importers, and cooperatives.[18] Molly Doane shows that "relationship coffee" allows consumers to feel a connection to production, but one that may bear little resemblance to how that relationship is felt by farmers.[19] Still, by personalizing the backstory, such narratives bolster the de-commodified image of micro-lot coffees. They create "cognitive proximity," virtual and vicarious connections to growers, in order to signal to consumers their commitment to alternative food ethics of smaller-scale production, sustainability, and direct relationships.[20] One study found that simply identifying a grower by name on packaging increases retail value by more than 20 percent.[21]

In late 2016 the Counter Culture website featured coffee from Finca El Puente in Honduras (twelve ounces for $17.25 plus shipping). Their description reads, "We met Moisés Herrera and Marysabel Caballero—the couple that runs Finca El Puente—in 2005. Since then, they have become like family and inspire us every year." (The coffee, a washed arabica grown at 1400 to 1653 masl, is described as a "mostly Catuai-variety lot lush with notes of Concord grape accented by a brown-sugar sweetness that finishes with a crisp, toasted nut character.") Around the same time Blue Bottle offered a "limited release" edition of a Honduras Guaimaca Miravalle coffee. The price was $12—for six ounces. The farmer, Don Miro, is described as exceptionally devoted to his coffee; harvested from high-altitude cloud forest land, "his mature coffee trees produce vibrant red fruit with dense seeds" that take longer to dry. Blue Bottle says the resulting quality is worth the extra cost: its "fragrant tea-like acidity" is punctuated by "orange blossoms and a syrupy mouth-feel." Such provenance and a sense of personal connection to a producer is a key element of de-commodified value.

Hanes Motsinger writes that small specialty roasters often "represent themselves as bearers of morality and social good through discourses of partnership, responsibility, and sustainability"; at the same time, as Paige West argues, such approaches usually elide structural problems. West describes how coffee shops play on various sorts of symbolic values to "infuse the coffee beans with a kind of veneer of meaning that connects the beans to the ways the consumers imagine themselves." She documents how images of producer "poverty and primitivity" are used to add value to coffee, with consumers imaging that they are contributing to farmers' dreams of a better life. She concludes that "with certified and single-origin coffees the images used to sell the products are also manipulated to make consumers feel as if they are making other people's lives better through the act of buying." Customers at the coffee shops West studied are mostly still learning about coffee quality, and they vaguely associate it with their imaginations of places like Papua New Guinea or Guatemala. The social narrative of exotic Otherness that traders attach would seem much less fungible than flavor descriptions, but it can become a blur for the distant consumer.[22] Through this affective side of the economy, cultural, moral, symbolic, and emotional values attach to the materiality of the beans and are used to add economic value, most of which does not reach the producers featured so prominently in marketing.

LEARNING TO TASTE QUALITY

For most who try them, it is clear that Third Wave coffees are different from run-of-the-mill joe. A whole range of subtle flavors come out in the clean, smooth, balanced profile of a well-brewed coffee. There is an objective, material distinction: they simply taste different, and in ways that must be based on molecular variances. Flavor, the overall sensory experience of food, results from the interaction of taste and smell. Taste refers to the perception of soluble compounds on the tongue activating receptors to identify sweet, salty, bitter, sour, and umami. With food and drink, we perceive aroma when volatile compounds (aromatics) travel retronasally from the mouth to the olfactory bulb, a bundle of receptors that can identify many thousands of unique molecular combinations that we perceive as smells.[23] But the biology can only tell us so much.[24] The values and labels we assign to particular tastes are learned; while we may realize this intellectually, they become embodied in a way that makes them seem natural.[25]

New tastes are "discovered," with some catching on among a cognoscenti and then, to the extent that they become stylish, learned by others. In the process, a common vocabulary gets established, one permeated with class and cultural associations. Research on quality conventions in global food chains illustrates how "different" can become "better" through turning subjective judgments into objective measurements.[26] In the case of high-end coffee, those who successfully define what "quality" is (researchers, coffee aficionados, marketers, trade associations) are able to translate symbolic and imaginative values into material gains.

A loosely coordinated network of institutions emerged in the 1990s to research, promote, and standardize Second and Third Wave coffees. At the center is the Specialty Coffee Association, which was founded in 1982 and hired its first full-time director (the famed Ted Lingle) in 1991.[27] Since 1989 the SCA has hosted the industry's most important trade show. The SCA's research arm, the Coffee Quality Institute, was founded in 1995 to promote uniformity of standards and quality benchmarks. The Coffee Quality Institute runs the industry standard cupping certification program (Q Grader) based on the SCA's one-hundred-point scale and flavor wheel. Founded in 2012 and loosely associated with Texas A&M University, World Coffee Research is funded by many of the same industry players that are behind the SCA and conducts research in the agronomy and organoleptic properties of coffee (including the *Sensory Lexicon* used by the SCA in building its flavor wheel). In 2014 the University of California at Davis launched a new interdisciplinary Coffee Center, combining agronomy, sensory science, and market research. The center developed from the research interest of chemical engineer Bill Ristenpart, and it was nurtured and supported by the SCA. The Alliance for Coffee Excellence, founded in 1999, holds annual Cup of Excellence competitions in producing countries and auctions off the highest-rated beans, often for significant premiums. The auctions have become a benchmark in the Third Wave quest for rarity and quality. These organizations are creating an infrastructure of valuation, developing conceptual devices and measurement apparatuses that frame market spaces and shape mental frameworks of value.

Cupping Protocols

Making the fine distinctions of taste and smell in coffee cuppings and competitions requires special training. Coffee tasting is a craft in that it requires mastery of a field that combines the intellectual aspects with the material and sensory; this must be built up over time, with the knowledge becoming tacit, embodied. Coffee cupping, like wine tasting, is a creative art, requiring both a perceptual sensitivity to the components of a taste (and smell) and the poetic ability to translate those into evocative adjectives. Until recently, cupping descriptors were mostly limited to broad attributes, such as "bold," "balanced," "bitter," or perhaps "elegant." With the rise of Second and Third Wave coffees, and the formation of the Specialty Coffee Association, cupping was transformed from a quirky talent into a formal skill, grounded in scientific replicability, that could be taught. In 1984 the SCA published Ted Lingle's *Coffee Cuppers' Handbook,* which integrated chemistry and sensory science into new cupping protocols designed "to make as objective an evaluation of the coffee's quality attributes as humanly possible."[28] Lingle's book marked a watershed in specialty coffee cupping, and, with a few modifications, the protocols he proposed remain the standard today. They provide the basis for the SCA's one-hundred-point scale, which is built from rating ten quality attributes: fragrance/aroma, flavor, aftertaste, acidity, body, uniformity, balance, clean cup, sweetness, and overall. The first five are based on the physical chemistry of coffee while the last five are grounded in sensory perceptions; the "overall" attribute is the only that allows for a cupper's more subjective appraisal. Some or all of these attribute scores may be represented as a spider graph (figure 4). While there are a few different cupping protocols, the SCA's one-hundred-point scale is the industry standard, with the added virtue of echoing Robert Parker's influential wine ratings.

Based on Lingle's work and the SCA cupping protocols, the Coffee Quality Institute developed and administers the Q Grader program. Being certified as a Q Grader is a badge of honor in the Third Wave coffee world, and in 2017 there were about 3500 around the world. It often takes years to pass the various tests of knowledge and skill, and some aspirants hire coaches to help them train. Successful applicants have to pass five "triangulation cuppings" to differentiate more than ninety coffees as well as complete other tests, such as identifying the addition of a specific acid (acetic, citric, malic, lactic, or phenol) to identical cups of coffee (see figure 5). It is a grueling and rigorous process, converting subjective impressions into replicable objective measures. Through such techniques, great care is taken to align the symbolic and the material, to

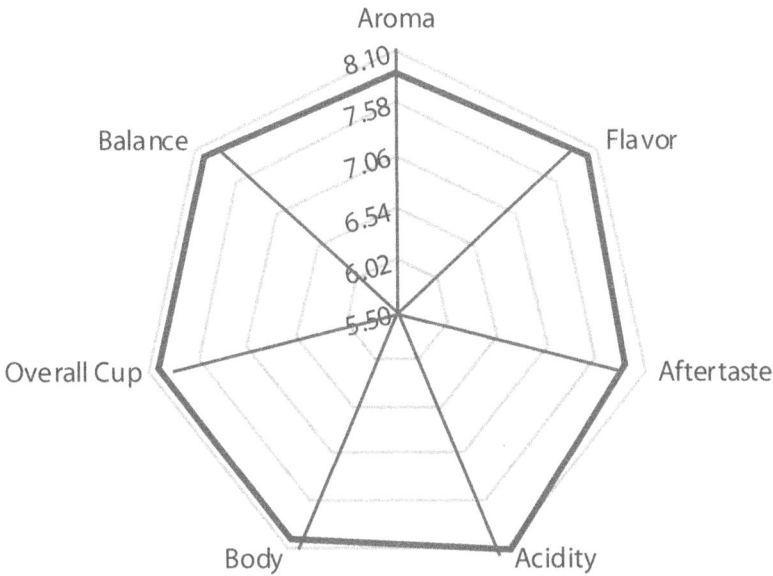

Figure 4. Spider graph of coffee cupping results, scoring 86.0.

ground conceptual values in science and solid, quantifiable metrics to the extent possible. This is central to the Third Wave notions of authenticity and legitimacy: getting cuppers to agree—at least most of the time and within a small margin of error—on a formal scale (while expressing their more idiosyncratic variability in the descriptors). Working with its Coffee Quality Institute, the SCA goes to great lengths to bolster the scientific credentials of its classifications and tasting protocols, stressing that they are documenting objective, measurable differences. The ultimate goal is to "understand which molecules in a coffee are connected to which flavors."[29] For now, they settle for replicability, creating a standard based not on one person's tastes, so that a cupping in Nairobi or Guatemala will produce the same results as one in New York or Nashville. It is a remarkably effective system, resulting in multijudge competition panels having little internal variation in scores.

Aaron Duckworth, a Q Grader and award-winning barista, observes that "you have to learn to taste coffee—some people are naturals, like

Figure 5. Triangulated cupping at the Anacafé headquarters, Guatemala City.

at music, but everybody has to learn to taste, to identify and distinguish the flavors, and that's not easy."[30] In a coffee cupping course, one first learns the basic protocol (let the grounds form a crust for 3 minutes, break it, and inhale to judge the fragrance/aroma score) and etiquette (slurping and spitting are encouraged). The taste of coffee changes significantly with temperature. One rookie mistake is drinking one's coffee too hot; it is most full bodied and flavorful around 40° to 50°C. In a formal judging, cuppers taste the coffee first at around 70°C, again as it cools toward 40°C, and finally at around 20°C. In one coffee

championship I guest judged, the barista described the Ethiopian varietal he was brewing as presenting "fresh jasmine undertones, with a
hint of caramelized sugar, and then tart black mulberry" at around
65°C and then metamorphosing into "lichi, 90% dark chocolate, and
jasmine undertones" when cooled to body temperature. Lo and behold,
those were the flavors I tasted, although I cannot say how much his
words influenced my framing of the sensory experience.

In a cupping course, novices are coached to identify and label certain
flavors, gently guided in the "right" direction. When I learned to cup, I
would tentatively identify a flavor (pomegranate?) and the master cupper might nudge me in a particular direction ("perhaps it is actually
raspberry ... or what do you think?"). While I might taste a distinct flavor in the cup, I was often unable to articulate it until prompted with the
proper vocabulary. I was never told what to taste, but guided in what to
taste for and nudged toward a common lexicon. More and more cuppers
are now using tablet-based electronic judging forms that come with
drop-down menus to suggest descriptors. In these ways, one becomes
trained to look out for certain flavors and to internalize a way of categorizing coffee. Such practices create the norms of Third Wave quality,
with its measures of excellence that reward virtuous practice. They also
create social divisions, with insiders who command the esoteric knowledge and outsiders who do not.

Taste Descriptors

Roasters and retailers rely on numerical metrics and the intersubjective
reliability of grading when buying bulk quantities—at least to make the
first cut, then they will usually sample their finalists. But at the very
high end of the scale, the numbers must be supplemented with more
evocative descriptors. The language used to talk about Third Wave coffee is inspired by the wine world, with exotic and evocative descriptors:
"Orange blossom, white tea, syrupy"; "Tangerine, brown sugar, lime";
"Caramel, nutty, round." The convention is to include three single-word

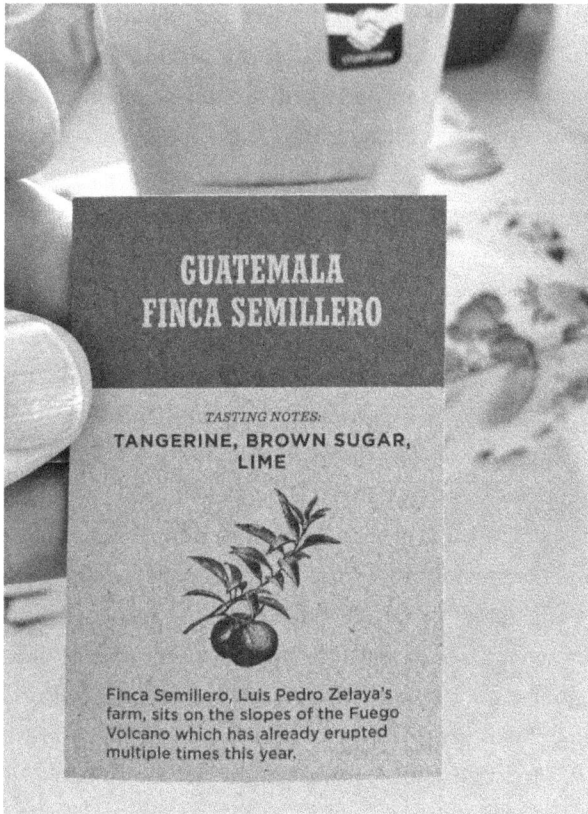

Figure 6. Descriptor card from Stumptown for Finca El
Semillero Beans.

descriptors on a label, and descriptors include specific flavors as well as a
range of sensory adjectives (smooth, juicy, creamy, complex, deep, clear,
clean, etc.). Cupping notes and taste descriptors help guide consumers to
certain flavor profiles, and these are often supplemented with evocative
biographical notes (figure 6).

In wine, sensory descriptions were revolutionized in the 1980s by
the adoption of Ann C. Noble's "aroma wheel," which established a
common vocabulary and level of specificity beyond vague adjectives
such as "velvety" or "smooth." Based on that example, the SCA worked

with researchers at the University of California at Davis and Kansas State University to develop the Coffee Taster's Flavor Wheel. First published in 2015, the chart offers a range of descriptors coming from "the frontiers of sensory science methods and analyses." The methodology is described using specialist technical language ("an Agglomerative Hierarchical Cluster [AHC] analysis was performed on the results from the sorting exercise to group the flavor attributes into different categories [or clusters] represented visually by a dendrogram").

With descriptors ranging from chamomile, rose, and jasmine to petroleum, skunk, and pipe tobacco, the flavor wheel is a remarkable study in the art and science of taste, an attempt to classify and categorize an ultimately subjective sensory experience through poetry and botany (see figure 7). Many coffee cuppers say that, in practice, they use the flavor wheel as a reference to help think about flavors but not as a strict categorization framework.[31] Many will work by first identifying a broad flavor (perhaps something malty), then they will systematically think through specific examples, comparing them with the recent sensory memory: beer (no), malted milk (no), these are too malty ... something more subtle ... gingerbread, perhaps.

Cupping is an art of improvisational practice. One must creatively engage an existing framework in a way that resonates with others' sensory connotations. Descriptors should be "projective," resonant with others' sensory experiences and memories. Tasters can stretch their metaphors and analogies, but only so far, for the plant's biochemical properties produce similar intersubjective sensory experiences. Nashville roaster and barista Tom Eisenbraun studied English in college at the University of Georgia, and, like many in the Third Wave world, forwent the usual college-graduate career path to pursue his life passion in coffee. In assigning flavor profiles, he calls on his love of poetry and prose; he sees it like writing a haiku, an act of creative expression exercised within the restricted structure of the descriptor trilogy. Eisenbraun adds that while poetic language is powerful, it is important not to let its seductions slip into affectation. Tasters have to keep in

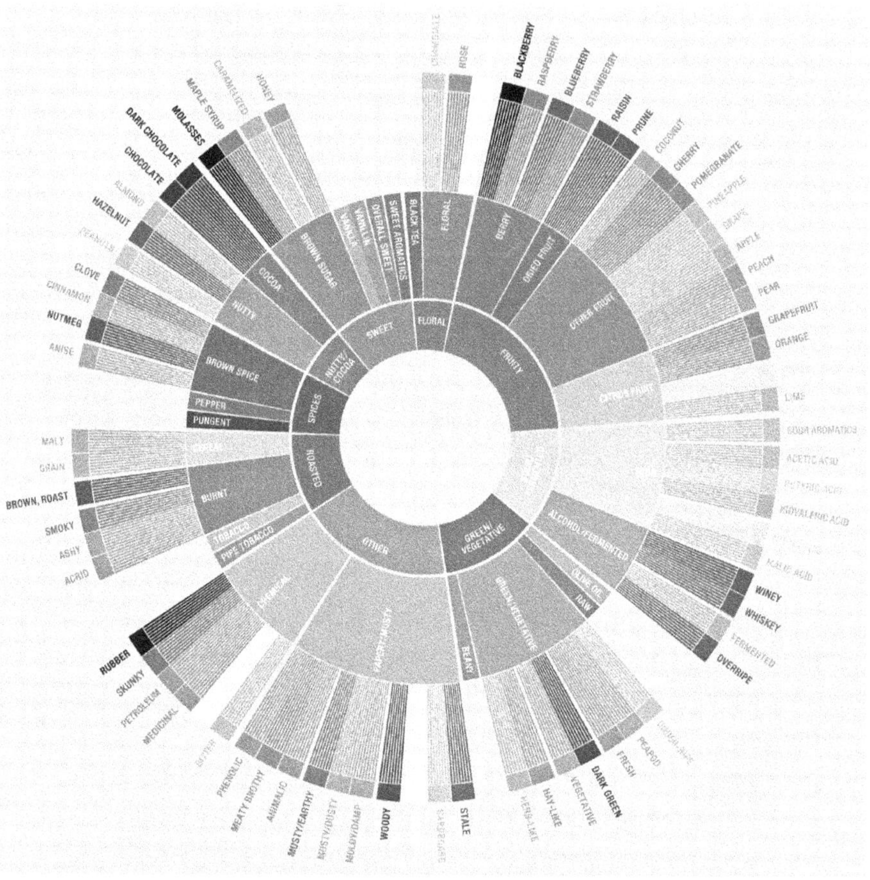

Figure 7. The Coffee Taster's Flavor Wheel by the Specialty Coffee Association, World Coffee Research, and University of California at Davis.

mind, he says, that the goal is to speak in a way that consumers can actually understand and to which they can relate.[32]

In terms of descriptors, even with a common vocabulary, there can be idiosyncratic differences and variability in judging intensity. Thus, there is a need for common reference points to ground the SCA flavor wheel. In order to calibrate the flavor wheel categories on a scale of intensity from zero to fifteen, World Coffee Research published the first-ever *Sensory Lexicon* for coffee in 2016. The lexicon provides a categorization of tastes that is descriptive, quantifiable, and, for those trained in its use, replicable: two trained tasters anywhere in the world should give the same score for any attribute based on a standard protocol. To give an example, the lexicon's calibration (on a ten-point scale) for honey (a "sweet, light brown, slightly spicy aromatic") reads:

REFERENCE: Busy Bee[™] Pure Clover Honey
  Aroma: 6.0
    Dissolve 1 tablespoon honey in 250 milliliters of hot water. Serve ¼ cup in a medium snifter. Cover.
  Flavor: 6.5
    Dissolve 1 tablespoon honey in 250 milliliters of hot water. Serve in a 1-ounce cup. Cover with a plastic lid.

Cup of Excellence

The rise of Third Wave coffees is neatly captured in the philosophy and market making of the successful Cup of Excellence program, which aims to reward farmers for producing high-quality coffee. The first Cup of Excellence competition took place in Brazil in 1999. It was the culmination of efforts by economically liberal elements of the International Coffee Organization to offer a market-friendly alternative to Fair Trade premiums and to counter efforts at reviving quotas. Building on the work of national coffee associations, such as Guatemala's Anacafé, the idea was to replace the charity premiums of Fair Trade with quality premiums based on objective measures, and to reward the small and medium-sized farmers producing the highest quality coffee—an apparent neoliberal meritocracy, with all of the promise and peril that entails.

In their quest for objective evaluation, Cup of Excellence competitions have taken cupping standardization to the next level, with each coffee blindly evaluated by several different cuppers. Only coffees that get consistently high scores advance in the competition; each country will have twenty-five to thirty-five ranked coffees (out of hundreds of

Figure 8. Cup of Excellence descriptors word cloud.

entrants), and these are sold through a live online auction. Prices for the top ten coffees in the 2016 Guatemala competition, with cupping scores from eighty-nine to ninety-two, ranged from $10 to $53 a pound. Bradley Wilson and colleagues examine the factors that contributed most to Cup of Excellence winners in Central America over a number of years. They found that the quality score is by far the most important attribute, followed by the number of descriptors (e.g., grapefruit, maple syrup, smooth) used by judges, and then altitude (the higher the altitude, the better the coffee).[33] Terroir plays a role, too, and Cup of Excellence–certified coffees (not just the winners) from Guatemala get an average premium of $3.33 per pound because of their country of origin. Nobert Wilson and colleagues have found that Cup of Excellence prices are largely determined by a lot's symbolic attributes.[34] Figure 8 represents the descriptors of coffees auctioned in Cup of Excellence competitions in eleven countries between 2004 and 2015.[35]

Cup of Excellence protocols are strict, enforcing a particular sort of merit to what is "in the cup." This builds on the Q Grader certification program, which in turn uses the SCA's one-hundred-point scale and

World Coffee Research's *Sensory Lexicon*. Working together and in concert with Third Wave roasters and retailers and journalists, these devices and conventions have made an effort to establish new taste criteria and to ground those value judgments in objective measurements. In this way, the means of symbolic production can work to make "different" into "better," employing science (agronomy, geography, climatology) to create categories of "objective" differences, upon which are built the cupping profiles, and values are assigned to these profiles on a scale that corresponds to price.

Third Wave coffee experts emphasize that quality is measurable—there is pride and trust in the objectivity of the blind cupping, the epitome of meritocratic process. At the same time, these conventions constitute a specialized knowledge that marks a certain kind of cultural capital. In coffee, there are objective empirical differences that we could trace to a multitude of compounds ("more complex than wine," the in-crowd likes to remind initiates) associated with particular varietals and terroirs. In recent years, the fruity acidity of natural processed coffees has become more valued; juicy is a frequent descriptor, and I heard one coffee described recently as like "angel cake with strawberry jam." In the language of the tastemakers, new flavors are "discovered," but, of course, we learn the differences that matter. Emil Holland and colleagues examine how quality gets determined through analyzing a specific negotiation between a grower and coffee importer; they conclude that tasting is always contingent, having to be constantly recalibrated in terms of intersubjective consensus. Consumers, in turn, must learn the relevant cultural and social fields of value to appreciate the evolving standards of fine coffee.[36]

TRANSLATING THIRD WAVE VALUES

Coffee enthusiasts and professionals have developed a vocabulary linked to a system of values and valuations with corresponding numeric scales and metrics, but their work is largely behind the scenes, insiders talking to other insiders. This gets translated into the consumer market by Third Wave coffee shops and internet operations. As with Nashville's Barista Parlor, most Third Wave stores stress the artisanal quality of their coffee and the virtues of particular terroir.

Baristas in Third Wave coffee shops often act as cultural intermediaries, at once seeking to meet their customer's wishes while also pushing them to try new things, to identify, and then hopefully desire, new flavors. Patricia Boaventura and colleagues show how the Third Wave represents a shift toward value co-creation, in which consumers actively participate in the value they pay for; in their analysis, consumers see buying and consuming as helping them support symbolic/moral/affective goals. John Manzo's study of Third Wave coffee shops illustrates the creative back-and-forth between baristas and customers that helps shape what is considered desirable.[37] Such dialectic encounters between desire and profit (the consumer having an idea about their preferences that is honed and given form and direction by the expert vendor) constitute the way symbolic value worlds are created and sustained at the grassroots level.

Tastes for high-end coffees are created by roasters and retailers through creative improvisation that calls on the emergent standards for measuring coffee quality. Baristas I have interviewed report that one of the most common customer requests is for a coffee with "low acidity" (other frequent customer descriptors include "bold" and "clean"). In fact, acidity is a key component of all coffee profiles. What the customers likely mean is that they prefer a coffee that is well balanced rather than low in acidity, a point on which they can be gently educated by a barista. In such ways (the consumer having an idea about their preferences that is honed and given form and direction by the expert), the market is constructed through dialectic encounters between desire and profit.

Third Wave tastemakers work to teach the market what to value and are constantly seeking out new markers of distinction for their brands and their coffees. In recent years there has been a move away from the deep chocolate flavors of Bourbon and toward the more citrus and floral notes of Maragogype beans and the bright complexities of Mocha and

Gesha varietals. Roasters are seeking the ever more exotic, as it is oddity and novelty that is most valued. As I was writing this, I received a promotional email for a Red Gesha offered by Stumptown with "juicy notes of watermelon and rose water with a hard candy sweetness." It is difficult for smallholding farmers to keep up with market tastes that shift so quickly, especially when they have to make decisions about what varietals to plant four or five years out.

As Third Wave retailing matures, we see slightly less emphasis on the narrative details of provenance and more on the sensory properties and the art of blending and roasting. The stress on blends may correspond to the pace of a roaster's expansion plans (as blends offer much more flexibility in supply chains). Paige West shows how importers distinguish particular coffees from the others on offer in terms of cup profile ("good acidity," "chocolaty and nutty"), and at the same time how they must be prepared to "make an alternative seem commensurable" in case a substitute is needed. One Hamburg importer describes the art of uniquely differentiating lots (e.g., Papua New Guinea's distinct fruity flavor from the bit of fermentation that happens when the beans are transported from remote highland plots to wet mills) while also needing to have backups with similar characteristics ("this Panamanian has a similar profile … "). They work hard to singularize the product, but also to leave the flexibility to substitute another coffee when needed, undermining the producer's market power.[38] In addition, many Third Wave coffee shops are chasing new flavors through technology and barista artisanry, with herbal infusions, coffee cocktails, nitrous cold brews, and a growing range of innovations. All of this diminishes the importance of terroir and the power of farmers.

MATERIAL AND SYMBOLIC MEANS
OF PRODUCTION

The rarefied price of high-end coffee is justified through the artful translation of qualities and connotations across symbolic and material value worlds. This is to say that the values of terroir and authenticity are created not just by the material conditions of the farms but also by the narratives of roasters, baristas, and tastemakers. It is the interplay of material use values and more affective and symbolic values—and how these come together in the meaningful and sensual act of consuming a craft coffee—that justify Third Wave prices.

Most in the specialty coffee world emphasize that the high prices paid for a Third Wave coffee is all about what is "in the cup." Their notion of quality strives for solidity and objectivity, with tasting certifications and blind cuppings. Yet tastes in coffee are always changing, especially in this market, where the objective is to sell a de-commoditized product, something singular, unusual, and unique. In pursuit of an ever-changing sense of quality, Third Wave organizations go to great lengths to make evaluations as objective as possible, to ground them in science and inter-subjective replicability. Yet quality itself is a social construction, an agreed-upon contrivance, with the devices of qualification (protocols, scales of measurement, intersubjective replicability) producing and reinforcing certain conventions. As Sarah Besky writes, "Quality is constantly being reproduced and rediscovered in fields, factories, laboratories, tasting rooms, and auction halls."[39]

To justify their price, specialty coffees have to carry symbolic values that distinguish them from other coffees—partly through cupping descriptors and numerical scores, partly by the lore that builds up around particular areas and farms. A big part of the economic value added in the Third Wave coffee market comes from the symbolic values produced through provenance narratives, often featuring farmers' personal histories, as told by roasters and baristas. Controlling the material means of production was at the heart of the distribution of power in a classic industrializing world system marked by core and periphery relations. In mature capitalist markets, however, needs and desires have to be manufactured along with their objects. In such contexts the greatest gains come not from controlling the *material* means of production but rather from influencing the narrative construction of *symbolic* value worlds that orient paths of desire and demand.[40]

Roasters and coffee shops, the SCA and its corporate partners, and coffee trendsetters around the world have built a system of coffee metrics and descriptors that anchors valuations and price; this symbolic valuation machine is deployed alongside the cultural capital provided by narratives of romanticized provenance and self-improvement; and apparatuses such as the SCA Flavor Wheel and the accompanying lexicon go to great lengths to ground their symbolic value creation in objective metrics. The bulk of surplus value accumulation takes place in the Global North, allowed not so much by control over productive capital as the ability to translate qualities across value worlds. Thus, we find coffee aficionados chasing the most unusual flavors, the most unique characteristics in the cup.

While apparently rewarding objective "quality," these fickle preferences structurally disadvantage smallholding Maya coffee farmers in Guatemala, as I detail in subsequent chapters. Maya farmers also attach moral imaginations for a better life and a better world to coffee. They may be blessed with the auspicious geographic and climatic conditions to grow high-end coffee, but they largely lack the social capital needed to translate their material endowments, technical expertise, and cultural capital into economic gain. In the value worlds of affluent Third Wave consumers, market-setting power rests with those controlling the symbolic and imaginative means of production.

At this point, some deeper background on coffee's origins and classifications is in order. The next chapter looks at the ways coffee consumption arose alongside scientific and commercial forms of classification, and how it contributed to the rise of liberal and neoliberal approaches to commerce.

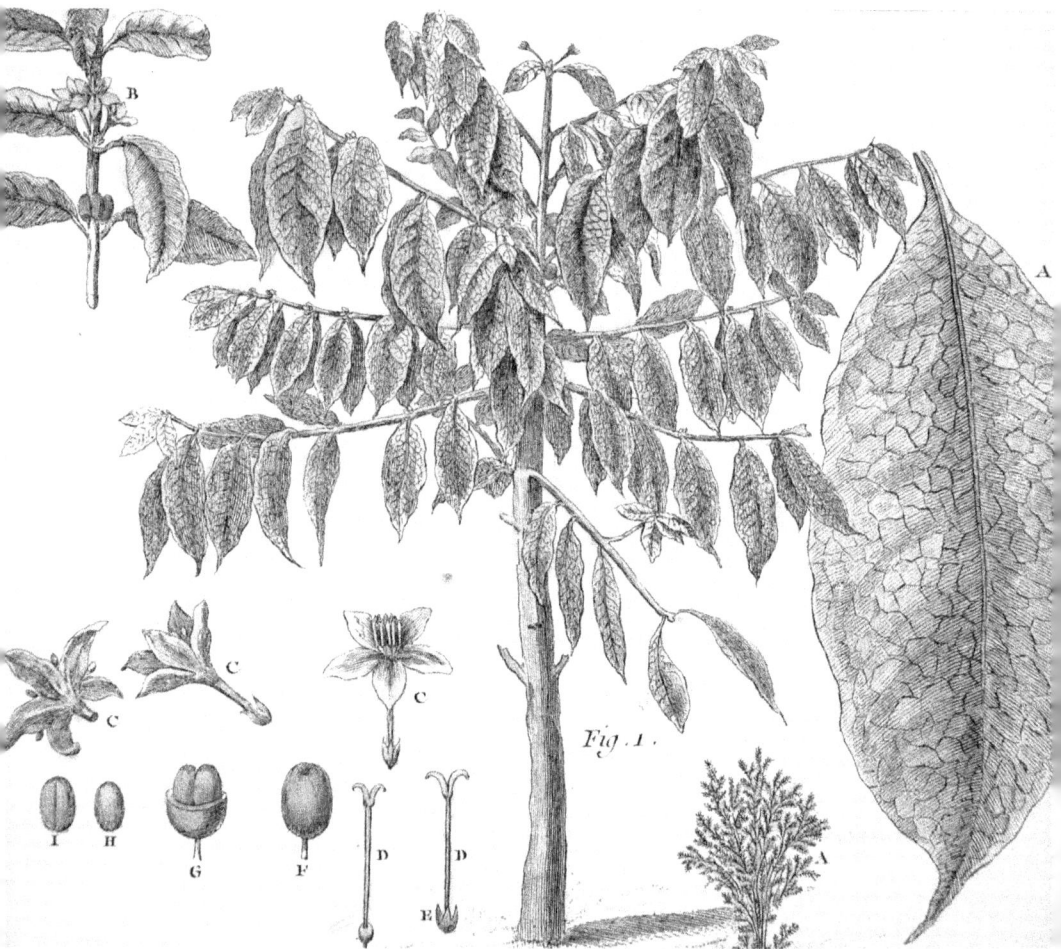

Figure 9. Botanical drawing of *Coffea arabica* from Diderot's 1751 *Encyclopédie*.

CHAPTER TWO

Plant Biology, Capitalist Trade, and the Colonial Histories of *Coffea arabica*

Carl Linnaeus got it wrong when attributing the geographic origins of *Coffea arabica*. It was 1737, the heady days of the Enlightenment, and the Swedish botanist was living outside Amsterdam, frequenting the botanical gardens and working on what would become his magnum opus, *Systema Naturae*. Dutch coffeehouses at the time, like those in London and Hamburg, were buzzing with radical ideas about science and progress, assertions that knowledge should be grounded in reason and measurable data rather than in faith, and stories of the great wealth to be made in global trade. Across Europe, a set of values was coalescing in coffeehouse debates around science, rationality, progress, democracy, and trade—ideas that Michel-Rolph Trouillot calls "North Atlantic universals" because, while claiming neutrality and universality, they prescribe a particular view of how things should be based on "cultural assumptions ranging from what it means to be a human being to the proper relationship between humans and the natural world."[1] Despite their lofty language, these Enlightened ideals were built on the cruelties of colonialism, the commodification of human bodies, and the establishment a system of power relations that continues to shape global inequalities.[2]

A key part of the modernist project involved categorizing the world into discreet units that could be measured, ordered, and compared—a first step in taming the chaos of nature and harnessing it toward human ends. While purporting to simply reflect reality, such categorizations created new realities, establishing cultural facts such as "race," the nation-state, and the "economy." For his part, Linnaeus developed a system of organizing the biological world with taxonomic designations based on phenotypic similarities—including an odious racial hierarchy of humans. Even with the rise of genetic understandings of evolutionary relationships, Linnaeus's nomenclature lives on, with many casual errors of naming ensconced in everyday practice, as with coffee (order: Rubiales; family: Rubiaceae; genus: Coffea; species: Arabica).[3] The mistake with coffee is understandable. In the early 1700s, most Europeans associated coffee with Arabia: coffee had been introduced to Europe through contact with the Muslim world; the port of Mocha held a monopoly on the global coffee trade; and most production came from the Yemeni highlands, assumed to be the ur-source of the plant. "Mocha" was the benchmark designation for quality that would have been familiar to Amsterdammers of the time. Given this, and with all those plants to classify, we can see why Linnaeus made the Arabian attribution. But, in fact, coffee traces its origins to the highlands of Ethiopia.

Classification schemes, Linnaeus's taxonomy included, are conceptual devices that encode value judgments, privileging some traits over others to create a seemingly homogenous group. Within categories, individual variation and nuance are elided to produce a useful, if imperfect, representation that helps people and states conceptually manage the complexity of life.[4] They also create artificial boundaries that break up the continuums of the natural world—such as the divide between green and blue, or the border between your land and mine. While often treated as objective reflections of reality, categories and classification help create the reality we perceive, framing the way people conceptualize and act in the world.

We may view taxonomies and other such classification schemes as sorts of "judgment devices" or "calculative devices," socio-cognitive conventions that frame relationships between things (or people or ideas).

Such devices set up particular comparisons and choices, as with spreadsheets, grocery store shelves, and online platforms.[5] Markets themselves, both physical and virtual, are calculative devices, creating fields in which a product can be compared with other items. As with categorizations, judgment devices simplify: they leave out parts of the story or diminish the importance of certain aspects, to set up a particular set of choices while not determining exactly what individuals will choose. Therein lies their power: in the supermarket as in the voting booth, people may be free to choose, but between options that have been framed by a complex, and often hidden, political-economic apparatus.

Calculative devices often rest on seemingly objective measurements, but, behind the numbers, always lurks a value judgement. Today we find ourselves inundated by calculative devices based on classification and quantification. It no longer raises a brow to numerically rate almost anything on a five-point scale, from headphones and hotel rooms to a therapist's efficacy or the service at a coffee shop.[6] Marion Fourcade has shown how ordinal classifications (based on relative position) have come to be used to determine judgments of essential worth.[7] Arjun Appadurai points out that privileging "hard" metrics reflects an ethical stance based on statistical probabilities and cost/benefit analyses whose "avalanche of numbers—about population, poverty, profit, and predation—threatens to kill all street-level optimism about life and the world."[8]

This chapter turns to the history of coffee. As an object of desire and profit, we find that coffee has played a significant role in the development of global capitalism and the modern world system—what some scholars term modernity/coloniality.[9] Looking at how coffee came to be classified botanically and commercially, I focus how devices such as taxonomies and commodity standards reflect and promote particular values and worldviews. I show how coffee's taxonomic designations map onto its spread around the world, leading to today's commodity trade and the Third Wave fascination with heirloom varietals. This is a story of colonial expansion and justifications of human enslavement, new conceptions of economic progress and scientific rationality, and arguments for individual liberty and free trade. Ideas and plans hatched in eighteenth-century European coffeehouses became part of a feedback loop in which the drink's caffeine stimulated debate and contributed to the development of classically liberal views of economics and politics; these ideas then propelled a burgeoning global trade in coffee and more broadly justified a system of capital accumulation in the Global North dependent on extracting surplus value from raw materials and labor in the Global South. This is a history very much alive today, reflected in contemporary patterns of trade, legacies of ethnic exclusion, and the neoliberal ideologies of the Guatemalan elite. Third Wave coffee has emerged as part of a late capitalist "economy of qualities," but it takes place in a neoliberal context of commodification and standardization that traces its roots to eighteenth- and nineteenth-century trade.

TAXONOMY AND TRADE: COFFEE'S SPECIATION AND SPREAD

The history of coffee shows how the plant's botanical traits and bio-chemical properties have intersected in consequential ways with human intentions and social arrangements, blurring human/nonhuman and natural/cultural divides.[10] The plant's speciation cannot be under-stood apart from global trade and colonial expansion, nor can its physi-ological effects be considered separate from market forces and com-mercial interests. Coffee has not been just an object of human desire, but an active protagonist: both as a living plant and as a beverage, it has influenced human affairs in ways mundane and profound. As a drug food, it produces discernable effects on human physiology, heightening attention, increasing stamina, and releasing the pleasure molecules of dopamine in the brain. The spread of *C. arabica* was propelled by its chemical and bioactive properties acting on human bodies and desires. Its mildly addictive properties and agreeable effects enticed people to start consuming it, planting it, and trading it. In this way, the botanical and material properties of coffee interacted with cultural, religious, and political value worlds.

Coffee comes from flowering plants of the genus *Coffea,* which today has two dominant species, *Coffea arabica* and *Coffea canephora* (Robusta).[11] *C. arabica* was the only widely known and cultivated species until the early twentieth century, and today it makes up about 70 percent of global production, including almost all Second and Third Wave coffees. Robusta, discovered in the Congo and only recognized as a species in 1897, has a high caffeine content (as much as double that of arabicas), grows at low elevations (as low as sea level), and is resilient to many pests and disease. Roasters generally consider its flavor inferior, an opinion reflected in market prices, although there is a preference for it in parts of Southeast Asia, and a few Third Wave pioneers have recently called for a reconsideration of its distinctive tastes. Vietnam and Brazil are the largest producers of Robusta, the bulk of which goes into instant coffees and coffee flavorings and as filler in low-cost brands.[12]

C. arabica only grows at certain altitudes and conditions, and while geography is not destiny, neither has it been inconsequential in the history of global trade and structural inequalities. Scientists and farmers can make adaptions with breeding and genetic engineering, but *C. arabica* still only grows between six hundred and two thousand meters above sea level in temperate climates (above freezing and below 27°C) that get a lot of rain (about 178 centimeters per year) but that also have a pronounced dry season.[13] Because of these properties, coffee cultivation is limited to the areas around the equator between the Tropics of Cancer and Capricorn (25° North and 30° South), mapping all too neatly onto areas that rank high today in terms of conflict, poverty, and malaria (map 3).[14]

The small bushes of *C. arabica* originated in the highlands of Ethiopia, where today we find the greatest diversity. Genetic mapping suggests that a speciation event involving *Coffea eugenioides* and *Coffea canephora* produced the first arabica; it was domesticated around either Harar, Ethiopia, or in the Yemeni highlands, from whence it spread

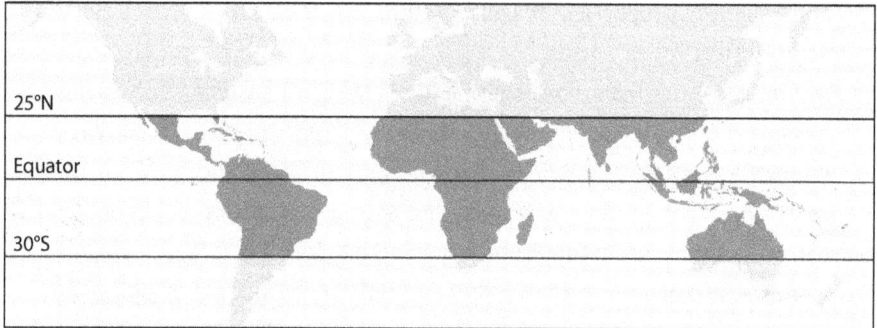

Map 3. The coffee production belt.

throughout the Middle East.[15] Coffee's expansion depended on its exemption from Muslim strictures against alcohol and other intoxicants, and this was not without controversy. Clerics issued periodic bans against the stimulant, including one in Mecca in 1525, but all failed in the face of popular sentiment, and eventually the drink was widely adopted across the Muslim world. Some suggested that the angel Gabriel revealed coffee's power to Muhammed, giving it the implicit blessing of the Prophet. The Shadhili, followers of a form of Sufism, promoted the use of coffee as a tool to allow the faithful to stay alert during nighttime prayers, producing a sort of devotional euphoria. Sufi communities also gave rise to the coffeehouse, a public space that was frequented by intellectuals and a broad swath of male society.[16]

By 1500 the Yemini port of Mocha was the center of the world's coffee supply, and it held a virtual monopoly on the trade for almost two centuries. At first the Yemenis had imported coffee from Ethiopia, but they soon began producing it themselves. This coffee was the source of what has come to be known as the Typica varietal of *C. arabica*. ("Varietal" refers to naturally occurring variations, whereas "cultivar" denotes a subspecies variation that is intentionally selected and bred.) Yemeni production took off after the Ottomans established control of the region in 1550, allowing them to monopolize both production and trade, and leading to Linnaeus's taxonomic attribution. To maintain its dominant position, Mocha outlawed the export of seedlings on pain of death, creating a genetic bottleneck that helps define *C. arabica*'s population biology to this day.

Coffeehouses spread rapidly through the Ottoman Empire in the fifteenth and sixteenth centuries, supplied with coffee from Yemen. The Ottomans would open coffee houses in conquered cities as a public sign of the new regime. As with later European coffeehouses, these were places for men to gather and talk and play chess; there was philosophical and intellectual debate, allowed by the openness of this space apart from the mosque and from the state. Men from different strata of society would sit side by side at coffeehouses, in juxtaposition to the normal rigidity of the social hierarchy, and they became known as places to float unorthodox ideas.[17]

Coffeehouses came to Constantinople in the 1550s, and European travelers took note of these "sober taverns" with the sociality and debate of a pub but fueled by the stimulant coffee rather than beer or gin. By the early 1600s Dutch merchants were importing coffee from Mocha, supplying coffeehouses in London, Venice, and Vienna. By 1657 London had as many as three thousand coffee shops.[18] At the time, northern Europeans were drinking about three liters of low-alcohol beer per day per person, as it was safer than water, widely available, and fairly cheap. After 1650, the massive expansion of coffeehouses in London and across northern Europe brought with it a literally sobering effect on society, lifting Europe out of a long-standing alcohol buzz.

CAFFEINE AND PSYCHOACTIVE EFFECTS

To understand the uptake of coffee across the Middle East and Europe, we need to consider the psychoactive effects of caffeine. Coffee literally changes people, not only affecting one's metabolism and neurochemistry but also modifying one's outlook on the world. It focuses the mind, sharpens perceptions, and enhances stamina and concentration. (Caffeine is the most widely used psychoactive drug in the world by far.)

Although not as addictive as tobacco or cocaine, the caffeine in coffee makes people want it, even crave it, leaving one feeling like a lesser self without it (as suggested by the excuse "Sorry, I haven't had my coffee yet"). Many coffee drinkers only feel fully human with coffee as a co-constituent part of their bodies and mental states; it is a key ingredient of their chemically enhanced subjectivity. We are what we drink, at least in part, and coffee makes many of us feel somewhat smarter, stronger, and happier. *It* acts on *us*. Caffeine presumably evolved as a toxin to protect plants, although it does not thwart all insects: recent research has shown that it can heighten bees' ability to collect pollen, much as it aids human efficiency.[19]

Wolfgang von Goethe, like many of his artistic contemporaries, was overly fond of coffee; although excessive consumption made him nervous and jittery, he continued to drink it. Fascinated by the strange hold the beverage had on him, he began researching its biological causes. In 1819 he enlisted Friedlieb Ferdinand Runge to explore the chemistry of coffee, resulting in the discovery of the alkaloid caffeine ($C_8H_{10}N_4O_2$). Runge would also go on to promote quinine, the key component in the bark of the cinchona tree used to fight malaria. In 1838 German chemist Hermann Emil Fischer demonstrated caffeine's similarities to quinine and strychnine, and he categorized it in a family he called purines. Fischer synthesized caffeine in 1895 and derived its structural formula in 1897, for which he won the 1902 Nobel Prize in Chemistry.[20]

When a person drinks coffee, caffeine quickly induces a number of physiological effects. Within an hour, caffeine and other molecules have been absorbed by the stomach and small intestine and spread to cells throughout the body. Much of the caffeine is metabolized in the liver, producing compounds that dilate blood vessels and stimulate the flow of oxygen to the brain. Caffeine also induces fat cells to release energy for muscle use, affecting proteins involved in thermoregulation while stimulating lipid oxidation. At the same time, caffeine travels directly to the brain, where its unusual molecular property as both water- and fat-soluble allow it to easily cross the blood/brain barrier.

The level of caffeine in the blood peaks a couple of hours after consumption, depending on one's metabolism and ability to break down caffeine, which varies greatly.

Once in the brain, caffeine reacts in ways that make us less tired, producing modest jolts of adrenaline and dopamine. It acts on the adenosine system, which is responsible for producing a sense of fatigue in our bodies. Adenosine builds up in the brain throughout the day, gradually reaching a tipping point at which point one starts to feel tired. Caffeine's molecular structure is close enough that it can lodge into adenosine receptors, thwarting the adenosine molecules from letting the brain know that, according to its circadian rhythm, the body is tired. A cascading effect then stimulates an adrenaline boost and an uptick in dopamine levels. When coffee is drunk in moderation, the result is a generally pleasurable effect that heightens concentration, attention, and mental acuity. Recent research also shows that a number of other compounds in coffee beyond caffeine, including various forms of chlorogenic acids, significantly improve health outcomes in moderate drinkers.[21]

EUROPEAN COFFEEHOUSES AND ENLIGHTENMENT LIBERALISM

These physiological effects played an important role in the development of Western Enlightenment liberalism, laying the groundwork for the neoliberal philosophies that frame contemporary trade and that underwrite values held by many of Guatemala's coffee oligarchy. Coffeehouses, as opposed to taverns and opium dens, offered sober spots of conviviality, creating new spaces that were fertile ground for philosophical debates and scientific discussions. Jules Michelet attributes coffee ("the sober liquor, powerfully cerebral, which, unlike alcohol, increases clarity and lucidity") with fueling the French Revolution.[22] Ideas about civil society, public opinion, and democracy all emerged from European coffeehouses of the 1700s. *The Economist* characterized

Figure 10. London Coffeehouse, ca. 1690–1700.

the interconnected network of European coffeehouses as "the internet of the Enlightenment era."

Replacing the dulling effects of beer with the stimulation of caffeine provided a cognitive context that, combined with the democratizing ethos of the coffeehouse, nurtured the rise of rational thought and its approach to ordering the world. Coffeehouses provided a venue conducive to the emergence of ideas about liberal trade, science, secular art, and civic organization. While there is never a single cause for social revolutions, the psychoactive properties of coffee were not insignificant to Enlightenment modernity.

London's coffeehouses were places to read newspapers and pamphlets and discuss ideas (see figure 10). Participation depended not so much on social rank as the ability to pay, part of a market-led liberalization of consumption that also gave rise to other sorts of democratizing ideas. Jürgen Habermas credits coffeehouse discourse communities with the emergence of public opinion and civil society.[23] Neither of the Crown nor of the Church, they were venues where the meritocracy of rational debate began to challenge the status of nobility.[24] In 1659 members of the Rota Club, one of the civic organizations that met at the Turk's Head Coffeehouse in London, participated in the first recorded use of a ballot box. The early trade in shares of merchant enterprises took place in coffeehouses, and, famously, Lloyd's of London grew out of insuring these ventures out of Lloyd's Coffeehouse. In 1675, sensing coffeeshop philosophies posed a threat to his authority, Charles II banned them, but protests forced him to reverse that decree within a matter of days. Later, Adam Smith's antimonarchical, liberal ideas would find fertile ground in the rational atmosphere of many coffeehouses. The Royal Society for the Encouragement of Arts, Manufactures and Commerce, which counted both Smith and Karl Marx as associates, traces its origins back to a 1754 meeting at Rawthmell's Coffee House in London.[25]

PLANT BIOLOGY AND TRADE

In coffee's early days, Dutch, and later French, producers and traders supplied the bulk of coffee for European demand. Starting in the early 1600s Dutch merchants established a regular trade route from Mocha to supply the market. The Dutch East India Company (VOC, the world's first common stock corporation) was founded in 1602 to provide financing that would last beyond the single voyage of a merchant ship, and coffee was a key part of its business. As European demand for coffee rose, the Yemenis were able to extract increasingly high prices based on their monopoly. In response, in the 1690s the Dutch successfully smuggled out a few seedlings, presumably the Typica varietal of *C. arabica*.[26] Those were taken to the Dutch colony of Java, where they were planted, and one of those plants was taken to Amsterdam in 1706 (map 4). Today there is surprisingly little genetic variation among cultivated arabicas, a legacy of the early Yemeni monopoly and smuggled Dutch seedlings that became the basic stock for Caribbean, Latin American, and South Asian production.

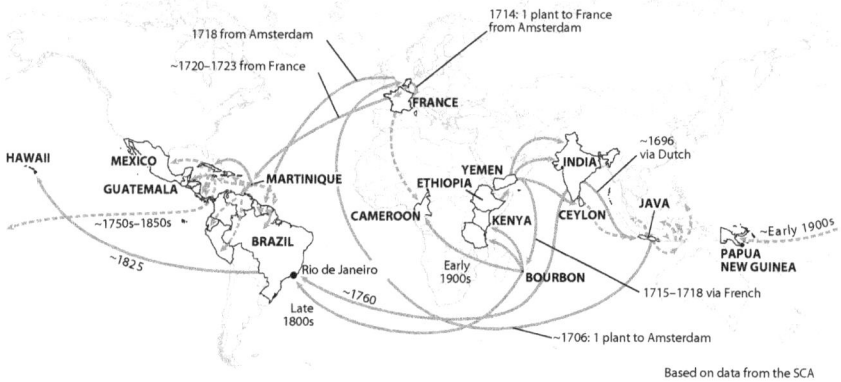

1714: 1 plant to France
from Amsterdam

1718 from Amsterdam

~1720–1723 from France

FRANCE

HAWAII

MEXICO

GUATEMALA

MARTINIQUE

~1750s–1850s

~1825

BRAZIL

Rio de Janeiro

~1760

Late 1800s

YEMEN

ETHIOPIA

CAMEROON

KENYA

Early 1900s

INDIA

~1696
via Dutch

JAVA

CEYLON

BOURBON

1715–1718 via French

~1706: 1 plant to Amsterdam

~Early 1900s

PAPUA
NEW GUINEA

Based on data from the SCA

Map 4. The historic spread of *Coffea arabica*.

The seedlings were cultivated in the greenhouses of Amsterdam's Hortus Botanicus and from there transported to Suriname and to French colonies. In the early 1700s Dutch production grew quickly, with the first public auction of Java coffee held in Amsterdam in 1712.[27] While Mocha beans from Yemen still commanded a premium, "Java" became a recognized category of coffee in the global trade. During this time, in Java, Sumatra, and neighboring territories the Dutch imposed a brutal system of forced cultivation that required farmers (including subsistence farmers) to produce certain quantities of export crops, notably coffee. This led to widespread food shortages and famines, and lasted until the mid-nineteenth century. The 1860 novel *Max Havelaar* exposed the cruelty and harsh conditions of Dutch coffee production, leading to major reforms. But for more than a hundred years, Indonesian production had allowed Dutch traders to sidestep Mocha's monopolistic prices and solidified Amsterdam as the center of the global coffee trade.[28]

The main rival to the Dutch VOC in the coffee trade was the French East India Company. The Dutch had fatefully gifted King Louis XIV with several coffee plants from the Hortus Botanicus in 1714. From this stock the French planted seedlings on the island of Bourbon (now known as La Réunion, located off the coast of Madagascar). A genetic mutation, or perhaps a happenstance crossbreeding, occurred on Bourbon, resulting in a varietal that had a sweeter, more balanced taste and produced a higher yield than Typica. This Bourbon varietal of *C. arabica* became widely recognized as superior and much sought-after by French connoisseurs. At the same time, the French began planting coffee on slave plantations in Martinique and Saint-Domingue (today's Haiti), and by 1788 Saint-Domingue supplied about half of the world's coffee with Typica and Bourbon stock.[29] Their dominance ended abruptly in 1791 with a slave revolt that ultimately resulted in the historic 1804 victory and Haitian independence. Following the Haitian revolution, production began to move to mainland Latin America, as Haitian products were blacklisted from many global markets (including France and the United States) in an effort to discourage other slave revolts.[30] Brazil was an early adopter, relying on slave labor to work the plantations. This gave Portugal a foothold in the coffee market, which until then had been dominated by the French and Dutch; England never had a significant coffee-producing colony, and by the mid-eighteenth century tea prevailed as the British beverage of choice.

Starting in the 1830s, Brazil became the world's most important supplier: by the end of the 1840s it was the source of almost 40 percent of the world's coffee, a share that continued to grow for another fifty years. Following the introduction of the higher-yielding Bourbon varietal (widely replacing Typica), Brazilian production accelerated in the 1870s, linked to increasing U.S. demand. By 1876, the United States consumed one-third of the world's coffee production, and 75 percent of that came from Brazil. In this period, most retail coffee was bought as green beans, roasted at home, and prepared in boiling water. By the late nineteenth century, however, large roasters had started selling prepackaged coffee, competing largely on brand integrity—quality blends, protective packaging, consistent roasting, and no added stretchers such as chicory or barley.[31] The 1907 U.S. Pure Food and Drug Act required coffee to be marked with its port of export, part of an effort to combat adulteration, and by 1935 90 percent of all coffee sold in the United States was roasted and packaged. This was the start of First Wave coffee, and Maxwell House, Folgers, Jacobs (Germany), Douwe Egberts (Netherlands), and other familiar brands trace their origin to this period. Facilitated by new classifications and standards, and mirroring the rise of Fordist mass production in the United States, coffee production moved toward ever-greater scales and efficiencies, led by Brazil.

By the late nineteenth century, the passion for measuring and creating standards and benchmarks was going strong in Europe and Latin America.[32] These classifications started with science but soon extended to the social, cultural, and political-economic realms. Brazil chose the motto "Order and Progress" to emblazon its flag, reflecting a commitment to the promise of a better future through science and rationality.[33] Looking at the political economy of "botanical biographies," Daniel Reichman shows how Brazil promoted a modernist approach to its coffee economy as it turned away from slave labor. (The legal importation of enslaved people was halted in Brazil in 1850 and abolition was declared in 1888.) Early on, Brazilian leaders promoted a view of development as inevitable and rational, best pursued through science and commerce.[34] In 1887 Emperor Dom Pedro founded the Instituto Agronômico de Campinas in an attempt to bring scientific rigor to the service of the nation's plantation economy through selective breeding and experimental agronomy. As Reichman shows, the institute developed and promoted a number of important *C. arabica* cultivars. Santos no. 4, a medium-grade Bourbon shipped from the port of Santos, became the trade benchmark for low-cost blending coffee.[35] Through all of this, Brazilian production emphasized quantity over quality, and, despite a rapidly growing number of Third Wave producers in Minas Gerais, Brazilian coffee still carries that reputation.[36]

Coffee spread from Brazil across Latin America in the mid-nineteenth century, becoming especially important in Colombia, Costa Rica, and Guatemala.[37] While planting the same Typica and Bourbon varietals of *C. arabica* as in Brazil, Guatemalan and other Central American growers took a different approach. They cultivated shade-grown coffee, interspersing the coffee bushes with a variety of taller trees. Counterintuitively, growing coffee in the shade improves photosynthesis in a way that produces larger and heavier fruits. Further, virtually all Guatemalan coffee was (and is) wet processed. Together, the techniques of shade growing and wet processing emphasized quality over quantity in Guatemalan and other Central American production, distinguishing it from the Brazilian competition.

Brazilian coffees are mostly grown in full sun and are natural (dry) processed. Natural processing simply allows the cherry to rot off the beans, which involves mild fermentation and enzymatic reactions that impart a fruity, acidic flavor. Wet processing requires more labor and water than the natural method, but it produces a cleaner cup. As we will see in the next chapter, the German market preferred the quality of Guatemalan beans, and German farmers in Guatemala oriented production toward the shade-grown washed arabicas.

Coffee requires a remarkable amount of labor to make it from plant to cup. Every bean is touched by multiple hands. For washed coffee, processing begins immediately after the harvest (figure 11). First pickers separate the fruit ("cherry") by color, selecting just the ripe red ones. The bags of cherry are taken to a processing mill (*beneficio*); larger plantations have their own beneficio, as do most cooperatives, but they are out of reach for most individual smallholders. The fruit is dumped into a large tank of water, with underripe ones floating to the top to be skimmed off. The ripe berries are then poured into a mechanical de-pulping mill that detaches the two interlocked seeds (each of which we would term a "whole bean"). Covered in a sticky film of mucilage, these ferment in water for twenty-four to forty-eight hours, after which the remaining pulp is washed off. The now separated beans are spread out to dry, usually on concrete patios, until they reach 11 to 12 percent moisture content. This normally takes a few days and requires the constant turning of the beans with special rakes to make sure they do not rot.[38]

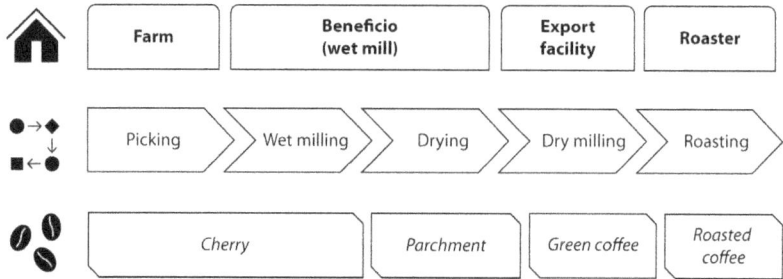

Figure 11. The stages of processing washed coffee, with locations and product designations.

At this stage, the coffee is classified as "parchment," with each bean covered in a thin, dry skin. Most beneficios sell parchment coffee to exporters, who remove the parchment skin with hulling machines in their dry mills, sometimes followed by polishing to make the beans shine. At this point the beans are classified as "green coffee" (*café oro*), which is sorted by size and density—traditionally by hand but increasingly with optical scanners—before being exported in sixty-kilogram burlap bags. Green coffee remains fresh for about a year (although some roasters in Japan swear by older vintage beans).

With its approach to science and development, Brazil was the source of several important varietals and cultivars. Maragogype emerged as a natural mutation of Typica in the 1870s in Bahia; it had larger fruits and beans, and thus a higher yield. In the 1910s in Minas Gerais, Caturra emerged as a mutant of Bourbon. With a Bourbon-like cup profile, Caturra has a higher yield and produces after just three years. This varietal was intentionally bred by Brazilian agronomists at the Instituto Agronômico de Campinas in the 1930s.[39] It spread slowly at first, but it came to be widely planted in Guatemala and elsewhere after the 1970s. Brazilian scientists proceeded to crossbreed Caturra with another Bourbon varietal, Mundo Novo, to produce Catuai, which remains to this day one of the most widely planted coffees in all of Latin America (figure 12).

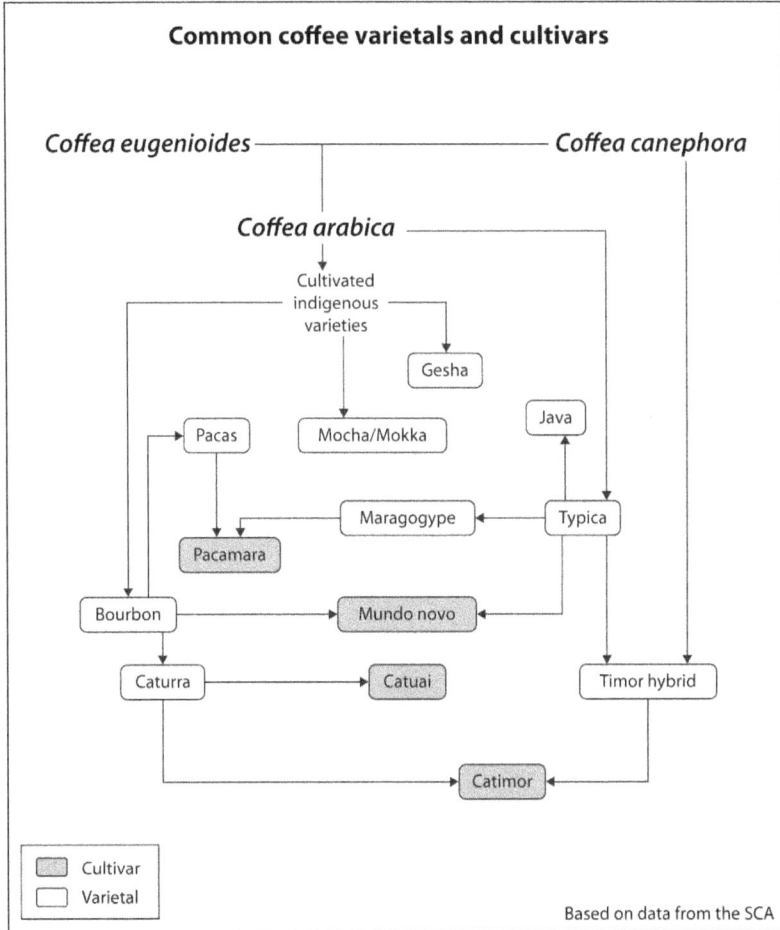

Figure 12. Taxonomic chart of common coffee varietals and cultivars.

The range of conditions coffee will grow under has been expanded by selective breeding and genetic modification, but there is always a tension between taste and productivity. Coffee plants are susceptible to a number of diseases and pathogens when closely spaced on orderly plantations. The most devastating threat comes from coffee rust (known as *roya* in Spanish). A parasitic fungus (*Hemileia vastatrix*), leaf rust likely coevolved with coffee in the Ethiopian highlands. It requires physical

contact with coffee to survive and spread, but once it infects an area
densely planted with members of the *Coffea* genus, it is difficult to eradi-
cate and can quickly devastate the crop. Temperature and humidity
affect the rate of spread, and some claim that El Niño events trigger
outbursts. In the 1870s the fungus reached Indonesia, and an epidemic
destroyed many Asian plantations. After its discovery in Congo, Asian
production largely shifted to Robusta. In Latin America, there was a
major outbreak of rust in 2012–13. A number of organic farms were
wiped out, although most smallholders were diversified enough to mitigate the impact. Most of the Guatemalan farmers I have spoken to realize the dangers of economic dependency on a single crop, and the
power of the natural world. To them, it is apparent that coffee has its
own form of agency that must be reckoned with.[40]

In one of its oddities, *C. arabica* self-pollinates, reducing the possible
range of genetic variation. This is not a trait shared with Robusta, and
in the 1940s a varietal emerged in Timor from a rare cross-species
(Robusta and arabica) hybridization. The Timor Hybrid offered a high
yield, was rust resistant, and grew at a range of elevation: thus, it offered
superior productivity all around. Yet, in terms of taste, it shared more
with Robusta's bitter cup profile. Agronomists then bred the Timor
Hybrid with Caturra stock, producing the Catimor cultivar that introduced more Bourbon influence into the line. Alas, the arabica taste profile was still overwhelmed by Robusta's bitterness. Still, its seductive
properties (so productive, so disease resistant) proved irresistible to
farmers, who are always looking to mitigate risks and uncertainty. First
Wave coffee brands in the 1950s, competing mainly on price, started
including more low-cost Robusta and Catimor, and instant coffees
(which used more Robusta) took off in popularity. By 1956 Robusta
made up 22 percent of the world market. In the 1950s the Catimor cultivar of arabica was widely adopted by producers. Farmers loved the productivity and resilience of the plants, and, despite the compromise in
taste, production spread widely and quickly. The rise of Timor and
Catimor are associated with the decline in coffee quality in the 1950s

and 1960s; coffee consumption also began its decades-long decline around this time, aided by the rise of soft drinks.[41] This was part of the Fordist zeitgeist—the agricultural corollary to mass production in factories—reflecting a move away from quality concerns to a singular focus on efficiency and price, serving a utilitarian bland good to the masses.

The Third Wave movement has renewed interest in a wider range of varietals. Some early varietals are now sought-after heirlooms, such as Gesha, named for its Ethiopian town of origin, and Mocha, which harkens back to the early Yemeni stock. Today Guatemalan smallholders mostly grow Typica, Bourbon, Caturra, and Catuai. The more diversified medium and large farms also plant Maragogype, Pache, and Pacamara, and the cutting-edge Third Wave growers have Gesha and other heirlooms and prized cultivars (see table 2).

COFFEE AND COMMODIFICATION

Coffee became a commodity in the markets of Amsterdam, Hamburg, and London in the early days of global trade. Such global markets demanded a way for distant actors to trade similar items without personally inspecting them, leading to the development of a system of classifications based around places, ports, and quality grades. Buying a Java or a Mocha or a Santos no. 4 gave buyers a good enough sense of what they would be getting to complete a transaction. Coffee's commodification was central to the rise of global trade. Coffee futures were among the first traded derivatives, starting in Amsterdam and then in Hamburg and New York, and reflected a remarkable shift in thinking: buying something sight unseen, and perhaps not even grown yet, based solely on a broad category of quality and appearance. Detached temporally from the material object, such futures allowed for speculation and helped build an infrastructure of global commerce.

Commodification negates particularities and differences, reducing the many meanings associated with a good to the numerical metrics of

TABLE 2

Varietals and Cultivars of *C. arabica* Grown in Guatemala

Varietal/cultivar	Tasting notes
Typica	Balanced, sweet, with citric acid notes; the "original" varietal from which most modern arabica production stems
Bourbon	Sweet, smooth, with good acidic balance; pronounced wine and chocolate undertones; classic coffee taste
Maragogype	Typica varietal discovered in Brazil in the 1870s; citrus and floral flavors; dwarf bushes with large fruit and beans
Caturra	Bourbon varietal discovered in Brazil in the 1910s, actively bred in the 1930s; a Bourbon-like cup profile with higher yield; produces after just three years
Catuai	Hybrid cultivar developed in Brazil in the 1940s; one of the most widely planted cultivars in Latin America
Catimor	Hybrid of the Timor cross-species varietal and Caturra; good yields and disease resistant, but plagued by a poor cupping profile
Pacamara	Hybrid of Pacas Bourbon with Maragogype; classic Bourbon profile with some of the citrus and floral notes of Maragogype
Gesha	Heirloom varietal named for the Ethiopian port; Stumptown's website describes it as "like a Szechuan peppercorn, or the Sun Ra Arkestra, complex and otherworldly"

price and quantity, making any one item interchangeable with others in the same nominal class (as in a "mild arabica"). Like Linnaean taxonomies, it is a particularly powerful calculative device to strip meaning and social relations from a thing, removing it from other value worlds.[42] In the case of coffee, commodification reduces the worth of green beans to the common denominators of price and grade, the easier to trade with across great distances. Of course, coffee beans mean something to those who grow and harvest them. They are part of producers' value worlds, from a grower's pride in a quality product or abundant crop to a worker's scourge at this agent of oppression. Still, for commodity products, these sorts of social, political, and emotional values get removed in the process of trade.

Marx was a coffee drinker, at least occasionally visiting coffeehouses. While he did not write about coffee, Marx did consider the implications of the shift away from individually produced artisanal goods to mass-produced capitalist commodities. In volume I of *Capital,* he described how capitalist relations alienated workers from the means of production: factory machinery replaced artisanal production and turned human labor itself into an interchangeable commodity—a commodity often enhanced by coffee and sugar consumption. From coffeehouse to shop floor, coffee biochemically integrated itself into capitalist formations of political economy and modernist notions of self and society. Not just a recreational drug, coffee was used to wean factory workers from drinking alcohol and increase productivity. Sidney Mintz calls these drug foods, when combined with sugar, "proletarian hunger killers," providing a cheap energy boost at the expense of more substantive nourishment.[43] In 1850 physiologist M. Gasparin argued to the Academy of Sciences of Paris that while the food regimen of Belgian miners consisted of a substantially low quantity and quality of foods, they maintained muscular strength thanks to the ability of coffee to decrease fatigue and hunger.[44] Modern biohacking and chemically enhanced workplaces started with the industrial coffee break.

Marx points out that with commodification, social relations and meanings are replaced by a singular monetary value, price. That is the genius of the commodity form: it is infinitely exchangeable, sight unseen, in a way that minimizes social and moral frictions.[45] Yet the commodity form is not the end of the line. Commodification strips away social, moral, and other symbolic values to make an item fungible, substitutable. Marketing often plays with these different meanings, reassembling and reassigning them; Marx wrote that value "does not have its description branded on its forehead; it rather transforms every product of labor into a social hieroglyphic. Later on, men try to

TABLE 3

Categories of Guatemalan Washed Arabicas by Altitude

Category	Altitude in feet	Altitude in meters
Strictly Hard Bean (SHB)	4500–ca. 6500	1350–ca.2000
Hard Bean, Semi-Hard Bean	3500–4500	1050–1350
Prime/Extra Prime	2500–3500	750–1050

decipher the hieroglyphic, to get behind the secret of their own social product."[46]

The material and economic value worlds of the coffee trade are built on certain calculative devices that privilege precise metrics: a pound of coffee has a certain price at the farm gate and another on the New York futures exchange, and along the chain from tree to cup, coffee is repeatedly weighed and measured. The ordering of commodity trade depends on weights and measures as mechanisms to make things equivalent with a category. The coffee trade employs a mix of evaluative metrics for weight and quality, some metric and others imperial. At the broadest level, the global coffee trade has four basic grades: Colombian milds, other milds, Brazilian naturals, and Robustas; "mild" denotes washed processing. Further distinctions are made based on altitude; in Guatemala "Strictly Hard Bean" coffee is grown above 4500 feet (1350 meters), a classification known as "Strictly High Bean" in other countries (table 3). A standard hundredweight is 100 pounds but a "long hundredweight" is 112 pounds, which is said to go back to the days of mules and carts when the overfilled sacks were used to compensate for spillage, to ensure that a full 100 pounds was registered at the destination. A standard "bag" of green coffee, according to the International Coffee Organization (ICO), is 60 kilograms (132 pounds), but in Guatemala a standard bag is 69 kilograms (152 pounds).[47]

The international benchmark price for First Wave coffee (the New York C price) is for future delivery of 37,500 pounds (17,000 kilograms, about 250 bags), meant to approximate a container load, as a standard twenty-foot equivalent (TEU) container can hold as much as 44,000 pounds. The New York coffee futures exchange began in 1882 and is today operated by Intercontinental Exchange (ICE, also the parent company of the New York Stock Exchange). The ICE contract stipulates that a "Lot of Coffee 'C' shall consist of 37,500 pounds of washed arabica coffee of the growths of Burundi, Colombia, Costa Rica, Dominican Republic, Ecuador, Guatemala, Honduras, India, Kenya, Mexico, Papua New Guinea, Nicaragua, Panama, Peru, Rwanda, Salvador, Tanzania, Uganda, or Venezuela." Coffees from Colombia get an automatic US $0.04 per pound premium, while coffees from Brazil are deducted $0.06 per pound, reflecting perceptions of national quality. The contract states that the coffee should be of "one (1) growth, in sound condition, sweet in the cup, of good roasting quality, and of bean size and color in accordance with criteria established by the Exchange." Colombian coffees may have no more than ten observable imperfections, and others no more than fifteen imperfections, per standard 350-gram sample.[48] Dealing with enormous volumes, the exchange employs an objective approach to grading, with uniform procedures to standardize quality evaluations. Such standardized quality grades can only distantly approximate final taste, and evaluations are based not on cupping but on visual inspection of defects—an approach accentuated in recent years by the advent of high-tech optical sorters that can identify anomalies and blow defective beans off a conveyor belt in dry mills before bagging, a task previously, if more imperfectly, done by hand.

In the 1960s and 1970s, world systems theorists described how colonial relations had produced a global structure of core and periphery economies based on differential access to capital-intensive means of production.[49] In many ways coffee is a classic case: countries in the tropics produced a raw commodity for sale to the core countries of the Global North, with most of the surplus value accruing in the core. This system depended on the cheap labor and continued underdevelopment of the periphery, a pattern of economic dependency mapped onto colonial legacies. Even today this geographic imbalance is encoded in the terms of C price futures, which designate that container loads of green

TABLE 4
Specialty Coffee Association Categories of Green Beans

Class Number and Grade Designation	Criteria
1. Specialty Coffee	0–5 defects + 1 distinctive attribute in aroma or taste
2. Premium Grade	6–8 defects + 1 distinctive attribute in aroma or taste
3. Exchange Grade	9–23 defects
4. Below Standard Grade	24–86 defects
5. Off Grade	More than 86 defects

beans originate in one of nineteen named countries (all in the Global South) for delivery to one of eight licensed warehouses in the United States and Europe (New York, New Orleans, Houston, Bremen, Hamburg, Antwerp, Miami, and Barcelona). While an estimated more than twenty million smallholders produce about 70 percent of the world's coffee, they earn only a small percentage of the final value. Green coffee exports (even accounting for all the middlemen and mills) make up only twenty billion dollars of the global two-hundred-billion-dollar coffee market.[50] Coffee producers may retain control over the means of agricultural production, but the bulk of value added comes from roasting, marketing, and distribution.[51] In the case of coffee, large buyers dominate the undifferentiated commodity-grade market, and the share of economic value realized increases the closer the seller is to the point of consumption.[52]

For Second and Third Wave specialty coffees, the SCA has developed its own rubric for grading green beans to supplement the C contract (table 4).[53] There is a tension at play here, for specialty coffees are often traded on their uniqueness, but as even this sector of the market is big business, standardized classifications are needed to frame the terms of trade.[54]

·　　·　　·

From its early days of cultivation, coffee insinuated itself into human affairs, changing individual diets and cognitive acuity while fueling a global system of trade and capitalist expansion. This history has been a dance between human intentions and plant biology, with the physical and biochemical properties of coffee becoming entangled in social, religious, political, and economic value worlds. Coffee's speciation, and the current geographic distribution of varietals, was formed in the contexts of European colonial expansion, and accelerated by modernist pursuits of efficiency through the application of scientific principles.

The drink's sobering effects first spread across the Muslim world and then throughout Europe, with coffeehouses providing a new sort of public space, more democratic and open, that gave rise to Enlightened modernity. Just as coffee is linked to the rise of modernity (historically and psycho-pharmacologically), it is also tied to colonialism and its political, economic, and racial legacies. From its earliest days, slave labor and other sorts of forced and coerced labor were used to produce coffee in the Caribbean and in the East Indies. As we will see in the next chapter, many of the social, political, and economic inequities built into the colonial plantation system persist today.

Coffee's emergence as a global commodity illustrates the ways individual diversity and geographic particularities can be converted into an undifferentiated category—reducing an item's many social, political, and botanical meanings to the simpler metrics of price and grade. On the one hand, coffee is just coffee. It has use value, it serves a function— it warms and stimulates and fills. But there is coffee to be drunk and coffee to be traded.[55] For the latter, worth must be reduced to exchange value.

Still, coffee, like all objects, is given social meaning by humans—it takes on both cultural values (as in a coffee break, for instance) and idiosyncratic meanings (as part of a morning ritual, for example). In this sense, coffee is not just coffee but a container of meaning and social relationships, part of value worlds tied to the material object but not limited to its material utility. In the late capitalist context of the Third

Wave market, these other values play an important role in justifying prices.

In the following chapters, we turn to Guatemala as a case study in the ways global trade has intersected with geography and ethnic relations to produce the situation we find today.

Figure 13. Finca El Porvenir (ca. 1886).

CHAPTER THREE

German Oligarchs, First Wave Coffee, and Guatemala's Enduring Structures of Inequality

Guatemala is a place where ancestry matters. While Maya peoples make up about half of the population—depending on how the category is drawn—they have been historically excluded from national political and economic power structures. That has changed somewhat over the last decades, as Maya activists have become increasingly organized following the end of civil war in 1996. Today, one sees Maya women wearing traditional dress at the university and in professional settings; Mayan-language advertisements and public service announcements are occasionally heard on the radio and seen on billboards; and Indigenous politicians have held a number of cabinet-level posts. But deep structural inequalities persist.

It is sometimes claimed that twenty families run Guatemala, and that is probably not far off the mark. Marta Casaús Arzú identifies twenty-two intermarried families, including her own, that play a dominant role in business and government, with another twenty-six families on the periphery of this inner circle. This concentration of political and economic power goes back centuries, although an early twenty-first-century influx of drug money has created a new and flashier elite vying for influence. Guatemala's traditional oligarchs tend to hold a staid, cosmopolitan view of their place in the world, seeing themselves as bearers of the European tradition of modernity, as much a part of a global elite as citizens of a nation. At the same time, they can be intensely parochial in terms of family and social ties; for most, kin clearly come before country. Among the traditional elite, German, English, and Spanish lineages and physiological markers are valued, often discussed in terms of blood (*sangre*), and relations between families are meticulously tracked.[1] While they may publicly celebrate ancient Maya heritage and the folkloric value of contemporary Indigenous languages and customs, many also see the largely rural Maya population as a hindrance to the country's progress.

Reflecting on this ethnic and class social structure, and the economic inequalities it reproduces, Demetrio Cojtí Cuxil, a prominent Maya public intellectual, claims that Guatemala can only be understood as a "neocolonial state." He means that the extractive relations between the elite and the masses, and between Indigenous and non-Indigenous peoples, laid down in the colonial period are perpetuated today through neoliberal economic structures, nominally democratic institutions, and insidious racial prejudices.[2] He observes that entrenched ethnic inequalities remain even after the end of dictatorships, the rush of market openings, and the shifting cast of players. Both Indigenous peoples and poor and middle-class non-Indigenous (*ladinos*) are marginalized in relation to structures of political and economic power, but Maya peoples endure a double discrimination based on racialized stereotypes that have their roots in colonial-era distinctions.[3]

In terms of wealth and income, Guatemala has one of the world's highest levels of inequality, a pattern that goes back to the late nineteenth-century establishment of the coffee economy. Building on Cojtí's analysis, this chapter links the history of plantation economies with the current situation of insecurity and inequality in Guatemala. It is a history of changing sorts of violences and structural exclusions, from labor abuses to civil war, with the one constant that Maya peoples bear the brunt of suffering. As Achille Mbembe observes for the African "postcolony," this has not been the progressive march of liberal modernity, but nonlinear entanglements of violences, politics, and capitalism.[4] The rise of First Wave commodity coffee and large-scale production in the late nineteenth and early twentieth centuries depended on labor coercion and ethnic discrimination, solidifying class and racial distinctions. On the plantations, patron-client relationships prevailed, using social, political, and economic dependency to create a system to supply cheap labor. This was at the expense of workers, but justified—often on both sides—by the small acts of patronage, such as a loan or money for a funeral, which, welcome as they may have been in the moment, reproduced the unequal power relations.

Early on, German traders came to dominate Guatemalan coffee production and trade, with their classically liberal ideas of progress—born in European coffeehouses—converging with Guatemalan elites' project "to forge a modern, unified and racially whitened nation out of a heterogeneous postcolonial society."[5] Living and working on their remote plantations, and yet with a native understanding of European tastes and quality conventions, the Guatemalan-German planters had a foot in both places. This gave them the social, cultural, and financial capital needed to translate their product across different value worlds. While justified in terms of philosophies of free trade, their profits depended on exploiting Indigenous labor to work lands stolen or coerced from Maya communities. Gladys Tzul Tzul argues that a modernist European worldview inhibited the colonizers from ever fully bridging the ontological divide between their individualism and more fluid forms of Maya collective agency.[6]

In reaction to the grossly unequal distribution of land and the brutal conditions of plantation labor, Maya communities frequently pushed back. Julie Gibbings shows how Q'eqchi' Maya strategically blended Western "liberal ideas of virtue, autonomy, and self-determination with Q'eqchi' principles of solidarity, reciprocity, and subsistence production, ideas that derived from entirely different sets of principles," to justify their sometimes violent resistance in the early twentieth century.[7] By the 1970s, with plantation conditions not much better, Marxist rebel forces formed in the Maya highlands seeking land reform and an end to the neocolonial relations of power. Using guerrilla tactics, they staged strategic attacks on army encampments, telephone towers, and, particularly, coffee plantations. These provocations were met with a disproportionate response, as the Guatemalan military, backed by the United States, waged scorched-earth campaigns against rural Maya communities. Peace accords were signed in 1996, but the postwar era has proven no less violent, with persistent inequality, endemic state corruption, and the rise of a narco-elite. Political scientists shy away from classifying the country as a "failed state," but it certainly teeters on the brink. Liberal policies have morphed into neoliberal policies, racist attitudes have transformed into a language of multicultural differences, and the main perpetrators of terror and violence have become nonstate actors, but in all too many ways the present is structured like the colonial past.[8]

But let us start the story in 1888.

1888 AND THE EMERGENCE OF THE COFFEE PLANTATION ECONOMY

In 1888 Erwin Paul Dieseldorff arrived in Guatemala. Son of a Hamburg merchant family, the twenty-year-old Dieseldorff was coming from a stint working at an uncle's London trading house. He was tasked with expanding the family business and determined to make his mark in this new land. Dieseldorff joined a growing wave of German immigrants— mostly merchants, engineers, and other professionals—who were beginning to dominate the Guatemalan coffee market. It was a small population—there were less than one thousand Germans in Guatemala at the time of Dieseldorff's arrival—but their economic and political influence was profound, and it is still felt to this day. Dieseldorff would go on to become the most influential member of the coffee oligarchy.[9] He and his compatriots benefited enormously from laissez-faire trade arrangements between Guatemala and Germany. They celebrated their commercial and political freedoms while presiding over a system of systematic exploitation of Indigenous labor, with all of the cruelties large and small that entailed. Today his old plantations are but a faint remnant of their glory days, but one can still buy Dieseldorff brand coffee in Guatemalan supermarkets and online.

In 1888 Alfred Krupp, then Germany's largest industrial employer, began selling coffee to his workers. Soon roasting over one thousand kilograms per day, he brewed coffee in the factory canteen and sold bags of beans at cost in the company store. A shrewd businessman, Krupp was willing to forgo a markup to stimulate his workers with caffeine; he saw it as the ideal tonic for an urbanizing, industrializing workforce unaccustomed to the discipline of factory life. He was not alone in this assessment. Just the previous year, Hamburg's chamber of commerce advised its members that "there is no more healthy and no more strengthening beverage than coffee for workers; that's why the efforts by the government and by private industrialists are intended to terminate the noxious abuse of liquor by installing coffee shops for workers."[10] By this time, coffee consumption in urban Germany had been rising sharply for several decades, and Hamburg had replaced Amsterdam and London as the primary port of entry for Latin American coffees. The Hamburg Coffee Exchange opened in 1887, and, building on its proudly held Hanseatic heritage, the city's trading houses, shipping lines, and merchant banks flourished. At the same time, coffee spread from being a luxury item of the bourgeoisie to a staple in worker households. Such democratization of consumption was heralded by coffeehouse liberals as proof of the virtues of free trade—the rationality of the market resulted in more stuff for more people. In this instance, it was also due to the visible hand of the state working through Otto von Bismarck's social welfare efforts to mollify unrest in the transition from an artisanal and agricultural to a wage-labor economy.

In 1888 Brazil abolished slavery. At the time, about half of the world's coffee supply came from slave plantations around Rio de Janeiro and São Paulo. One of history's many ironies is that the coffee beans that fueled the development of liberal ideas of liberty and rationality in European coffeehouses were largely grown with slave (and other sorts of coerced) labor. Late on the heels of Haiti's successful revolution (which ended in independence in 1804), Brazilian emancipation marked a turning point in New World production. The end of large-scale and legal slavery forced a move toward modern, capitalist agriculture. Befitting the 1889 motto of their new Republic (*Ordem e progresso*), Brazilians took a rational, scientific approach to national development, looking for inspiration in Comte's positivism. As Daniel Reichman recounts, Brazil started research centers to develop new agricultural technologies and coffee cultivars; in the spirit of such progress, by 1889 the superior Bourbon varietal of *C. arabica* had overtaken Typica as the most widely planted in Brazil. And not only in Brazil, for coffee production had by this time spread north to Colombia, Costa Rica, and Guatemala, all of which quickly developed reputations for higher-quality beans than Brazil.[11]

· · ·

Nineteenth-century Guatemalan coffee plantations were intensely local—their own little societies—and yet they were also existentially oriented toward international markets and distant political economies. As a mode of not just production but also existence, plantation life exhibited many contradictions.[12] The *cafetaleros'* livelihoods were built on a flourishing "free" trade that depended on state coercion of labor; there was a Humboldtian appreciation for cultural differences, and a simultaneous willingness to subjugate the Maya; there was a strong sense of German identity and yet an openness to recognizing interracial unions with Indigenous women. These contradictions did not negate one another but coexisted, intertwined in morally complicated arrangements. The history of coffee in Guatemala is replete with villains and heroes, and sometimes they are the same person.

In the absence of large gold or silver deposits, the Spanish conquistadores in Guatemala sought to build their fortunes on agricultural exports. The resources they required were land and labor, both of which had to be wrested away from the Maya inhabitants. Natural dyes destined for Europe were the dominant crops until the mid-nineteenth century. At first it was indigo, although by 1824 the country's top export earner was cochineal, a deep red hue extracted from insects that feed on the nopal cactus. Trade in both continued at a great volume until the advent of synthetic dyes.[13]

Following independence in 1821 (as part of the Federal Republic of Central America) and then again in 1847 (as an independent country), Guatemala's commercial and political elite recognized the risk of dependency on a single export crop. Borrowing an idea from successful European competitions for innovation, such as Napoleon's Food Preservation Prize, which led to canning technology, President Mariano Gálvez in 1834 offered two hundred pesos to the first person to harvest a hundred hundredweights of coffee, and then a hundred pesos for the next three to accomplish that feat.[14] In the mid-1800s, two influential organizations, the Consulado de Comercio (made up mostly of Spaniards who exported agricultural products) and the Sociedad Económica de Amigos del País (with a base of politicians and intellectuals), threw their weight behind coffee. They promoted early cultivation by setting up seedling nurseries, a model *beneficio,* and a significant fund to buy coffee (as a guarantee for hesitant farmers). Such interventions, coordinated with the government and grounded in liberal and positivist ideas birthed in Europe's coffeehouses, applied science and reason to promote economic and social progress. Thanks to these efforts, by 1870 coffee had become Guatemala's single most important export. In 1860 coffee represented 1 percent of Guatemalan exports, but by 1870 it was 44 percent; this did not reduce dependency on a single crop, it just made that crop coffee (table 5). Coffee retained its place as the country's single most important export for most of the twentieth century, and Guatemala's coffee oligarchy played a central role in national politics over that period.[15]

MAYA COMMUNITIES AND FORCED LABOR

For students of Guatemala, coffee has a deservedly bad reputation, associated with exploitative labor relations and the concentration of political

TABLE 5

Coffee and Cochineal Exports from Guatemala, in Pesos

Year	Coffee	Cochineal
1867	415,878	1,068,047
1868	788,035	891,513
1869	790,227	1,266,613
1870	1,132,298	865,414
1871	1,312,129	876,025

and economic power. Commodity coffee is both labor- and capital-intensive, requiring sufficiently large and efficient plantations to be able to compete with the prices of other producers around the world (namely, Brazil). Such production imposes high barriers to market entry, which keep both economic and political capital restricted to a small class of wealthy, well-connected, and inevitably non-Indigenous landowners. Throughout the nineteenth and twentieth centuries, the Guatemalan coffee elite controlled production more tightly than its peers in other countries (except for El Salvador) and exerted their influence over the affairs of state, as with the labor laws mentioned above.[16] This tightly held, large-plantation political economy was closely associated with self-serving legal, political, and social structures; it also replicated a global pattern of core and periphery relations within the periphery itself.[17]

Most Maya communities and individuals did not have title to their land; they had simply occupied and used it for generations. Liberal policies sought to stimulate market growth by expanding private property, allowing "unproductive" land to be surveyed and auctioned off by the state. Indigenous communities, many of which held communal lands, were taken advantage of in this process, as their traditional rights were not recognized as legitimate ownership and their subsistence agriculture was not considered "productive" in a modernist sense. As a result, many Maya communities had their lands stolen or appropriated and sold.

Figure 14. Eadweard Muybridge's *Commencement of the Harvest* (1875).

Nineteenth-century coffee plantations in Guatemala were concentrated on the Pacific coast piedmont (the Boca Costa) of the highlands and in the region of Alta Verapaz, on the Atlantic side of the Sierra Madre. In 1877 the liberal government of Justo Rufino Barrios passed a law allowing for the appropriation of "unused" lands. This resulted in a massive land grab, displacing Maya families and communities to higher altitudes and to less desirable lands.[18] In Alta Verapaz, displaced communities often remained as *colonos,* meaning that they labored on the *finca* in return for being allowed to live and grow subsistence crops on undeveloped parts of the plantation (figure 14). By 1921, a remarkable 40 percent of the Alta Verapaz population were living as *mozos colonos.*[19]

Historian David McCreery distinguishes Guatemalan coffee plantations from other Latin American producers by their size, largely foreign ownership, and capital-intensive technologies.[20] German machinery was the gold standard in coffee production, and German engineers working on plantations pieced together all the equipment used to produce quality washed coffees, including de-pulpers, mills, dryers, and separators. To this day German equipment is held in high esteem, and some fincas proudly continue to use hundred-year-old machines. This pattern illustrates the dependency built into the system of trade, with raw materials, in the form of coffee beans, traveling to Germany, where capital- and knowledge-intensive industrial goods are produced and sent to Guatemala. Even with the mechanization of washed processing, coffee production still depended on cheap and abundant seasonal labor. For quality coffee, the cherry has to be handpicked, requiring many people going through the fields day after day, returning over and over to the same tree, during the months of harvest.

A recurrent complaint of plantation owners was the lack of workers, and this was often linked to racist stereotypes of the Maya as lazy and indolent. For example, J. C. Cambranes cites one grower who complained that "the difficulties which we have had to face have not been few, the Indians' local spirit being the main one; they always look suspiciously upon the one who tries to turn the lands they keep abandoned into productive one."[21]

In fact, they probably just did not want to work on the plantations. They were largely able to meet their own subsistence needs with plots of maize and beans (*milpa*) and kitchen gardens. Working conditions on plantations were abysmal, and employment on them was resisted by many Maya communities. Workers had to travel to the plantations, pay was low, food was scarce, and housing and sanitation conditions poor. Malaria, dysentery, and smallpox spread among migrant workers. To add insult to such illnesses, the work was backbreaking, and workers were often cheated on the weight of cherries picked (or through accounting fraud, as their illiteracy made them easy targets). Few, if any, would choose such work, especially since most were able to supply their subsistence needs with production at home.[22]

As a result, large landowners lobbied the government for laws compelling labor from Maya (and other peasant) communities. In response, the government instituted *mandamiento* laws that required rural peasants to work a certain numbers of days per year for the state, which could then assign their labor to plantations. Major forced labor laws were enacted in 1830, 1877, 1878, 1894, and 1934. These varied in their specifics, but the aims were consistent: to force Maya to work for wages on pain of imprisonment or corporal punishment. In the late nineteenth century, tens of thousands of seasonal Maya migrant laborers were forced to work on Boca Costa plantations during the harvest; Greg Grandin reports that the numbers had climbed to around 250,000 by 1921. In this way, the liberal economic practice idealized by Hanseatic merchants and coffee-shop intellectuals ended up relying on state-enforced coerced labor from largely Indigenous communities.[23] Employers could legally pursue runaway workers; plantations often had stocks and prisons; corporal punishment was common; and many owners and administrators considered it their right to have sex with any of the women workers (or workers' spouses or daughters) on the finca.

Plantation owners discovered that debt could be even more effective—less bureaucratic and more efficient—than the state's forced labor system and that poor peasants were always in need of advanced wages. They employed unscrupulous labor recruiters who would make the rounds in highland Maya communities, offering loans in the months before harvest, when food reserves were lowest, and supplying alcohol, especially during town fiestas. Larger fincas would pay workers in a sort of company script, but with minted coins (*fichas de finca*) that had to be used in company stores or with surrounding businesses that could trade with the finca. Fichas de finca were finally outlawed in 1945.

Maya workers resisted in various ways. One common demand of Indigenous workers was to be paid in advance for their labor. More than once owners had to relent in the face of unified Maya resistance. There were significant coffee worker uprisings in 1865, 1877, 1886, and 1905. David McCreery sums the situation up: "The government and employers had the coercive power of the army, the telegraph, and the repeating rifle on their side. But the Indigenous population had the numbers and an awareness that without their participation the export economy would collapse."[24]

ERWIN PAUL DIESELDORFF AND
JOSÉ ANGEL ICÓ

When young Erwin Paul Dieseldorff arrived in Guatemala, he spent time learning the coffee business on the Boca Costa before heading to Alta Verapaz, where an uncle had established a trading business.[25] With money from his family in Hamburg, Dieseldorff systematically bought up a number of existing coffee farms and Maya lands. In one instance, in 1890, he paid for 580 acres of Q'eqchi' Maya lands to be surveyed; he then outbid 123 Q'eqchi's to take title of the land in a public auction.[26]

Dieseldorff's story reflects the ideological contradictions typical among German coffee growers of the time. He stole land from Q'eqchi' farmers, making them his peons on their ancestral lands; he fought attempts to educate the Maya, fearing that they would cease to be good laborers; and he vigorously lobbied government officials to crack down on Maya labor activists. It is, therefore, surprising to learn that Dieseldorff was also an eager student of the Q'eqchi' Mayan language and local customs. He published works on the traditional medicinal plants of Alta Verapaz and on the ancient Mesoamerican calendrical system. Indeed, he championed the need to understand and work with Indigenous communities—and this seems to have been out of intellectual curiosity, a felt paternalistic duty to promote betterment, and a pragmatic instrumentalism in the service of maintaining a supply of willing workers.[27] He wrote that "the Indian in the Alta Verapaz should be treated as a child. To gain authority, the administrator has to be resolute and vigorous; he must have definite views and avoid changing his mind several times. On the other hand, he has to be friendly and fair-minded to gain the heart of his people."[28] His view was that a serious and sustained engagement with local culture could help improve labor relations while increasing productivity and quality.

Dieseldorff would have been familiar with the adventurous descriptions that had made Alexander von Humboldt a leading figure of the nineteenth century. He probably saw in Humboldt a kindred spirit, as

Dieseldorff had a similarly wide-ranging intellectual interest in the natural world, from geology and botany to linguistics and archaeology. He collaborated with the geographer Karl Sapper and even presented his research at the academic International Congress of Americanists. H. Glenn Penny argues that the coffee capitalism of Dieseldorff and other Germans "brought more to Guatemala than debt peonage. It brought migrants who served as intermediaries between knowledge cultures, produced a great deal of knowledge about their adopted homeland, and shaped intellectual and political debates about its future and its past for generations."[29]

Dieseldorff was married to a German woman. That was somewhat rare, as not many German women made the trip to Alta Verapaz in the nineteenth century, and it was commonly accepted among the Germans for men to have Q'eqchi' sexual partners and relationships short of formal marriage. In addition to two children with his wife, Dieseldorff recognized a daughter by his Q'eqchi' consort. That daughter, Matilde Dieseldorff Cú, went on to marry the plantation owner Max Quirin, taking over his operation after he died and becoming a grande dame of Cobán society.[30]

José Angel Icó was an unlikely nemesis for Dieseldorff. Born in 1875 in a small Q'eqchi' village in Alta Verapaz, Icó was raised in a family whose modest circumstances passed for affluence by local standards, nurturing the boy's ambitions. In the historical record, we get to know Dieseldorff and other prominent growers as individuals, but most Maya remain nameless in a way that diminishes their role as protagonists. Icó is an exception thanks to historians Greg Grandin and Julie Gibbings, who have mined archival records to flesh out the story of Icó's life and his rise to become a Maya labor activist. Angered by the exploitation of Maya workers on Alta Verpaz's coffee fincas, Icó became radicalized as a young man, and his writing provides a vivid glimpse into the hardships of plantation labor. Through passion and rhetorical flourish, he was at times able to mobilize strikes of thousands of workers. In a sort of rhetorical jujitsu, Icó used the idiom of liberalism and national pride to press his case for Indigenous workers' rights. Grandin shows how he petitioned the government, garnered newspaper coverage, and started a peasant union to demand that employers at least abide by the laws as written. Icó used the language of "slavery" to describe plantation conditions, and he called out forced labor for what it was, eschewing the polite euphemisms preferred by legislators.[31]

All of this earned the ire of Dieseldorff, notwithstanding his multicultural intellectual interests. Dieseldorff accused Icó of "hypnotizing" the Indians, called him a Bolshevik, and repeatedly petitioned the government to put a stop to his insurgencies. As Grandin describes, their conflict came to a head in 1920, when Icó led a strike of Dieseldorff workers and a subsequent land invasion of forty-five Q'eqchi workers on Dieseldorff's land. Icó eventually went to jail, losing the land he invaded; he died six years after his release in 1944. Although he did not live to realize his dream of freeing forced Maya labor on the coffee plantations, he was able to witness the election of Jacobo Arbenz—a leftist who campaigned on a platform of land reform—as president of Guatemala.

GERMAN CONSUMERS AND GUATEMALAN PRODUCTION

The liberal values and politics espoused in Europe's cafes in the nineteenth century manifest in the great merchant houses, transport firms, and democratic chambers of Bremen, Lübeck, and Hamburg; while Adam Smith *wrote* of the wealth of nations, the Hanseatic merchants and financiers actually made it happen. Hamburg is still today proudly the "Free and Hanseatic City-State of Hamburg." These merchants' tastes and values, grounded in a northern European Protestant *Weltanschauung,* shaped the formation of the coffee economy in Guatemala. Up until 1900 Guatemala exported most of its coffee to Germany, where the market demanded especially high-quality beans. While most nineteenth-century coffee would be considered unremarkable in the contemporary specialty market, Guatemalan washed arabica was some of the best available at the time (as evidenced by the various awards it earned at world expositions). In 1868 the German counsel in Guatemala wrote to Bismarck, the German head of state, extolling the "excellent quality" of Guatemalan coffees and noting that they are "particularly appreciated in Germany."[32]

The German preference for quality coffee stems from the refinement of a bourgeois aspirational taste. Drinking their own product, which was often stored in rooms underneath their formal parlors, the families that ran merchant houses were in a unique position to define quality conventions. They also made quality distinctions part of an explicit and coordinated commercial effort. Justus Fenner writes that "the strategy of the Hanseatic coffee firms to assure steady profits had three components. First, they would step up importation of low-quality coffee from Brazil. At the same time, they would make a direct incursion into high-quality coffee production in order to control that part of the coffee commodity chain. Third, they would create a bifurcated consumer market in Germany, where more profitable sales of high-quality coffee would compensate the lower prices and potential risks of importing lower-grade coffee."[33] In this, Guatemalan coffee was considered especially well suited to the refined German palate.[34]

Hamburg, and to a lesser extent Bremen and Lübeck, heirs to the Hanseatic tradition, became the key points of entry for Latin American coffees. By 1890 Hamburg had replaced Amsterdam and London as the primary port of entry for coffee destined for the European market.

As their home ports were growing and the German market was demanding higher-quality coffees, German planters in Guatemala were specializing in shade-grown, washed arabicas planted mostly in the 1000–1500 meters above sea level (masl) range. The Germans who came to dominate Guatemala's coffee industry, like Dieseldorff, were mostly from the city-states of Hamburg and Bremen. Their farms were concentrated along the Boca Costa Pacific piedmont and in Alta Verapaz, on the Atlantic side of the highlands. At first, it was individual merchants and families setting up farms, but by the late nineteenth century firms such as the Compañia Hamburguesa de Plantaciones and the Hanseatic Plantation Corporation owned large numbers of farms. And yet the total number of German immigrants was quite small. At the end of the nineteenth century there were only about nine hundred Germans in Guatemala, but they controlled one-third of production and two-thirds of coffee exports; they owned plantations, had control over the best engineering and technology, and built the transport and finance infrastructure.[35]

Crucially, they also kept ties and allegiances to their home cities through kinship, finance, and trade ties.[36] This was not a generic "German" identity but a specific link to their home ports and their Hanseatic heritage. Largely professionals, scientists, and merchants, the Germans in Guatemala sought to establish a sort of *Heimat* (homeland) abroad. Through their communities, they created a sort of Germanness appropriate for the context, one that, in Alta Verapaz, encouraged Germans, more than others, to learn Mayan languages and integrate themselves into local social structures, including through marriage and offspring.[37] It was not uncommon for children to grow up in Alta Verapaz speaking German and Q'eqchi', and settlers often divided their time between the plantation and Guatemala City or Hamburg. The Germans had to depend on local authorities to supply their workforce, but they often circumvented local power to get things done through their networks with the president and other high officials in Guatemala City.

Building on the liberal bourgeois value worlds of northern Europe, many of the professionals and merchants who made up the German immigrant community found meaning in their enterprises beyond accumulating capital, seeing themselves as a civilizing force, bringing order and progress to a backward land and peoples.[38] Christiane Berth illustrates how German plantation owners saw Guatemala as a wild, uncivilized space that they could convert into ordered and productive purpose. Regina Wagner reports that many Maya preferred to work for German owners, although most accounts present devastating portrayals of coffee labor in the nineteenth century across the board. As Glenn Penny notes, while many German owners were progressive (for the time) in their view of Maya workers and their social and cultural traditions, they were also often cruel and racist.[39]

The Hanseatic mission of taming the wilds converged with the proto-eugenic views of Guatemalan elites. In particular, Guatemala's elite classes worried about the country's "Indian problem," namely, that there were too many of them and that their presumed premodern ways held back the country's development as an Enlightened national state. In contrast, German immigrants were seen as a source of industriousness, scientific and engineering skills, and commercial networks. It was hoped that these light-skinned entrepreneurs would jump-start the country's rural economy. An 1887 agreement between imperial Germany and Guatemala gave Germans in Guatemala expansive rights. Children born of German parents were considered German citizens by birth (and could apply for Guatemalan citizenship if desired), and Germans were given broad grants of free trade with their home ports.[40]

It was mostly German men who came to Guatemala, and Q'eqchi' women were often used as domestic and sexual servants; rape of plantation workers was common. A significant number of Q'eqchi' women became common-law wives to German owners and administrators; their offspring were often recognized as such and used as intermediaries between German owners and Q'eqchi' workers.[41] Marta Casaús Arzú reports that one plantation owner claimed that "the only solution for Guatemala is to improve the race, to bring in Aryan seed to improve it. On my plantation I had a German administrator for many years, and for every Indian he got pregnant I would pay him an extra fifty dollars."[42] This attitude toward Maya bodies was justified by ideals of progress, betterment, and the German notion of *bildung,* self-cultivation through industriousness. It was widely held, as Dieseldorff argued, that the Maya should be viewed as children in need of benevolent guidance—but benevolence should never get in the way of industry, and when the two came into conflict, the Maya suffered.

WARS, COUPS, AND REVOLUTIONARIES

After World War I, another, larger wave of German immigrants came to Guatemala, and many became engineers, accountants, or administrators for the more established German farms and trading houses. The new immigrants tended to be more nationalist and were quick to switch to National Socialism after 1933. That year, of the eight largest coffee producers in Guatemala, five were German and three were English. Julie Gibbings reports that the Cobán German Club (the oldest such club in Central America) was the first to endorse the Nazis, complicating the accepted norm of German-Q'eqchi' unions. By 1936, when a visiting warship allowed Germans in Guatemala to vote in the German election, 98.79 percent voted for Hitler.[43]

With few interruptions, Guatemala was led by military rulers from the time it gained independence in 1821 all the way up until 1985. From 1930 to 1944, Jorge Ubico, an admirer of fascism and equal parts tyrant and populist, governed the country. He solidified the position of large plantations, including those of the U.S.-based United Fruit Company, which acquired a huge percentage of the country's arable land as stock for banana production. At the same time he proclaimed an end to the most egregious forms of exploitative debt and forced labor, to much acclaim from Indigenous communities.[44] Coffee continued to be the engine of the national economy, however, and rural plantation labor remained scarce. Thus, in 1934 Ubico introduced a new vagrancy law, cloaked in the language of a free market and with the Orwellian moniker *trabajo libre* (free work). Maya and ladino campesinos were proclaimed free to sell their labor to whomever they chose, a seemingly Enlightened, liberal position, but the illiberal rub was that they had to sell their labor to someone. The law required men of working age without a "profession"—and self-sufficient subsistence farmers were considered unemployed—to work 100 to 150 days a year, often assigned to coffee fincas. This was widely remembered by rural workers as a period of great hardship ("we were slaves" was a common refrain).[45]

After entering World War II, the United States pressured Guatemala to join the Allies' effort and clamp down on Nazi supporters. Although Ubico had been sympathetic to Hitler and Mussolini, he quickly changed course and targeted German citizens, confiscating property and sending many to internment camps in the United States. Through legal maneuvers and the dual citizenship of those who had been born in Guatemala (as enshrined in the 1887 treaty), several families, including the Dieseldorffs, were able to hold onto their lands, but for most it was a devastating blow.

In 1944 a group of military officers brought to an end to the long series of dictatorships. The following year, progressive Juan José Arévalo was elected president, solidifying a period that has come to be known as the "ten years of spring" in Guatemalan democratic politics. As part of his reforms Arévalo overturned vagrancy laws, the use of company script, and the corporal punishment of workers (all of this at least on paper, as government directives were often not put into practice on remote plantations). Arévalo was succeeded in 1951 by the even more progressive Jacobo Arbenz. Arbenz, the candidate dreamed of by José Angel Icó, instituted one of the most ambitious programs of land reform in Latin American history. Many coffee fincas lost lands to workers, and peasant unions were much emboldened by the reforms.[46]

A CIA-orchestrated coup deposed Arbenz in 1954 and installed an anti-communist government that would define Guatemala's Cold War trajectory for the coming decades. Land reform halted, and in many cases reversed, and the state targeted campesino and Indigenous activists for retribution and repression. One lasting impact of the 1945–154 period was the abolishment of forced labor laws. As a result, fincas began to rely more on other forms of coercive recruitment of seasonal labor (such as loans, pay advances, and other forms of debt, often fueled by alcohol).

The 1954 coup and subsequent military rule gave rise to the decades of civil war that characterized Guatemala of the 1960s, 1970s, and 1980s. In the early 1960s, disaffected military officers joined with leftist university students and professors to start a Marxist insurgency. The state reacted with a massive counterinsurgency campaign, introducing a new level of violence and fear into the country's long-simmering social tensions. This early rebellion was decisively crushed by the late 1960s. In the early 1970s a new wave of campesino movements emerged to fight for higher wages and better conditions. At the same time, guerrilla groups reemerged in Guatemala's western highlands. By 1972 the Ejército Guerrillero de los Pobres (EGP) had organized a column of combatants in the jungles of El Quiché, winning converts by attempting to speak native languages and assassinating especially cruel plantation owners. The state responded by intensifying its anti-guerrilla military campaigns and its use of extrajudicial death squads throughout the 1970s and early 1980s.[47]

1978: LA VIOLENCIA AND COFFEE PLANTATION ECONOMY

In 1978 General Romeo Lucas García took control of the government, installing his brother as defense minister and escalating military actions against the guerrillas and all those living in the largely Maya, rural areas where they operated. Elites' Cold War–inspired anxiety of Marxist revolutionaries converged with their long-smoldering fears of an Indigenous uprising, creating the ideological justification for ethnocidal campaigns directed by the military.

In 1978 the Comité de Unidad Campesina (Committee for Campesino Unity), or CUC, formed, quickly becoming a powerful national force in organizing workers on coffee, sugar, and cotton plantations. The group was crucial in forcing a tripling of the legal minimum daily wage in 1980, from a little more than US $1 per day to $3.20 per day. The CUC was largely viewed by the military and elites as a beachhead of communism, and its leaders were targeted for violent reprisals.

In 1978 Q'eqchi' campesinos in the Alta Verapaz town of Panzos began to demand higher wages and access to lands from local plantation owners. Panzos is on the far Atlantic edge of Alta Verapaz, where the coffee-growing highlands descend into tropical jungle and banana plantations. Its river port was key for coffee exports starting in the 1880s. On 29 May 1978, hundreds of campesinos marched in the central plaza, demanding a return of stolen lands and greater political representation. They were met by soldiers who opened fire, killing as many as one hundred. The killings at Panzos ushered in Guatemala's most intense period of violence (1978–83), marked by massacres of entire villages, death squads and torture, and a genocidal impunity. The hardest hit areas were those that sent the majority of seasonal workers to plantations.

Greg Grandin traces a direct link between the violent domination of the Maya by coffee oligarchs in the late nineteenth and early twentieth centuries to Guatemala's intense Cold War violence in the 1970s and 1980s, likewise directed largely at Maya communities. Ostensibly, the military aimed to stamp out guerrillas, but they targeted not only active subversives but also potential subversives, a category often understood to include all Indigenous communities. More than just a military conflict, this was a war of values. The army's explicit goal was to change the hearts and minds of potential and actual revolutionary sympathizers, but this also involved exterminating those they perceived as resistant. Michael Richards shows how the army cultivated a particular cosmopolitan value world that viewed society as divided into a modern ladino urban sector and an antimodern rural Indigenous sector.[48] From this perspective, the march of progress required eliminating the primitive ballast that held the country back.

Revolutionary groups such as the Guerrilla Army of the Poor, consisting of thousands of armed combatants and rural supporters, sought to overthrow the elite establishment and institute massive land reform. Coffee plantations, as representations of ensconced inequalities and historical injustices as well as actual sites of labor exploitation, became flashpoints (figures 15 and 16). In his book *Silence on the Mountain*, Daniel Wilkinson unravels a single telling event: in December 1983, rebel forces burned down the plantation house on the La Patria coffee finca in San Marcos. The mountains around this region were one of the strongholds

Figure 15. Jean-Marie Simon's 1981 image of a woman and children picking coffee.

of the guerrilla forces of the Organización Revolucionario del Pueblo en Armas (ORPA), and coffee plantations were prime targets, the physical manifestation of the inequality and exploitation they were fighting. Guerrilla forces based in the mountains would regularly descend to the plantations and the town, collecting war taxes and giving speeches to workers about their fight and the causes of exploitation. These visits were often followed by incursions by the army, whose regional base kept an eye on guerrilla movements and any sign of sympathy for the rebels in surrounding communities. At one point in this fraught environment, the army suspected that La Patria was overly sympathetic to the guerrillas and sent troops to occupy the finca for several months.

As Wilkinson describes, the German-Guatemalan Endler family, who owned La Patria, felt caught in the middle of the conflict. While the sympathies of the Endlers and their administrators were certainly with the status quo over revolution driven by land reform, they tried to

Figure 16. Jean-Marie Simon's 1981 image of end-of-the-day weighing on a coffee plantation.

treat their workers well and had felt coerced to host the army. Nonetheless, the guerrillas saw the occupation as active collaboration with the army, and so when the army decamped, ORPA fighters returned, called the workers to the plantation house, threw open the liquor cabinet, and told the assembled workers that they were now free and should take what they wanted from the plantation house. They then burned it down.

Over the course of the civil war in Guatemala, as many as 200,000 were killed, many in horrific ways; kidnappings, secret prisons, and torture were widespread, as was the network of informants that reported suspected subversives. Everyone's lives were touched. Fighting a hemispheric battle against communism provided the Guatemalan state with not only U.S. support but also a moral justification for attacking Maya culture at its roots (even razing towns and villages where it found expression), thus forcing their integration once and for all into an envisioned post-Indigenous nation-state. A United Nations peace commission determined that the vast majority of atrocities were attributable to the military over the thirty-six years of conflict and that this was a case of genocide, intentionally targeting the Maya population for extermination through scorched-earth policies and tactics. This claim of genocide is rejected by most of the (non-Indigenous) elite and the coffee oligarchy; a well-funded "No Hubo Genocidio" (There Was No Genocide) billboard and bus stop ad campaign took the stance that Guatemala was the front line in the global battle against communism, and that while there were excesses and unfortunate massacres, it was a legitimate war and not a genocidal campaign. In 1996 the government and revolutionary forces signed a peace accord, and while the political conflict has since died down, the country remains a violent place. The underlying problems of inequality, institutionalized discrimination, weak governance, and structural violence continue.

NARCO DOLLARS AND INEQUALITIES: GUATEMALAN POLITICAL ECONOMY IN THE TWENTY-FIRST CENTURY

With gross national income of about $3400 per capita in 2019, Guatemala is not a poor country, at least according to the World Bank. By their standards, Guatemala ranks solidly in the category of middle-income countries. But these averages hide vast inequalities. Guatemala's Gini coefficient (an index of inequality) ranks among the highest in the world table 6). According to the United Nations Development Programme, the top quintile of the population receives 57.3 percent of per capita family income. In an economy highly dependent on subsistence agriculture, just 3 percent of Guatemalan landowners control 69 percent of arable land while 95 percent of (mostly Maya) smallholding farmers control 28 percent of the land. Wealth and income inequality in Guatemala map closely onto ethnic divisions. By virtually any measure, the rural Maya suffer disproportionately from poverty and lack of

TABLE 6

Key Social and Economic Indicators for Guatemala, the United States, and Germany

	2019 human development index rank*	Gross national income per capita, in US dollars	Life expectancy	Average height in meters	Gini index of inequality	Murder rate per 100,000	Traffic deaths per 100,000
Guatemala	127	$3,356	73.7	1.59	55.9	26.1	114.7
United States	17	$62,850	79.5	1.77	40.8	5.3	12.9
Germany	6	$47,180	81.2	1.81	28.3	1	6.8

* Out of 189 countries (data from World Bank, UND, UNODC).

access to land, education, and health care.[49] Poverty levels are highest in coffee-producing regions of the country.

In 2019 the New York commodity price for coffee fell to $0.87 per pound, down from a high of $2.99 a pound less than eight years earlier. Not coincidentally, in 2019 Guatemala was the largest sender of undocumented migrants to the United States, and many of these were Maya from coffee-growing regions. Vivid images of families and children held behind bars covered the media, but the humanitarian crisis did not start at the border. Its causes were further upstream, when families decided that upending their lives and making the perilous journey northward would give them their best chances in life. There has been a surge in the number of Guatemalans who would like to migrate as coffee prices drop below the cost of production. Reporting in the *Washington Post*, Kevin Sieff concluded that "the migration problem is a coffee problem." Sieff tells the story of forty-eight-year-old Rodrigo Carillo, whose entire wealth was in his plot of coffee trees. He had done well with the growth in coffee demand over the last decade, and belonged to a cooperative that received Fair Trade premiums. Still, with prices below $0.90 per pound, he did not see a future. He told Sieff that he planned on crossing into the United States with his five-year-old son.[50]

Guatemala's postwar political economy has been marked by shifting power relations and new actors. While precise figures are hard to come by, in 2019 Guatemala's main sources of foreign income were likely 1) drug trafficking, 2) remittances from migrants abroad (which accounted for 66 percent of legal foreign revenue), and then 3) coffee and bananas. The old-school elites, identifying closely with their Spanish or German heritage, are still a force to be reckoned with. But while they look down on gauche displays of wealth, the old guard's economic power has become overshadowed by the flashy narco dollars flowing into the country. With its weak governance, remote stretches of jungle, and strategic location, Guatemala emerged in the 2000s as the primary transshipment point for cocaine traveling to the United States. While it is just one link along the chain, the amount of money it generates dwarfs even stalwart exports such as coffee. Guatemala boasts an inordinate number of banks for a country its size, and the 2000s saw a massive building boom in Guatemala City that seems to be based on luxury apartment towers. Guatemala also has one of the world's highest murder rates, competing for last place with neighboring Honduras and El Salvador.[51]

While the narcos have particularly gruesome preferences for murder, from hanging severed heads from an overpass to melting bodies in vats of chemicals, they are not the only source of violence. There are also street gangs, *maras,* such as Calle 18 and the Salvatruchas, which are linked to El Salvadoran networks and specialize in extortion. Operating at another level, shadowy organizations run by former military and intelligence officers, such as the Cofradía and El Sindicato, focus on customs fraud and high-level government corruption. Very few murders are brought to justice, with fewer than 2 percent ever making it to trial. Impunity largely reigns, especially for those with means.

Corruption in government in rampant; it would be farcical if not so tragic, and it perversely provides a justification for a neoliberal tactic of starving the state of resources. Many Guatemalan elites see taxes as feeding the waste and corruption of the state, claiming that they would gladly pay higher taxes if they could trust the government to be good stewards of their money. This becomes a vicious circle, as the government is starved of resources to provide key services, and the lack of those services is used to justify keeping taxes low. Guatemala devotes the lowest percentage of GDP to taxes of any country in the region (9.8 percent).

Vanderbilt's Latin American Public Opinion Project (LAPOP) conducts biannual representative surveys of public sentiment across Latin America. Their 2019 survey in Guatemala found low levels of support for democracy as a form of governance (less than 50 percent), and 48.6 percent expressed an openness to a return to authoritarian rule.[52] More than 64 percent do not believe the judicial system punishes the guilty, and 61 percent see government corruption as endemic. In terms of confidence in institutions, only churches, the army, and the United Nations' International Commission Against Impunity (CICIG) top 50 percent in the LAPOP data.[53] But the most pressing concern for most Guatemalans, by far, is security. More than 50 percent report not feeling safe in their neighborhoods, and one in five reported being a victim of crime in last year.[54] Over 69 percent of respondents do not let their children play outside for fear of violence. In this context, it is not surprising that many want to flee. About 1 percent of Guatemalans live in the United States, and, according to LAPOP, just over 25 percent report a desire to migrate.

Emerging on the national stage in the 1990s, a movement of Maya organizations has been pushing for Indigenous rights. Led by Maya scholars and activists, many educated abroad, a loose conglomeration of NGOs and political organizations has successfully fought for Indigenous rights legislation, although the government's implementation has been halfhearted at best. The pan-Maya movement has become a minor political force, with an influential public voice promoting multicultural development.[55] Major newspapers cover their activities in some depth, and there is indeed a greater awareness of cultural issues and less tolerance for blatant public discrimination, and yet leaders have been unable to convert this into a unified voting bloc. Maya peoples are divided by language and geography, and many of their pressing concerns are intensely local, even if they are sympathetic with the message of Maya cultural rights. In 1999 a Consulta Popular seeking constitutional changes to implement elements of the 1996 peace accords, including the progressive Agreement on Indigenous Rights and Identity, was soundly defeated (with an abstention rate of more than 80 percent, which tells its own story). Likewise, in 2006 Rigoberta Menchú (a polarizing figure in Guatemala, but the first serious Indigenous contender for the presidency) received only 3 percent of the national vote, in a country where Maya make up about half of the population.[56] In the countryside, deep local attachments and weak national attachments exist concomitantly. Maya peoples still primarily identify with their home communities rather than as a unified ethnic political bloc.

Demetrio Cojtí's analysis of Guatemala as a neocolonial state certainly holds true for the large First Wave coffee plantations. Despite its small size, Guatemala produces 2.5 percent of the world's coffee, exporting almost 75 percent of it to just four countries: the United States (40 percent), Japan (16 percent), Germany (9 percent), and Canada (9 percent).[57] There are more than 270,000 hectares of coffee planted in Guatemala, and 98 percent of it is shade-grown washed arabica. While the growing Second Wave market offers an alternative to smallholders with access to land, on the big coffee fincas, we still find extremely harsh working conditions and the widespread use of debt to indenture workers. About half of plantation workers are recruited through labor contractors, and a 2012 Verité study found that using labor brokers resulted in lower pay, worse conditions for workers, and frequently fraud. In 2019 the minimum legal agricultural daily wage labor rate was 90 quetzals (about $11.50), although the actual day rate is often much lower. Verité found that 78 percent of coffee finca workers reported earning less than the daily minimum wage (and 68 percent reported earning below subsistence wages). That study also found that Maya workers were paid an average of 60 percent of what non-Maya workers made for same tasks, and that the larger the finca, the worse the conditions. At the same time, the worst abuses of the previous centuries are much less common: the Verité study found extremely low levels of reported physical violence, confinement, or the confiscation of identification documents.[58] Child labor is still employed on many farms, with children's harvest usually counted toward their parents' total weight. After seeing children in the fields on a tour of a coffee finca, I asked the successful and educated owner of the farm about them; his response was to explain that Maya children do not like school and are not well suited to studies, and so working in the fields with their parents is actually the most culturally appropriate thing for them.

COLONIAL LEGACIES AND COMMODITY COFFEE

As commodities are made and traded, they act to anchor distinct, often distant, value worlds to the same material object. With standardized grading and an established futures market in place by the late 1800s, coffee became an undifferentiated commodity produced in tropical regions and exported largely to Northern hemisphere markets—a poster child for the sort of economic dependency observed in world systems models. This was the First Wave market supplied by Guatemala's large plantations with their Indigenous workforces, built on land seizures, labor coercion, and human cruelties. There was little or no Northern consumer regard for the lives and livelihood of coffee workers.

Coffee's role in Guatemalan society and political economy has built up through a series of events,[59] conjunctures of worldviews and material circumstances linked by networks of thought and structures of trade. The Guatemalan elite used coffee to pursue a particular vision of liberal modernity. Crucial to their success was an ability to translate across vastly different value worlds. Ideologies of racial superiority and policies of economic progress connected the bourgeois tastes of Germans to the dispossession of Maya lands for coffee farms. Dieseldorff and others learned Q'eqchi' and tried to cultivate a reliable and skilled workforce to produce their quality coffees. Moreover, they used their understanding of the burgeoning middle classes in the context of liberalizing and industrializing northern Europe to position their washed arabicas as valuable product for the German market, thus translating the worth of coffee across value worlds. As Glenn Penny argues, "The cultural and social capital German migrants brought from merchant colonies was as critical to their success as the liquid capital that came from their ties to German finance."[60]

The structural and ethnic inequalities of the coffee economy established in Guatemala in the late nineteenth century continue to define the country. As Grandin argues, there is a direct link between coffee plantation exploitation and the formation of revolutionary groups in the 1970s and 1980s, and the resulting genocidal violence. Histories often portray the Maya masses as pawns in the games of state, but Maya individuals have long actively resisted the impositions of the plantation economy and forced labor, sometimes using what James Scott terms "weapons of the weak," and sometimes through outright rebellion.[61] Deep structural inequalities persist, gang and drug violence runs high, and cynicism about the political system and government institutions runs deep.

Still, all is not bleak. The growing market in high-value specialty coffee has benefited a large number of smallholding Maya farmers in the remote areas of Guatemala's western highlands whose lands are ideally suited to the quality tastes of today. The next chapter looks at how the Guatemalan coffee oligarchy's ideological commitment to Austrian economics set the conditions for a Second Wave revolution that largely benefited small and medium-sized producers.

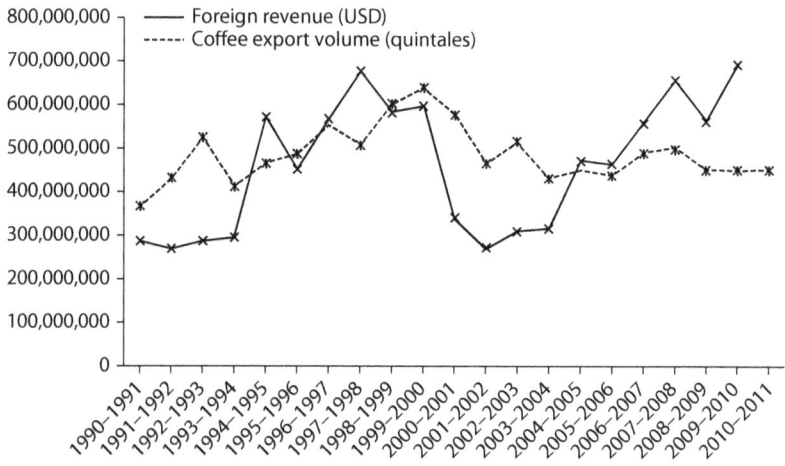

Figure 17. Guatemalan coffee export revenues and volumes.

CHAPTER FOUR

Austrian Economics and the
Quality Turn in Guatemala Coffee

Starting in the late 1990s, an odd thing happened. Guatemala's volume of coffee exports began to drop and yet foreign earnings, after reaching an all-time low in 2001, steadily increased. It was a graph illustrating just that point that led me to start researching the impact of specialty coffee on Maya farmers.

Bart Victor and I were meeting with Bill Hempstead in 2009 in a conference room at the headquarters of Anacafé (the Asociación Nacional del Café of Guatemala, the Guatemalan producers' association). Situated on the edge of one of Guatemala City's tonier neighborhoods, the modern, redbrick Anacafé building conveys a sense of corporate affluence, with a nod to its agricultural roots. It is also just blocks away from the airport's private hangars, which is convenient for the large coffee growers who still maintain plantations but prefer to live in Guatemala City and occasionally fly out to their farms by small plane or helicopter. Anacafé has a reputation as being the voice of the old guard elite and is viewed with suspicion by many on the left. A mutual friend had suggested a meeting with Hempstead to discuss a malnutrition project we were starting, and we took it out of courtesy. In that meeting he showed us a version of the chart shown here in figure 17.

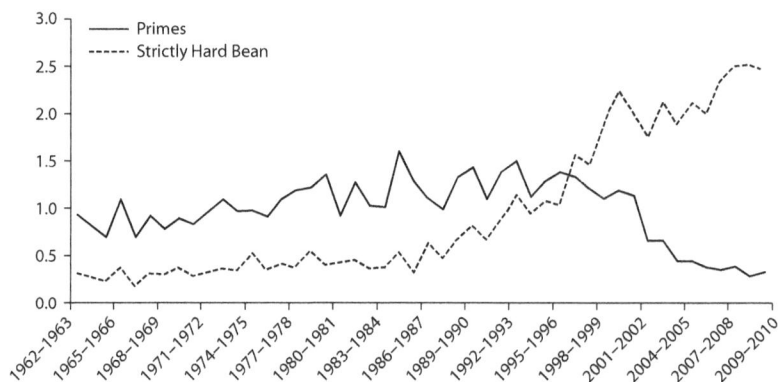

Figure 18. Guatemalan export volumes of Prime and Strictly Hard Bean coffees.

Hempstead—at once understated and charismatic—captivated us with a story of Guatemala's changing coffee market and the role of smallholding producers. At that point I associated coffee in Guatemala with its history of exploitative labor conditions and an unhealthy concentration of political power. Yet, Hempstead argued, it is not like that anymore. An amateur historian, Hempstead is always ready with a graph or a reference to buttress his arguments. He asked an assistant to pull up a version of figure 18, explaining the apparent paradox of falling volumes and rising revenues as a consequence of the decline of commodity-grade Prime and Extra Prime production (grown at 750 to 1350 masl) and the rise of higher-quality and higher-value Strictly Hard Bean (SHB) coffees (grown at 1350–2000 masl).

Bart immediately grasped the implication: this simple PowerPoint chart was showing a market transition with major social and political-economic ramifications. Guatemala's large legacy plantations are on relatively low lands that mostly produced Extra Primes for the First Wave market, but the shift in tastes for high-end coffee moved the market toward the higher-altitude Strictly Hard Bean coffee, mostly grown in the Maya highlands. This resulted in a rapid proliferation in the number of small producers—we estimate at least fifty thousand new growers over the last twenty or so years, many Maya smallholders. Hempstead was extolling a strategy that had slowly killed off his own family plantations, and happily claiming that Anacafé should get a lot of credit for making this happen.[1] He described the Second Wave impact on Guatemalan production as resulting from the conjuncture of a number of forces, including a U.S. market shift toward quality coffee, environmental limitations on where quality coffee would grow, a history of pushing Indigenous communities into the far reaches of the highland areas, and a commitment to a neoliberal economic and moral value world.

This chapter turns to the role of Anacafé and the coffee oligarchy in reorienting Guatemalan production toward the high-value specialty market. The liberal ideas that underwrote First Wave expansion transmogrified into a neoliberal ideology of Austrian economics that justified the move to Second Wave production. Guatemalan oligarchs have a reputation for the ruthless pursuit of self-interest, but their motivations are complicated, also involving a sense of honor and what they see as a virtuous fidelity to an ideal of liberty. Extolling individual freedom and meritocracy may be disingenuous when one is starting from a position of privilege built up over generations, having benefited from structured disparities in material capital (such as land and wealth) and human capital (including education and social networks). Nonetheless, as we see in the next chapter, the move to Second Wave production created a boom in many Maya communities.

DON BILLY

When we met with him, Hempstead kept a sizable office hidden away in a corner on the ground floor of the Anacafé headquarters, close to the cupping rooms and brewing labs and far from the bustle of the top-floor executive suites. His desk and side table were piled with books, papers, and maps—he had recently published a volume on Central American cartography, and he was working on a history of coffee in Guatemala viewed through his own family genealogy. The floor-to-ceiling bookcase on one wall displayed samples of Guatemalan coffees bought around the world, from Japanese canned drinks to bags of single-origin beans from small roasters in Portland, London, and Shanghai. Hempstead is always on the lookout for the latest thing in coffee, and he saw the quality turn in specialty coffee coming early on, in the late 1980s. He also saw Guatemala's particular competitive advantage: the country's producers had long grown high-quality washed arabicas, starting with early exports to Germany's demanding market and evidenced in the various prizes awarded to Guatemalan beans at world expositions in the late nineteenth and early twentieth centuries. Hempstead believed that this quality tradition combined with the country's varied altitudes and microclimates could position Guatemalan coffees to take a greater percentage of the growing high-value market. He was no fan of the international quota system that governed from 1962 to 1989, seeing such attempts to regulate and tame the market as futile, antiliberal efforts that do more harm than good. Citing Milton Friedman and Friedrich Hayek, he said that Guatemala needs more, not less, market competition to improve the lives of all.

Hempstead himself traces his lineage to two of Guatemala's most prominent coffee families. It is easy to portray the coffee oligarchy as villains, and they have given plenty of cause to reach that conclusion. But it is also important to distinguish between structures of exploitation and the motivations of individuals enacting them—and we need to understand both to capture the full complexity of how such systems work. Most coffee oligarchs do not see themselves as cruel or uncaring but as good people driven by moral values and political beliefs. Hempstead and his wife still live in his family's old house—modest by today's extravagant nouveau riche standards—with its large stretch of manicured lawn in the middle of the city, hidden by imposing walls and security gates, not far from the Anacafé building. He takes his position as steward of the family's legacy seriously, even as he has had to oversee the move to close down coffee production, a victim of the very processes he put into play. I got to know Billy, as he is known to his friends—

and that would be "Don Billy" to acquaintances and subordinates—over the course of this research, relying on him for insider information and socializing over meals at his home. He arranged for Anacafé to provide logistical support for our first round of surveys of smallholding coffee producers, and he clearly saw a value in having Bart and me independently document the changes he was extolling within the organization.

Hempstead was born and grew up in Cobán, the urban hub for coffee producers whose plantations were spread across Alta Verapaz. In the early twentieth century Cobán had been a cosmopolitan boomtown, and the Hempsteads were already major coffee producers when Bill's father married into the powerful Dieseldorff family. Among the last of the generations that grew up in this milieu, Hempstead was raised speaking English at home and Q'eqchi' Mayan with workers in the house and in the fields. Neighboring families similarly spoke German and Q'eqchi', with little need to master Spanish until adulthood. As an adolescent Hempstead went to boarding school in the United States, where he remained to do his undergraduate degree and then to get a Masters in Economic Development from George Washington University. He recalls this time as his "leftist youth," when he read the work of Andre Gunder Frank, Immanuel Wallerstein, and other critics of the global political economy, before coming back to Guatemala in his midtwenties. As his nickname suggests, Don Billy is quintessentially Guatemalan and yet speaks Spanish with a gringo accent. Upon returning to Guatemala, Hempstead worked first in banking before moving to what he now says was his destiny all along, coffee. Along the way he also became a skeptic of the sort of centrally planned interventions he had studied in graduate school, and a firm believer in the power of markets, seeing them as something of a natural force that governments futilely try to control.

In the wake of the civil war violence, parts of the Hempstead plantation were invaded by landless peasants and returned refugees. After a protracted legal battle, they negotiated a settlement, with the family giving up a portion of their finca. Losing that land still hurts Bill—it felt like a failure of his filial obligations despite the country's broad need for restorative justice—but the family has since largely abandoned coffee production. They now cultivate timber, experiment with mini hydro-electric generators, and look for other ways to earn income from the lands that once produced coffee in such abundance. Hempstead attributes his farm's demise to the success of Guatemala's shift to higher-quality, higher-altitude coffee, and to the rise of smallholding producers. He is wistful about what he has lost, and he loves looking at photos from the plantation's glory days. Still, he feels like he did the right thing, and, in any case, his kids are now living abroad and pursuing other professions.

Hempstead early vision of coffee's Third Wave potential earned him the 2011 Specialty Coffee Association Lifetime Achievement Award. He long served on the Anacafé board, with one term as its president, and has spent much of the past two decades working as a vaguely titled "senior advisor" to the organization, which gives him great leeway to pursue coffee research and special projects. Hempstead seems comfortable moving the agenda behind the scenes, happy to leave the day-to-day operations and politics to the elected leaders. He is well regarded and persuasive, and was able to push a reluctant Anacafé board, full of old-school Prime and Extra Prime producers, to embrace the quality turn in specialty coffee.

More than once he said that Anacafé had to simply "follow the market." And this was a refrain we heard repeatedly from past and current leadership of Anacafé, as much a moral as an economic justification. But, of course, markets are not ever "free" but depend on a range of formal institutions and informal customs to allow them to work. And, as in the case of Third Wave coffee production in Guatemala, Hempstead's efforts to *follow* the market also helped *make* the market.

ANACAFÉ

Anacafé has a reputation in Guatemala as a vehicle for the coffee oligarchy, which is associated with the anti-communist stance of the political right. An early convert to privatizing state functions, Guatemala closed the government Oficina Central de Café in 1960 and handed its role to Anacafé, a private nongovernmental organization. Anacafé forms part of the powerful Agricultural, Commercial, Industrial, and Financial Chamber of Commerce, whose acronym, CACIF, is used in casual conversation as shorthand for right-wing political interests. Anacafé and CACIF illustrate the entanglements of private and public interests characteristic of the Guatemalan state, with government policy in key areas largely outsourced to these private interests. By law, CACIF has guaranteed seats on twenty-three government policy-setting boards.[2]

The privatizing of government functions extends to taxation: Anacafé collects 1 percent of all coffee export earnings to support and promote the sector. Those funds have been used to subsidize farmers in times of crisis, to provide technical and marketing support, and to position Guatemalan coffee in the international market. This is essentially a tax that bypasses state coffers, a fact in which Anacafé leaders take great pride. Their stance reflects a widespread elite distrust of the political system and the well-documented corruption at all levels of government; paying taxes to a corrupt system is seen as feeding the beast. Sidestepping the bureaucracy, Anacafé presents itself as a success story of Guatemala's particular form of neoliberal outsourcing of state functions.

In 2011 and 2012, Bart and I conducted interviews with the then-current board members of Anacafé and with all of the living past presidents of the organization. Conversations moved comfortably from mentions of a new pastry shop on New York City's Upper West Side that we really should try to a recent Parisian opera that exceeded all expectations. Meeting them in various settings—offices, restaurants, homes—and seeing how they interact in the world gave the impression of comfortable, unapologetic privilege. With Guatemala City's homicide and kidnapping rates among the highest in the world, security is a concern for the wealthy. While wealthy narco tastes in transportation run to caravans of black SUVs with lots of guys in cheap black suits and earpieces

that snake under the collar, the old guard scoffs at such displays, preferring the simplicity of a discreetly armored car and perhaps a driver,
along with the usual retinue of gardeners and household servants, mostly
young Maya women.

Seeing the coffee oligarchy balance moral and ideological values with
self-interest sometimes reinforced and sometimes complicated our pre-
conceptions, and there were many uncomfortable moments during our
fieldwork. Bart would catch my eye to stifle a reaction when we heard
remarks of casual racism, often insidiously polite, about "the Indians,"
and especially the singular emblem of the "bad Indian," Rigoberta
Menchú, the Maya rights activist, Nobel Peace Prize laureate, and pres-
idential candidate in 2011. This was a time when there was a concerted
effort to bring military leaders to justice for atrocities perpetrated during the civil war. Charges were being prepared against General Efraín
Ríos Montt, the charismatic evangelical former dictator who oversaw
the massacres and massive scorched-earth campaigns of 1982–83. Not
long after, a billboard and bus advertising campaign, presumably funded
by the right (CACIF), declared *No Hubo Genocidio* (There Was No Genocide) to mobilize opinion against the charge that the military intentionally targeted Maya communities because of their ethnic heritage.
Almost all of the former Anacafé leaders were firmly in the "No Hubo
Genocidio" camp. The semantics here have real legal and historical
implications and can be used to distract from the fact that tens of thousands died horrific and unjustifiable deaths, and that millions had their
lives and livelihoods upended.

Anacafé has been changing over the last thirty years, and it became
clear in our interviews that this shift owed much to Bill Hempstead's
efforts, even though he prefers the background to the limelight. To
understand Anacafé we must look not only to its role as a conservative
voice in national politics, but also as an arena of different interests. The
Anacafé board's twenty members are elected within divisions to represent different segments of producers; these are unpaid positions, and
the board actively cultivates a sense that this is a public service and not

a source of personal enrichment. In recent years there has been an effort to diversify the board. Still, notably, there is largely an ideological consensus, with Anacafé officers almost uniformly conveying a strong free market orientation.

HAYEK IN GUATEMALA

Just as liberal thought emerged from the coffeehouses of eighteenth- and nineteenth-century Europe, Austrian venues in the mid-twentieth century saw the rise of a fervent neoliberal ideology among an influential circle of economists and political philosophers. Stressing the virtues of individual liberty and private property, this Austrian school viewed the post–World War II emergence of social democracy and state regulation with skepticism. Friedrich von Hayek's (1944) *The Road to Serfdom* had made the case against central planning and other government regulation of the market as not only inefficient but as threats to liberty. He argued that markets provide the best way of aligning need (demand) and supply, claiming they were infinitely superior to the projections of bureaucrats in an office in Moscow, or Berlin, or Washington. Hayek imagined a global system of governance that could protect capitalist markets and property rights from political interference ("distortions"). His view of economic liberty and consumer sovereignty, combined with an understanding of value as a subjective judgment, gained increasing traction in certain academic and political circles during the Cold War and was popularized by Ayn Rand's novels. Such influence was the plan all along.

In 1947 Hayek and a small group, including Ludwig von Mises, Milton Friedman, and Karl Popper, founded the Mont Pelerin Society. Its founding statement warns of the dangers to civilization of the emerging world order that had been "fostered by a decline of belief in private property and the competitive market; for without the diffused power and initiative associated with these institutions it is difficult to imagine a society in which freedom may be effectively preserved."[3] They saw markets as better information-sharing and distribution mechanisms than central planners, whose efforts they characterized as robbing freedom from individuals. They argued that capitalist free markets were inherently anti-imperialist and color-blind, going so far as to reject race as a category. Seen as a neutral information-gathering machine, the market was understood to reflect what individuals "really" want, not what others decide is best for them.[4] Driven by intellectual and political zeal, the members of the Mont Pelerin Society devised a strategy of winning over influential converts in academia and governments around the world. The rise of the Chicago school of economic thought serves as a testament to its success.

The plan also succeeded in Guatemala. Among the Guatemalan elite there is widespread admiration for Austrian economics, an affinity for Ayn Randian libertarianism, and a connection with the Mont Pelerin Society. This is largely due to the efforts of Manuel Ayau (1925–2010), a Guatemalan who became the first non-European president of the Mont Pelerin Society. Ayau, who came from oligarchical family lines, studied engineering at Louisiana State University and was a strong supporter of the counterrevolutionary Carlos Castillo Armas, the dictator installed by a CIA-led coup in 1954.[5] Ayau discovered Ayn Rand's novels, which lead him to read Hayek and von Mises. He became a fervent convert to the Austrian school, participating in seminars organized by the Foundation for Economic Freedom. In 1959, Ayau founded the Center for Economic and Social Sciences in Guatemala, an economically liberal think tank founded to "study and promote the idea of freedom."

Ayau effectively spread the Austrian school gospel in Guatemala, orchestrating visits by von Mises in the 1960s and Hayek in the 1970s. He actively lobbied politicians and had his think tank staff closely track legislation. But his most consequential legacy is the 1972 founding of the Universidad Francisco Marroquín, an entire institution (today with close to five thousand students) organized around the principles of Austrian economics and neoliberal tenets. With Ayau as the new university's rector, the reading list required that all students read the core works of Hayek, von Mises, Milton Freidman, and others. To this day the university does not take funding from the government—limiting its research revenue—and to the extent possible eschews any governmental contracts. The goal is to create a small-scale space of libertarian ideals, a "Libertópolis." The expansive campus is well landscaped, with low-slung modern brick architecture. The parking lots brim with new cars, and buildings include the von Mises Library and the Adam Smith Plaza; behind one structure is a large sculpture of Atlas carrying the world, a nod to *Atlas Shrugged*. Video screens on the walls of the business school flash rotating quotes from von Mises, Schumpeter, Friedman, and others, and one hallway is flanked by a large-scale timeline of Austrian school thinkers. (One could argue that Guatemala already offers an image of what a libertarian, almost stateless, society might actually look like: heavily armed, with those who can afford it hidden behind walls topped with broken bottles or coils of razor wire, a place that, as Avery Dickins de Girón points out, has many more private security guards than police officers.)[6]

Francisco Marroquín's business and economics faculties are the most prestigious in the country, and it is the university of choice for the children of the well-heeled who do not want to study abroad. The university has trained several generations of businesspeople, economists, and doctors. It is a direct success of the Mont Pelerin Society's strategy of building influence through the academy and policy making. This form of Ayn Rand–inflected Austrian economics provided the ideological justification for Guatemala's neoliberal turn in the 1990s and early 2000s and it feeds a mistrust in government and a resistance to taxes among the elite. It provides moral justification for a privileged class position while glossing over of the history that led to that position. All the same, these are also sincerely and deeply held beliefs, not just, or only, cynical rationalizations.

THE INTERNATIONAL COFFEE AGREEMENT

Since its earliest days, the coffee market was marked by the dramatic boom and bust cycles of primary commodities. Given this volatility, most producer countries have supported quota and price guarantee systems.[7] In the post–World War II era, this preference converged with international efforts to rationalize and regulate the global economy (through the Bretton Woods institutions and the United Nations structure) and to bolster developing countries. Contra Austrian market fundamentalism, the consensus in development economics at the time acknowledged that there was an unfair dependency of primary product–exporting countries of the "periphery" on the markets of the more economically developed and industrialized "core" countries. As an antidote, the structures of the postwar global political economy sought to bolster the autonomy of peripheral countries through regulated quota systems and import substitution regimes.

In 1940 Brazil, Colombia, and other Latin producers came together with the United States to sign the Inter-American Coffee Agreement, divvying up U.S. demand. In the 1950s Colombia and Brazil began working with the U.S. National Coffee Association (of roasters and distributors) and the State Department to look for other ways to stabilize coffee prices and provide some immunity from communism. The result, in 1962, was the International Coffee Agreement (ICA), which created the International Coffee Organization. Part of the post–World War II spirit of rational global governance, the ICA sought to stabilize prices and establish production quotas for each of the fifty signatory countries (representing 99 percent of global production) and import targets for the twenty-five signing consumer countries (90 percent of the consumer market). This quota system was in force until 1989, when the ICA broke down, a triumph of neoliberal deregulation that ended First Wave coffee's comfortable status quo.[8]

Under the ICA quota system, Guatemalan producers had benefited from relative price stability, but many also felt they were not getting the quality premiums their coffees merited. (Each country or region receives a premium or discount from the New York C price depending on quality; Colombian coffee regularly gets a four-point premium, but Guatemala trades at par.) While the large coffee growers in Guatemala benefited from the stability of the ICA system, they also had an uneasy ideological relationship with such international regulatory bodies and regimes, seeing themselves, like the Austrian economists, as defenders of the free market in the face of state and multilateral regulation. Anacafé, representing Guatemala, along with the United States, had consistently argued against quotas, arguing that they should let the market, rather than a central planning body, make the decisions. In 1989, with neoliberal winds in their sails, they finally prevailed, and the ICA quota system was effectively abolished, opening the market to greater competition. After the disintegration of the quota system, there was a move to more quality-based pricing for washed arabicas (classified as "Colombian milds" and "other milds" on the New York exchange). As a result, David Johnson shows, large farms in Guatemala quickly lost their competitive advantage.[9]

ANACAFÉ AND THE QUALITY TURN

To understand Anacafé's subsequent role in the shift toward small-holder production, Bart honed in on the importance of two particular decisions. He posed them in the style of a business school case study, detailing the choices behind a major decision and following the consequences. What follows is based on Bart's framing and turns of phrase. The central players in the drama are Bill Hempstead; Max Quirin, a descendant of Edwin Paul Dieseldorff, whose sympathies were with the traditional landed elite; and José Ángel López, a Jakaltek Maya cooperative leader turned businessman whose election as president marked a major shift in Anacafé history—a Maya running the coffee association long associated with the oligarchy.

At a crucial Anacafé board meeting in late 1995, the mood was tense; the collapsing commodity price was threatening the survival of coffee production in Guatemala and the Pacaya volcano, visible from the conference room, was billowing smoke. World coffee prices had collapsed in the 1992/1993 season, dropping to their lowest point in decades, and the leadership of Anacafé had to confront the possibility that this time the drop was not just the latest fluctuation in prices. Coffee prices had always been volatile. It was such volatility that encouraged global producers to try quota programs such as the ICA. But this time the drop was likely a step on a structural decline, one that threatened the survival of the country's most important export.

At the prices offered in the early 1990s it was simply uneconomical to grow coffee. Growers could not survive unless prices were supported or subsidized. But Anacafé had always resisted any such measures, preferring the let the market mete out punishments as well as rewards. In global coffee politics, Guatemala was often the lone producer country voice for freer markets. In 1994 and 1995 there had been a modest uptick in the market, but by late 1995 the future was at best uncertain. The Anacafé board had to determine what, if any, future coffee production might have in Guatemala. The leadership was made up of producers like the president, Max Erwin Quirin. Quirin was a fourth-generation coffee farmer whose German family had been in the Guatemala coffee business since 1885. His namesake grandfather, Max Quirin, a large plantation owner, had married Matilde Dieseldorff Cú, a daughter of Erwin Paul Dieseldorff. He speaks proudly of his volunteering his plane and services as a pilot to the military during the civil war of the 1980s and is a vocal proponent of open markets. He saw his position in the 1995 meeting as a defender of "a completely free market," meaning that Anacafé should "allow as many exporters as possible in the country."

(Through his role at Anacafé, Quirin served as the CACIF representative on the board of the Guatemalan Social Security Institute. In 2015 an expansive corruption investigation known as La Linea uncovered massive abuse in the institute.[10] Along with several other board members, Quirin was arrested in 2015 for failure of oversight, and he was held without bail, as a flight risk, for several years. The *Wall Street Journal* ran an opinion piece calling for his release. In 2019 Quirin was convicted and sentenced to the three and a half years of prison time already served.)[11]

Critics describe Quirin's politics as reactionary, emblematic of traditional oligarchical privilege, yet in the 1995 meeting his commitment to laissez-faire economics converged with Bill Hempstead's belief that top-quality coffee could be grown profitably in the country. Hempstead pointed out that over the past few years European and American roasters had been willing to pay a significant premium for specialty-grade Strictly Hard Bean coffees. Thus, he argued, Guatemala had the opportunity to decouple its production from the rollercoaster of the New York C price. Hempstead made the case to the Anacafé board that they needed to turn their back on propping up production of Primes and Extra Primes and go all in on the quality turn. His was a bold and compelling strategic vision, but also one that threatened the livelihoods of many on the board. Hempstead had won over Quirin. With a few other allies, they pushed for the idea of marketing differentiated regions and sending Anacafé to the specialty meetings and trade shows—in other words, for spending more on marketing than on artificially propping up prices.

The Anacafé board tends to be fiscally conservative, perhaps due to their familiarity with the vagaries of the seasons and the markets. Some of the traditional constituency was opposed to spending money on marketing and promoting the Second Wave coffees. They argued that what was needed was a return to the quota system. Anacafé had been closely observing the strategy of Colombia's National Federation of Coffee Producers and its successful Café de Colombia and Juan Valdez marketing campaigns. Colombia promoted a single national brand and central control for production and exports. Some in Anacafé argued that to save their farms and save the history and structure of the Guatemalan industry they needed to follow the Colombian example of centralization, price controls, and state subsidies. Hempstead argued that Guatemala should turn its focus to the quality segment and promote regionalization in branding.

In July 1995 Anacafé received the final report of a study commissioned by the European Union, "The Coffee Chain Project," identifying five potential regional coffees to promote. While the climate and soils were right for the potential crop in these regions, it was unclear to the Anacafé board who would grow the coffee. Anacafé had the expertise and experience to build the capacity of new growers, but this would be different from anything they had done before. The new smallholders would likely be very different from the traditional *finqueros*. They would be scattered across the remote hillsides, cultivating a few hectares of land rather than the vast fincas, and would speak Mayan languages. Many would also still be deeply affected by the brutal civil war that had devastated many of their communities. In the past Anacafé had focused on technical assistance and agricultural support for growers, but the new plan would demand a massive investment in marketing. This presented a financial challenge as well as a historic strategic shift for the organization that many felt went against its origins.

Hempstead and others argued that Guatemala had the potential to be the main supplier of specialty coffee in the world. As Hempstead recalled, "We knew that Guatemalan growing regions are truly unique—it is not that way in other countries and that is our competitive advantage." They argued that coffee, a perishable product that takes a long time to start up production, cannot follow cartel strategies. Further, in order to compete in the specialty coffee market they had to shift their perceptions of and interaction with importers and roasters, seeing them as allies rather than enemies.

Quirin remembers thinking about a lesson he learned from Erna Knutsen, a Portland, Oregon, coffee roaster who had recently visited his finca in Cobán. She told him to "get me quality, and don't worry about the price." In the end, that view carried the day. The Anacafé board voted to endorse the new quality strategy, investing a majority of its funds to promoting (among farmers and roasters) high-altitude Strictly Hard Bean coffees. It was decided to promote regional varieties rather than "Guatemalan coffee," and what started as five regions grew to eight in the association's successful "8 Regions, 8 Cups" program, a model of specialty coffee marketing (map 5).

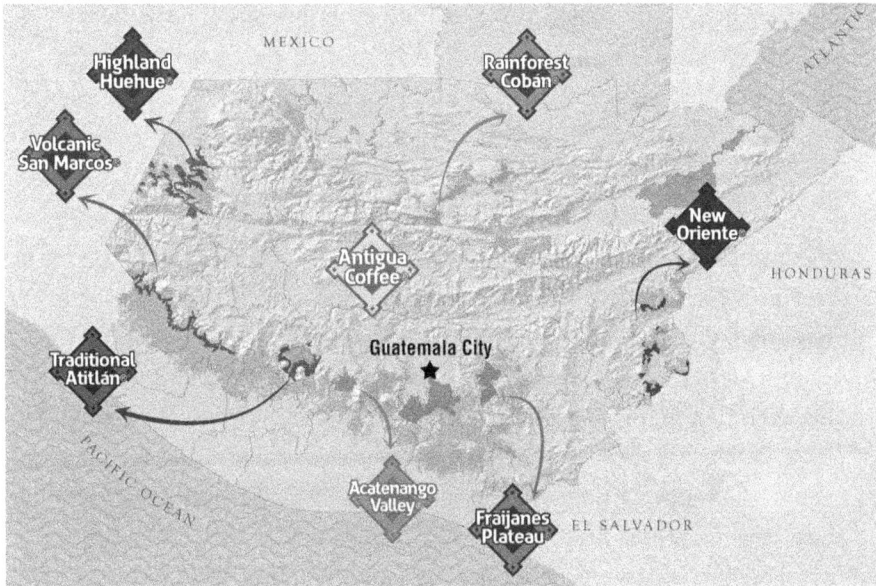

Map 5. 8 regions, 8 cups.

2001 PRICE COLLAPSE AND STAYING
THE COURSE

On 7 July 2011 at 6 a.m., at the Anacafé headquarters, the ninth annual Guatemalan Cup of Excellence coffee auction was held. In attendance were small and medium-scale producers from around the country. Their coffees, in lots of only tens and hundreds of pounds, had been judged by a global panel of cuppers to be the best of the harvest that year. Online, gourmet coffee roasters from around the world were bidding on the lots. Every two minutes the price was updated. The auction for each lot would end when the bidding stopped for two minutes. The New York C price on this day was under $2 per pound, but no one was paying any attention to the commodity price. This was an auction of high-quality coffee, each lot distinguished by its cupping scores and tasting notes. The taster described the "cup" for each lot in terms that recalled a fine wine. The last bid was placed at 11:30 a.m. The harvest of a Caturra varietal from the farm El Socorro, near the town of Palencia, was purchased for $20.12 per pound. It was described by the tasters as uniquely balanced in sweetness and body, characterized by notes of champagne, vanilla, and jasmine.

This auction was a direct result of the initial decision made in 1995 in the boardroom at Anacafé. In the intervening years tens of thousands of new producers began growing the high-quality Strictly Hard Bean coffees for the Second Wave market. Although First Wave giants such as Philip Morris, Nestlé, Sara Lee, and Procter and Gamble controlled about 60 percent of the world market and 73 percent of the U.S. market, by 2000 specialty coffees comprised about 10 percent of world coffee exports and approximately 15 percent of U.S. volume.[12] Significantly, Second Wave coffees did not follow the C price fluctuations. Their prices continued to increase even when C prices were down. The majority of these higher-altitude coffee producers in Guatemala are smallholders with fewer than five hectares under production. They represented about 30 percent of total coffee production in 2000, up from 16 percent in 1979.[13]

Then, in 2001, there was an international collapse in the coffee market, brought about by increasing Vietnamese production, a bumper Brazilian crop, and declining demand volumes. In 2000, coffee exports from Guatemala totaled some US $600 million; in 2001, that had fallen to $320 million. Coffee prices dropped to a historic low of $0.45 per pound, far less than the cost of production. In the following years most of the country's large coffee growers (who planted Prime and Extra Prime coffees) left the market, transitioning into rubber, macadamia nuts, palm oil, and sugarcane on their plantations. There were a number of land invasions of the large fincas; banks foreclosed on coffee properties unable to make their payments on capital or interest.

In 2003 José Ángel López was elected president of Anacafé. His rise marked a significant shift from past leaders in that he did not come from a traditional coffee family or one of the powerful private coffee associations. Indeed, he was an Indigenous coffee grower from the town of

Jacaltenango. Maryknoll missionaries arrived in Jacaltenango in the 1940s, intent on nurturing the spiritual and economic lives of the Maya Popti'-Jakaltek population. They encouraged cooperative organizations, and in 1967 residents created the Cooperativa Río Azul to promote coffee production as an alternative to seasonal wage labor on plantations and to subsistence agriculture. López's father was active in the cooperative and went on to become mayor of the town. As a youth López was introduced to coffee by his father, and he worked in the cooperative's *beneficio,* yet feeling limited by the lack of opportunity in Jacaltenango, at the age of sixteen he emigrated to Guatemala City to seek his fortune. Enrolling in the public Universidad de San Carlos, known as a bastion of leftist thinking, he studied political science. He remained active in the cooperative movement and was eventually was elected president of the national association of coffee cooperatives, FEDECOCAGUA. In that capacity he held a seat on the Anacafé board of directors. Smart, ambitious, and politically pragmatic, he quickly earned the respect of his fellow board members and was elected president of the association. López went on to run the country's rural development bank, serve on numerous corporate and public boards, and run for president in 2015. In 2020 he was named Guatemala's minister of agriculture.[14] López frequently cites the formative influence of the cooperative movement, and while he is a successful businessman and politician, he considers himself a voice for workers and smallholders.

As his tenure began López faced a crucial decision. With the 2001 price bust, growers worried that this could be the final death blow for Guatemalan coffee. López was faced with the challenging decision of whether to stick to the strategy of marketing regional specialty coffees mostly grown by smallholding producers to gain a high premium, or to reverse course and began creating price supports, perhaps issuing bonds against future production. López sided with Hempstead and argued that Anacafé needed to double down on its commitment to the new high-quality producers. This position prevailed, and the board adopted a new competitiveness plan focused on nurturing quality and differentiation (including a mapping system with GIS coordinates of farmers to trace micro-provenances). Lopez saw this as a huge win for small producers and cooperatives, such as those in Jacaltenango.

This turned out to be the right move. Rapidly evolving specialty markets have kept coffee export value growing in Guatemala even as total volumes have decreased. In the past, the only price was the New York C price for commodity coffee. Now specialty coffee buyers are paying significantly more than the C price for quality lots. For the large First Wave plantations, the strategy was to keep costs low and volumes high. Prime coffee beans were harvested, processed, and sold to wholesalers who in turn consolidated them with similar beans from all over the world. These large lots of commodity beans were then sold to a few global coffee roasters.

Now the quality "in the cup" and certifications of various types translate into Second Wave profitability even if the yield is low. Premiums are earned for organic, socially responsible, and environmentally sustainable practices. In an industry with a history that includes periods of forced labor, violence, and discrimination, some coffee growers now can choose from a number of opportunities to add a premium to the price farmers receive for their crop.

NEOLIBERAL VALUE WORLDS AND SECOND WAVE PRODUCTION

A belief in Austrian-inspired free market economics led Guatemala's coffee producers to oppose the system of ICA quotas and embrace the vision of small-lot specialty coffee championed by Bill Hempstead and José Ángel López. It may be that the large producers came to see that the Prime grade coffee they grew was not going to produce the returns it once did. It turns out that they were right, but at the time the decision was full of risk and uncertainty. We could easily imagine the coffee oligarchy clamping down during the market shift, brutally protecting their declining market shares and marshaling Anacafé's resources to prop up Prime coffee production. Instead, they reoriented the machinery of

Anacafé to support the growing volume and profitability of the specialty coffee market.

Past and present leaders of Anacafé explain their decision not as an attempt to aid small famers but as an effort to follow where the market leads: "We just follow the market" was a mantra we heard again and again. More than just a business tactic, this deeply held laissez-faire position is at once antistatist (and antiregulation) and pro–free trade ("we should be able to sell to anyone we want," as one large grower explained). Truth be told, they were not just following the market: their marketing, branding, and system of provenance fueled as well as followed Northern market trends toward Second Wave coffee.

In the next chapter, we explore the implications of the market shift toward specialty coffee on smallholding Maya farmers in the Guatemalan highlands.

Figure 19. Farmers washing cherry, Finca Rosma, San Pedro Necta, Huehuetenango.

CHAPTER FIVE

Maya Farmers and Second Wave Coffee

Carlos Cuyuch, a forty-six-year-old farmer who lives in a hamlet on the outskirts of La Democracia in Huehuetenango, started growing coffee in the early 2000s. While his native language is Mam, Cuyuch speaks Spanish fluently, if with a Mayan accent (an ethnic marker to which Guatemalan ears are attuned). He and his wife Ana live with their four children in a three-room cinderblock house with a corrugated tin roof, which sets them apart as one of the more affluent households in the community. An adobe wood-burning stove anchors the kitchen and serves as the family gathering spot. The kitchen opens onto a patio with a waist-high concrete water basin—the *pila,* which is used for washing clothes and dishes, for quick baths, and as a repository for water. The pila and the toilet connect to a municipal water system, but the supply is spotty, usually only running for a few hours a day. As a backup, Ana leaves the pila's tap dripping to keep the central basin full. The house has electricity, and both Carlos and Ana have basic prepaid cell phones. Their kids are all still in school, a fact of which they are proud, but they are also expected to work, to contribute to the household by helping in the fields, selling in the market, and working around the house. Carlos and Ana are doing very well by local standards, but it is still a precarious existence.

Carlos recalls that both as a child, when he worked with his parents, and later, on his own as a young man, he worked as a migrant laborer on coffee plantations. He explains, "We were poor, we didn't have anywhere else to work, anywhere to live, we did not have our own land to farm." The family labored seasonally on coffee plantations and used communal land to grow *milpa,* plots of maize and black beans that are at the heart of Maya subsistence and cosmology. Carlos yearned to have his own land, to enjoy the material and psychological security that it would provide. He saved what little money he could with that end in mind. "Around this time I had a *patrón* who loaned me some money to give me enough to buy half a *cuerda* of land," Carlos recounts.[1] "And so we were able to buy the land that we grow coffee on. Now I have six cuerdas and a house. It is hard work, but I have been able to do it."

Carlos's story is exemplary of the how the Second Wave coffee boom has been experienced in many highland Maya communities. The quality turn in consumption in the United States and elsewhere during the 1980s and 1990s increased demand for the Strictly Hard Bean (SHB) coffees grown on land above 1350 meters above sea level (masl). In Guatemala, that meant a geographic shift in production away from the mid-altitude estates of the Germans to lands in the Maya majority highlands. The move toward SHBs opened new markets and increased incomes for many families in historically marginalized Maya communities. Today a large number of former coffee laborers and subsistence farmers are supporting their families by growing and selling their own coffee. These producers cultivate increasingly differentiated varietals of arabicas on their own parcels of land using family labor and hiring day workers. A majority process and sell their coffee through a cooperative, and many of these are part of the fair trade system, which rose hand in hand with the Second Wave. Sometimes these farmers are able to sell their crop as domain-specific lots directly to small and medium-sized roasters around the world rather than having it disappear into the vast, undifferentiated market for commodity coffee.

Like most in their community, Carlos and Ana are Catholic, but they also participate in traditional Maya ceremonies around planting and harvest. They occasionally consult with one of Ana's cousins, who is a daykeeper, a Maya religious specialist charged with maintaining the count of a sacred 260-day calendar. Although they are not especially religious, they regularly attend mass, are conscientious about keeping up with agricultural rituals, and invoke these moral frameworks in justifying ideas and actions. In Maya spirituality, making a living from the land is seen as especially virtuous, linked to the cosmological cycles of regeneration and reciprocity. Other livelihoods can certainly be honorable, but there is a sense that *real* worth comes from the earth.

The rise in demand for Second Wave coffee has had profound and complex impacts on the lives and livelihoods of Maya producers. It entails new sorts of risks, both of crop failure and of market fluctuations, as well as new possibilities for financial gain and social change.[2] Farmers largely see this new market as positive, increasing incomes and fueling optimism. As Carlos and Ana describe it, coffee represents an opportunity in a context of few opportunities, an imperfect means to a marginally better life. They say that coffee has been a benefit to their family and their community, providing more income and a sense that things are getting better. In town, people no longer migrate to work as seasonal plantation labor. Those without land work locally for smallholding producers who need extra help at harvest. Still, even the successful live in modest circumstances with limited resources and opportunities. Most families, if they have land or not, employ a variety of economic strategies to get by, from growing subsistence crops to selling items in the market to working as day laborers. Carlos and Ana, for example, grow their own staple crops (maize tortillas and black beans are served at virtually every meal) and, after expenses, they earn around US $4000 a year from coffee. This is significantly more than the local average, and yet it is not yet enough to afford for their eldest daughter to go to university in Cobán or Xela, which she longs to do.

As a means to other ends, growing coffee provides a route for pursuing values-laden aspirations and economic security. From the angle of a capabilities approach to development, the Second Wave coffee boom in

Maya communities increases the ability of people to envision and pursue goals that they themselves value.[3] Yet in looking at the lives of Guatemalan coffee producers, we find that desires and preferences are shaped by power relations, social norms, and institutional structures. That is to say, what these producers value does not naturally flow from purely endogenous sources, but rather emerges in the context of community norms and cultural traditions engaging with the neoliberal structures of an international market.[4] What these farmers want, what matters to them, is not natural or neutral. The pull of desiring moves them, as individuals and collectively, to take up stakes in projects that are compelling because they embody certain moral, economic, or symbolic worth.[5] In the case of Guatemalan coffee's Second Wave boom, a number of external factors have created a particular opportunity structure in the form of the coffee market. Smallholding coffee farmers engage this imperfect structure as a route to a marginally better life, even as they realize they are excluded from the market's largest rewards.

This chapter turns to the experiences of Maya smallholding producers in highland Guatemala, focusing on how the growing market for specialty coffees intersects with local value worlds. This class of new producers emerged from a particular confluence of environmental endowments, consumer trends, market dynamics, actions of the traditional Guatemalan coffee elite, and historical legacies of violence and marginalization. But it was the smallholders' choices, framed by community values and individual aspirations, that determined just how this coffee would be cultivated, harvested, and processed. These farmers are concerned with improving their lives, exploring new options, and seeking more secure livelihoods for themselves and their children. They are also driven by values and aspirations that go beyond material needs, and they engage in the coffee market to pursue their own imagined futures. Understanding such desires only in terms of individual agency and utility maximization fails to reveal the complex cultural trajectories and value worlds that frame farmers' economic choices.

FIELDWORK WITH COFFEE PRODUCERS

In 2011 and then again in 2014, Bart Victor, Linda Asturias de Barrios, and I, along with a team of students, conducted surveys of a total of 397 households in fourteen coffee-growing communities in ten *municipios* in the Guatemalan highlands (map 6).[6] Our sampling targeted smallholders (with less than 2.2 hectares), and the data were collected when Second Wave production was booming and Third Wave demand was just beginning to impact the market.[7] Interviews were lengthy, taking more than two hours: we elicited growers' personal histories and asked about the role of coffee in their lives and its meaning for their families and communities, gathering data on cultivation practices, market relationships, participation in cooperatives, financing, and labor practices. In addition, we held focus groups of farmers and cooperative members in order to stimulate a more free-flowing conversation and a greater diversity of viewpoints, as well as to gauge the breadth and intensity of community sentiment.

On average, the producers in our sample reported that they had been cultivating coffee for slightly longer than twenty years, meaning that they started in the mid-1990s. Many entered the market gradually, and it was often hard for them to put an exact date on when they began. In the early days of the Second Wave boom, cooperatives working with Fair Trade and other certification regimes were able to pay significant premiums, attracting new producers and buffering them against global market slumps. Government projects and international aid played an important role in getting new producers into the market, and 81 percent of our sample had received some sort of assistance from these programs. Guatemala, through its main coffee cooperative association (FEDE-COCAGUA), was also an early player in the Fair Trade coffee movement, having worked with SOS Holland and its German partners to market "Indio-Kaffee aus Guatemala" (Indian Coffee from Guatemala) in Germany and the Netherlands in the early 1970s. The Fair Trade system, which guarantees minimum prices above the market norm,

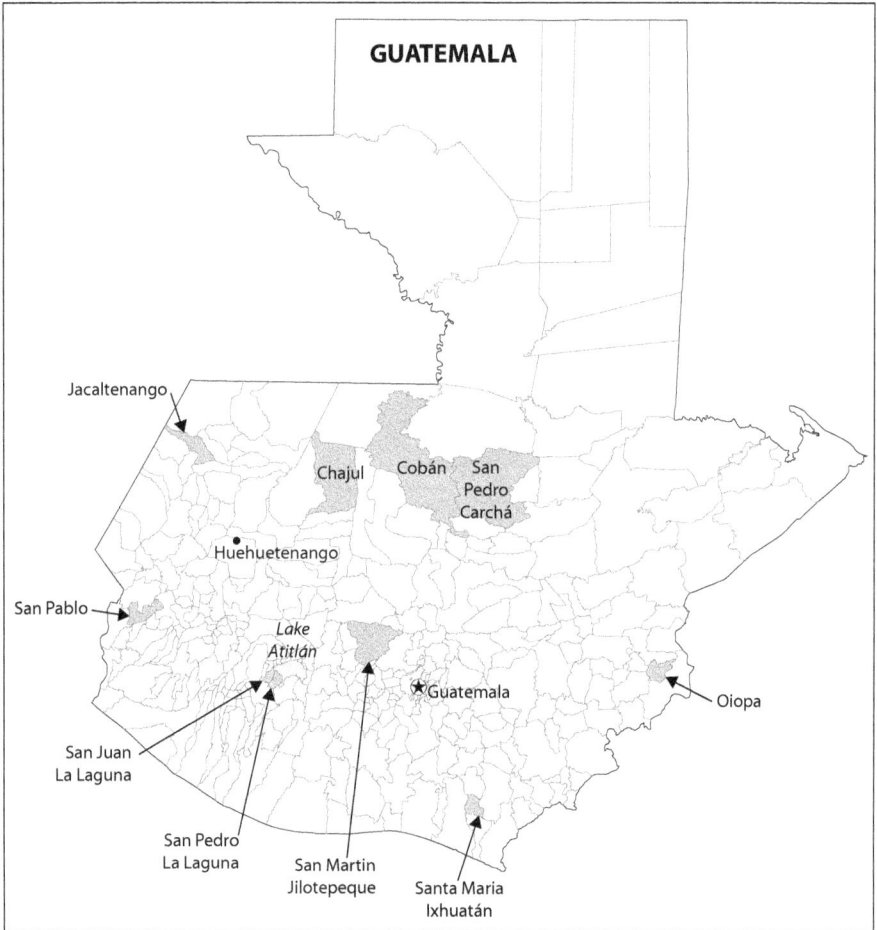

Map 6. Sampled communities.

played an important role in enticing smallholder cooperatives to enter the coffee market, an important capacity-building mechanism for the growth in SHB coffees. Still, it was not until the late 1990s that the Fair Trade market began to provide significant volume (U.S. consumption increased from about two million pounds per year to almost forty-five million between 1999 and 2005). In 2000–2001, when commodity coffee prices dropped to historic lows, Fair Trade premiums and a Starbucks program that paid almost double market rates helped sustain many farmers.[8]

The producers we interviewed were drawn to coffee production for a range of reasons, including family agricultural traditions, knowledge of the production process from working on plantations, and expected material gains. Those who had worked on coffee *fincas* learned the basic process of planting and caring for coffee there. Often they had kept a few coffee trees for decoration and some domestic consumption. Especially in Huehuetenango, but also in other parts of the western highlands, a significant number had family members who had worked in the United States and sent home remittances.[9] As demand began to rise in the 1990s for the high-elevation SHB coffees, they expanded their plots to devote more to coffee. One twenty-one-year-old Q'eqchi' man told us, "I learned about growing coffee from my father. As kids we used to play 'planting coffee.' I have been growing on my own for a few years now. Before there wasn't an opportunity for us Indigenous people to plant our own coffee, it was just for the Germans." Other respondents likewise commented that they had taken up coffee production after "the Germans" (a frequently used shorthand for the coffee oligarchy) had given up production. This conceptual reframing of who grows coffee represents an historically significant shift in Indigenous views of ethnic relations and perceived opportunity structures.

Starting small, with just a few coffee plants, and expanding gradually is a risk-averse and non–capital intensive strategy. Smallholder coffee production is a family enterprise, with spouses and children providing important labor inputs. Households in our sample averaged 5.8 members, with three of those working in the family coffee fields. Coffee is labor intensive, and global markets are always searching for cheaper labor. The family-run smallholding producers rely on unpaid family labor to compete, a pattern common in Latin America.[10] María, a thirty-two-year-old woman who works with her husband on their six acres, observes that "coffee is different from the other crops we plant around here. It is a form of self-employment that proves some income for people, sometimes enough to invest. When growers are very poor, they don't contract others for the harvest, the family just does it all. And this income stays in the community. Maize isn't very profitable, but coffee income lets us buy maize, or even maintain our milpa." If they do expand, smallholders may hire temporary workers for harvest. In our sample, small producers who hired workers would employ from two to ten employees, all of whom they hired locally.

The ability to own and expand one's landholdings is a primary attraction of cultivating coffee. In the minds of many, worth ultimately derives from the land, and investing in it is seen as security against an uncertain future. Significantly, our respondents generally defined poverty as not having land, and thus having to work on fincas, which several compared to being slaves. In our surveys 78 percent of farmers owned the land on which they grew coffee, and all planned to invest future surpluses in buying more land. Coffee has provided a way for these farmers to maintain control over the land, and perhaps even expand their holdings. It is also a way to earn extra cash income while maintaining an agricultural lifestyle, which, as tiresome as it can be, is also deeply meaningful for many.[11]

Debt is a pressing issue for small producers. Every respondent in our sample has taken out loans, and most do so almost annually. The majority of loans come from cooperatives and from banks (especially Banrural, whose state-sponsored mission is to service farmers). These loans pay for fertilizer and other inputs as well as help tide families over until the harvest, but they are also viewed as a hindrance to getting ahead. Almost all the farmers we talked to complained of the burden of debt that they were constantly working to pay off.

A surprising 94 percent of our sample was literate, well above the national average of 71 percent. The mean years of education was 2.9 for males and 4.8 for females; this is somewhat below the national average for men (3.5 years) and significantly above for women.[12] Female coffee growers are still very much the exception, and their relatively high education levels may reflect the sort of women who pursue this path.

Since the Spanish invasion, Guatemala has been historically Catholic in terms of religion, although that has coexisted (sometimes harmoniously, sometimes not) with traditions of Maya spirituality. Our sample was 59 percent Catholic and 31 percent Protestant. Since the mid-twentieth century, Guatemala has been the target of a number of Protestant missionary efforts, and conversion rates took off in the 1970s. General Efraín Ríos Montt, who ruled the country for a bloody eighteen months starting in 1982, was a fervent born-again evangelical Christian. Today Guatemala has one of Latin America's highest rates of Protestantism, most of the evangelical variety that eschews alcohol and Indigenous religious practices.[13]

Over 80 percent of respondents self-identified as Indigenous, reflecting the region's ethnic demography, and a majority of those spoke a Mayan language. Although 64 percent of our sample spoke a Mayan language, none were monolingual Mayan speakers—unsurprising, since trading coffee requires a least a rudimentary command of Spanish. Along with language, dress has traditionally been the most apparent marker of Maya identity, although things are rapidly changing, with younger generations improvising hybrid styles of speech and fashion. Many Maya women—and in some places the men as well—wear distinctive woven dress (*traje*). With designs and palettes associated with particular communities, traje is a visible marker of both ethnic and local identity. It is also a source of fascination for tourists and scholars as well as a target of discriminatory policies and attitudes. While traje is often described as the traditional clothing of the Maya, using the word "traditional" can be misleading. Carol Hendrickson observes that traje design and weaving are living, vibrant arts, with new patterns being developed all the time, some becoming trendy and others not. Today women commonly mix and match traje patterns from different towns, and they also combine them with Western clothes to create their own styles.[14] Kedron Thomas shows how Indigenous communities in highland Guatemala are in dialogue with global fashion trends: in wearing branded Nike or Coke T-shirts, Maya peoples are not simply mimicking North American fashion but are appropriating symbols and meaning to creatively express and contest constructions of race, ethnicity, gender, and class.[15] This work reminds us that we should take care not to reduce the Maya to just a list of traits, such as their clothing, and to view style choices in the context of larger political-economic histories and processes.[16]

The traditional large-scale coffee producers usually refer to themselves as *cafetaleros,* denoting both their occupation and social identity. Among the coffee growers in our sample, only 24 percent describe themselves with the cafetalero moniker, with a majority preferring the more generic (and less class-laden) term *agricultor.* Coffee is not as connected to identity for these smallholders as it is for the large producers; for those we talked to, coffee holds an instrumental and utilitarian role, one among several sources of income for most families. At the same time, whereas coffee exporting was once thought to be the exclusive domain of the elite—and this was a powerful psychological barrier to market entry—it is now seen as a viable option for small producers.

All the smallholders in our sample engage in other economic activities in addition to producing coffee, ranging from weaving and occasionally working as a day laborer to running a small store or tending another's fields. Most also grow subsistence milpa plots. Some plant coffee on land they own and then rent additional land for milpa. They also grow truck crops (54.6 percent) and work as day laborers (13 percent) on nearby plantations when needed. Nonetheless, coffee provides a growing share of household income ("most" income for 64.1 percent and "about half" for 22.5 percent), and it was universally recognized as the most profitable crop they could grow on their land at that time (recall that these surveys were done during a booming market period). One farmer notes that "with one quintal [a hundredweight] of coffee I can buy five quintales of maize," although the tendency of many to keep some milpa crops also shows a recognition that this equation can quickly turn upside down if coffee prices fall and maize prices continue upward.

For most small producers the combination of cash crops and subsistence crops is a way of balancing the desire for security with dreams of getting ahead. Manuel, a fifty-five-year-old Mam Maya man from Huehuetenango, explained, "I used to just grow milpa and work on the fincas, but then I saw people here start making money from their own coffee, and I decided to take it up too. I still plant maize and beans for the family, but the coffee gives us more income to cover the expenses that maize production cannot cover." We heard variations on this story over and over again. Sergio, a fifty-one-year-old K'iche' man, commented, "My parents just grew milpa, nobody grew coffee, it wasn't our custom. We grew milpa and went to work on the coffee and cotton plantations for money. But now we can make money from coffee—I even used it to send my son to work in the United States."

VALUE WORLDS OF MAIZE AND COFFEE

Maya farmers tend to have a special relationship with the land and its harvest. In part, this is the nature of farming. Growing milpa, coffee, or any crop can create a tight bond between farmer and the fruit of their labors. Watching the plants grow, caring for them in good times and bad, protecting the seedlings from the weather and pests—all of this creates a sensual connection between producer and product, one based on touch and sight, on emotion and sacrifice. For most Maya farmers, there is a spiritual relationship with maize and milpa, one linked to identity and informed by cosmological beliefs and cultural traditions as well as practical necessities.

The coffee-growing communities we studied still depend on subsistence milpa agriculture for a large portion of household staples. For most rural Maya families the milpa provides more than biological sustenance; it is also linked to metaphysical and ontological principles of regeneration and change. Maya origin stories relate that humans were created from maize, and the regenerative element central to much Maya spirituality is explicitly linked to the death and regrowth of the agricultural cycle. Every household has a corncrib to store dried corn on the cob, and for most people maize tortillas are obligatory staples of every meal.[17] Maya friends tell me that they do not feel full from wheat bread or rice alone and that their Maya bodies demand maize to be satiated. It is taboo to waste or throw away maize, and for those who practice traditional Maya spirituality, maize plays a central role in many rites.

As described by Victor Montejo, a "Maya-logical" ontology emerges from the relationship between the natural world, the spiritual world, and the human world. At its heart is a reciprocal covenant between humans and cosmic forces that animates life through agriculture.[18] Reflected in the 260-day sacred calendar and the cycles of plant rejuvenation—including the annual practice of burning the dried maize stalks after harvest to replenish the soil—this reciprocity sustains a healthy spiritual and material equilibrium. In this view, a good life depends on balance and centeredness—the primordial maize stalk is often envisioned as the axis mundi—and places a high value on "fairness," a form of balance between individual self-interests. Fairness as a social value is expressed in many ways, but in most communities it is reinforced through institutions governing communal lands, agricultural cooperatives, and Catholic brotherhoods (*cofradías*).[19] Most of the Maya farmers we interviewed are not opposed to individual success based on hard work justly rewarded, but there is a moral suspicion of those whose wealth derives from the labor of others or from unequal access to resources.

In fact, as Montejo argues, Maya views would not parse out the material and the spiritual as separate realms of existence, as I have done.[20] Rather, they see the natural world and the social and political and economic worlds as parts of an integrated system of symbolic and spiritual as well as economic and material values. By both necessity and predilection, Maya livelihoods reflect what some social scientists refer to as the "hybrid collectif," a fluid assemblage of connections that eschew the human/nonhuman and natural/cultural divides.[21]

In focusing on the spiritual dimension of milpa agriculture, I do not want to romanticize subsistence agriculture. It is hard work, a precarious existence; most farmers value the connection to the land, but also aspire to something more. These are not the closed communities of yore: even remote areas now have cell phone access, lively Facebook and WhatsApp activity, and residents who have gone to the United States to send home remittances.[22] This is a connected class of Maya farmers, linked to the global ecumene and yet limited in their aspirational horizons by the pervasive realities of structural exclusion.

Maya consumers talk about the provenance of maize with the precision of connoisseurs, almost inevitably preferring the terroir of their own community. The preference for maize from one's own milpa reflects its flavor profile but also its value as an unalienated product— the opposite of a commodity. While maize is grown for both material and spiritual sustenance, coffee is grown as a commodity to be sold.

Coffee, as a cash crop, occupies an ambiguous role within Maya agricultural and moral value worlds. While less venerated than maize, coffee production fits with the annual rhythms of community life and with the moral values associated with agriculture. Coffee means something to the farmers who grow and harvest it: it is a real part of who they are, of their material existence and their social identities. Farmers generally take pride in their crops, and they often use kinship terms to refer to their coffee seedlings and trees, speaking of them endearingly as they would offspring. Coffee presents a potentially lucrative route to getting ahead that depends on the familiar work of agriculture. It also feeds into the singular dignity that comes from earning one's livelihood from the land, which is recognized as the ultimate source of all worth ("including oil," as one traditional daykeeper told me). From this perspective, coffee provides a way to maintain the social, cultural, spiritual, and agricultural rhythms that are valued while also earning a little extra money.

Still, coffee, as opposed to maize, holds a distinctly less elevated position in moral terms. Coffee does not feed into the local diet in a significant way. Most households drink coffee, but generally it is boiled grounds, served weak with a lot of sugar—not a quality cup of coffee by SCA standards, even if the drinkers are growing specialty-grade beans. Coffee is viewed more as a source of money than of sustenance, grown to be alienated from local value worlds in a way that maize is not. In the K'iche' town of Nahuala people tell stories of coffee as antagonistic to maize, a threat to traditional orders. It is said that, once upon a time, maize plants refused to produce for the people as punishment for drinking coffee after eating maize. A famine resulted, and so a delegation of elders was sent to the Lord of Maize, who led them through a milpa and a coffee field. Their eyes were opened, and they realized how they had been abusing the coffee cherries: "The coffee looked burnt, because when it is roasted it dies. It suffers greatly. And when the people roast it in the skillet the poor coffee starts crying. After that it is ground: its whole body is ground up, which causes it great pain. And not only that: then there is a pot, ready with hot water. There is even more pain when the coffee is thrown into it." The famine had resulted because the maize was offended at being contaminated by such a tormented, dark substance. The Lord of Maize led the people to understand that "coffee was not really food and is only there to be sold for cash. Coffee is a means to buy our clothes, but corn is there for food."[23]

This story offers a vivid commentary on how commodities are created by stripping goods of their social and moral worth, reducing particular items down to the common denominator of price. The advent of the modern commodity form allowed for the emergence of global trade, with the ability to buy goods sight unseen, as with those first Dutch coffee futures traders. The cost of commodification, Marx observed, is social alienation. Whereas in agricultural and artisanal economies, products were embedded in local values worlds, with industrial and commodity production, that embeddedness is intentionally elided. In reaction to the alienation of opaque global supply chains, late capitalist markets have moved toward artisanal products that seek to re-embed production in an imagined social world, de-commodifying products such as specialty coffee to highlight their singularity and moral virtues. For smallholding Maya farmers, coffee is a commodity, produced to be sold for money, and, yet, increasingly, consumers are looking for de-commodified and provenanced products. In this context, it would seem that Maya farmer biographies would offer an advantage. But to realize the gains of the high-end artisanal market requires particular sorts of social and cultural capital and the ability to translate across symbolic value worlds.

GROWING AND SELLING SECOND WAVE COFFEE

It takes three to five years from planting seedlings for *C. arabica* to produce a decent crop; trees then produce for about fifteen more years before yields significantly decline. Coffee thus requires farmers to plan ahead and think about the future in particular ways. The crop's temporal and physiological needs interact with cultural value worlds to frame farmers' time horizons and future orientations. Since coffee requires a significant investment of land and labor, most new small producers hedged their bets by expanding production very gradually.

Most farmers say they are committed to coffee for the long term, even as they acknowledge prices are likely to fall at some point. They vividly recall the drop of 2000–2001, when prices reached historic lows on the world market, below even basic production costs. It was then that many medium and large producers left the market. Still, the small producers who have diversified income sources claim that they can hold out during a price drop because coffee production has the benefit of being able to adapt to variable inputs over several years. If prices are low, coffee fields can be left more or less unattended for a year or two without much harm done. Then, when prices rise, it can be cleaned up and harvested.

The type of connection farmers have to markets is crucial to their relative success. Small producers sell their coffee in cherry form to a cooperative (if they belong to one), which will have its own *beneficio* (wet

Figure 20. Intermediary buying coffee on the side of road.

mill), or to an intermediary who will transport it in a pickup truck to the local mill to sell for a markup figure 20). Some intermediaries are viewed positively, providing advice and loans; others are seen as predatory "coyotes," loaning money against harvest at extortionate rates and paying below market prices. Smallholding coffee farmers generally cannot do their own wet milling. That requires a large capital investment to build the tanks and buy the equipment, and the volume of smallholders cannot justify it. As a result, they have to sell their harvest as cherry, which needs to be processed as soon as possible after harvest. This gives a lot of power to intermediaries to set prices on the side of the road with bags of cherry that will not last more than forty-eight hours.

In our sample, more than half of the smallholding producers belong to a cooperative that runs a wet mill, and a majority of the rest say that they would like to join one. Due to steadily rising demand for SHB coffees, prices have gone up substantially season after season since 2001. For most of the early 2000s, market prices for SHB exceeded fair trade premiums, leading some growers to try to get out of their cooperative contracts and sell to intermediaries paying more (the focus of the next chapter). Overall, producers see being part of a cooperative or an association as a clear advantage; 74.4 percent of our sample belonged to an association, and most that did not said that they would like to. The cooperatives provide better terms for loans and a guaranteed buyer for production, and they make the transfer of technical and market information more efficient. Some producers complain that their cooperative operates too much like a private beneficio and also point to specific leadership and participation issues, but overall cooperatives are seen as advantageous.

Farmers normally get their price information from buyers (the cooperative, the beneficio, or the intermediary). Anacafé has a program to send out text messages of the daily New York futures price (the C price) to any farmer who signs up, an effort to make the market more transparent. Still, none of the farmers we spoke to found it useful in the negotiating process: the dollar-denominated C price for green beans on the New York futures exchange is only indirectly related to farm gate prices in highland Guatemala, and the going rate for specialty coffees has become decoupled from the C price.

COFFEE'S LABOR EMBODIED

Just as consuming coffee affects people's physiology and cognitive outlook, growing coffee shapes farmers' bodies. While many Brazilian plantations use mechanized harvesters, the higher-altitude shade-grown coffees in Guatemala require a lot of manual labor. Maya smallholders usually rely on familial labor, augmented by hiring neighbors as day workers for harvest. (Coffee requires labor year-round for fertilizing, weeding, pruning, and replanting, but most of the work is required for a couple of months of harvesting annually.)

Only ripe, red cherries should be picked for quality coffee, and these have to be selected individually from a branch's cluster that will have

Figure 21. Basket of coffee cherry.

fruit at various stages of maturation on it. Although picking coffee is considered unskilled labor, there is an art to it, a form of embodied knowledge that takes months or years to perfect: registering the subtle differences in refracted light to identify the ripe-enough fruit, gently grabbing and twisting it with a particular turn of the wrist to release the fruit, and dropping it in the basket as the eye searches for another ripe cherry (see figure 21). All this takes place in seconds, many times a minute, countless times a day, all the while the picker tries to come away unscathed by the prickly leaves. There is a delicate balance between speed (picking as many as you can) and selectivity (just getting the ripe ones) that requires constant evaluation and the ability to determine the worth of each cherry based on visual clues.

Trees are pruned to better facilitate picking, but it still takes a toll on the body. The slopes are often so steep that it is difficult—for a clumsy anthropologist, at least—to stay balanced. Harvesting involves carrying a large basket around one's neck, filling it with ripe cherry, dumping those into large bags, and repeating. Workers are paid by the pound on plantations, and their already-meager wages are docked if they pick too many unripe fruits. Workers will sometimes try to sneak rocks into their baskets to increase the weight, but these covert aggressions are usually no match for the overseers' finger on the scale.

Smallholders are more casual with their labor, but a premium is placed on getting the ripest fruit. Hands become calloused, and back and hip problems abound. Harvesting coffee shapes bodies in ways that are visible, especially in the stoop of older workers. Women and men participate in the harvest, as do children, the youngest of which will be strapped to their mother's back. Coffee requires heavy inputs of chemical fertilizers, pesticides, and fungicides. Smallholders often mix these in proportions based on observed practice, gut feel, and household finances. Anecdotally, there are high rates of pulmonary disease and cancers, and it would not be surprising if farmers and their families showed high levels of some of these chemicals in their bodies.

In these very physical ways (carrying the heavy baskets, picking the berries, hauling children, inhaling pesticides), growing coffee shapes the bodies of Maya farmers and their families (see figure 22). The proximate reasons are the mechanics of coffee production, but, as Paul Farmer shows, such public health issues are symptoms of deeper pathologies of power that determine who gets ill and who stays well. Coffee-growing regions of Guatemala are areas of heightened food insecurity, as well as drug trafficking and migration to the United States. In Guatemala almost half of all children under five years of age suffer from chronic malnutrition, one of the highest rates in the world. In rural Maya communities and in coffee-growing regions, malnutrition rates routinely top 75 percent. Indeed, stunted height—the primary indicator of chronic malnutrition—has become the norm in most Maya communities to the extent that most residents do not recognize it as anything extraordinary or as an indicator of underlying health issues. Maya men average 1.59 meters, and Maya women are an even more diminutive

Figure 22. Man hauling coffee.

1.47 meters (the U.S. average is 1.77 meters for men and 1.63 meters for women, and the Dutch male averages 1.83 meters and females average 1.68 meters). Comparing Maya children born in Guatemala with the children of Maya immigrants born in the United States, Barry Bogin and his colleagues found that Maya American children were on average 11.54 centimeters taller than their counterparts in Guatemala. This provides clear evidence that environmental and structural conditions in Guatemala produce the rates of malnutrition rather than genetic ancestry.[24]

Growing coffee does not directly cause malnutrition. At the same time, it is not just coincidence that some of the highest rates of malnutrition are found in Maya communities in coffee-growing regions. Structures of exclusion, justified by ideological and cultural values, produce these conditions. It is no *one*'s fault, and that is the insidious nature of structural violence: it seems to be just the way things are. Paul Farmer writes that this "suffering is 'structured' by historically given (and often economically driven) processes and forces that conspire—whether through routine, ritual, or, as is more commonly the case, the hard surfaces of life—to constrain agency." In this way, it is no accident that migrant labor in Guatemala comes from poor, rural, and largely Maya communities, and forms of structural violence frame coffee producers' health and the horizons of their aspirations. Many non-Maya Guatemalans see Maya shortness as something natural (an inherent racial trait), making them well suited to the low-to-the-ground work of agriculture. As Seth Holmes writes of migrant workers on berry farms in Washington State, the social structure of agricultural labor becomes literally embodied in workers' physical and psychological health.[25] According to plantation owners, Maya bodies are better suited than their own to harvesting sugar, cotton, and coffee, and to carrying the heavy loads of product.

THE MORAL COMPLEXITIES OF HOPE

Ixcanul, an award-winning 2015 film by director Jayro Bustamante, takes place in a Maya community in highland Guatemala where most of the adults and many of the children work at the neighboring coffee plantation. It appears to be one of the traditional elite-owned fincas, dependent on cheap seasonal labor to deliver a high-volume, but still hand-picked, commodity. The finca is portrayed as a part of daily life, but also as a place of hardship and suffering.

The movie, the first feature film shot in Kaqchikel Mayan, follows the tragic story of María, a young woman torn between her betrothal to an older overseer and her love for a young man yearning to go north to the United States. *Ixcanul* garnered accolades for its moving portrayal of the hardships of Indigenous life in Guatemala, and while those of us who know the area well had a few quibbles over particulars, most thought it accurately captured the reality of Maya communities.

When my wife, Mareike Sattler, showed the movie to residents of the Maya town Nahuala in 2017, however, many of the viewers reacted less enthusiastically. While they found the basic tragedy believable and appreciated the dialogue in their native language, they also noted that the movie made it look as if their lives were devoid of happiness and joy. Yes, there is pain and sorrow and discrimination, as they know all too well, but, they said, there is also hope and happiness. With the best of intentions, we often view those living in material poverty as driven primarily by need, whereas we assume those living in the affluent world are driven by desire. But, in reducing people to one dimension of their existence (such as poverty), we lose something important in our understanding. Maya farmers see themselves as more than poor, and not simply as victims. They are clear-eyed about the power differences that define the outlines of their existence, but they are still driven by desire as much as by need, and they aspire to a better future for themselves and their families.

Imaginings of the good and aspirations for something better give meaning to the actions of Maya coffee farmers and to specialty coffee connoisseurs alike. Recognizing this should not elide the inequities between their circumstances or ignore the structural conditions that lead to the poverty of one and the affluence of the other. Yet, in our attention to hard-edged material inequalities, anthropologists too often overlook the role of hope, optimism, and aspiration in the lives of those we study.[26] Arguing for greater attention to "the good," Joel Robbins writes, "We need to be attentive to the way people orientate to and act in a world that outstrips the one most concretely present to them, and to avoid dismissing their ideals as unimportant or, worse, as bad-faith alibis for the worlds they actually create."[27]

The farmers in our sample view seasonal plantation labor as a form of dependency, wrought with the hardships of being separated from one's family that they want to avoid if at all possible. They prefer to hold wealth in land and see coffee production as a way of expanding their landholding or enabling them to make their first purchase of land. They want to get ahead, to achieve *algo más* (something more, something better) in their lives, to see their children flourish. They are realistic in their expectations of coffee but also value the possibilities if offers, even if they are limited. The farmers in our sample overwhelmingly saw coffee as a net positive in their lives and in the vitality of their communities. They lamented the fluctuating prices, the danger from crop diseases and rainfall patterns, and how little of the final value came to them. Still, the booming market in recent years for high-altitude coffee has pushed prices up, raising material standards of living.

The rise of small producers provides a positive alternative to plantation labor. Now laborers can work locally and not have to migrate to the large fincas. Workers report that conditions with smallholders are markedly better than on plantations. Most small producers pay a day rate rather than paying by weight, which is seen as more fair. Workers report more casual and convivial work conditions. One man explained, "Before, when we worked on the finca, families got separated, but now we have the chance to be more together and more independent. You can see the benefits of this change, even those who don't have land; everybody now has better work conditions."

Lazaro Cuj, a forty-nine-year-old K'iche' Maya farmer in Chajul, sees coffee as his best chance to get ahead. Although he only attended school until the third grade, Cuj speaks Spanish fairly well and has made a good living selling his coffee to the large cooperative, the Asociación Chajulense. He explains, "Coffee is our only way to get ahead. I'm not a professional, I don't have an education, I don't have any skills beyond farming. Without coffee, I would be a peon. I want my son to study agronomy in the university, and with the money I'm making from coffee, we just might do it." The income coffee brings is important, but it is generally talked about in instrumental terms, linked to larger life projects and value worlds. Farmers talk about wanting to send their kids to school, maybe even on to high school in one of the larger towns, so that they can have more opportunities than farming can provide. They talk of buying a pickup, a way to cut out the middleman but also a powerful symbol of self-determination. These aspirations are grounded in values that extend beyond economic calculation, as Peter Benson and I have argued elsewhere.[28]

Coffee is seen not as a way to get rich but as a significant source of income that can keep a family out of absolute poverty. For most small-scale growers, coffee income is not sufficient to sustain their families, but it is an important source of additional income, one strategy among several in the household economy. Miguel, a forty-one-year-old *ladino* farmer from Huehuetenango, observed, "We have to put food on the table, but we would also like other things, for our children to go to school, and for this it [coffee] isn't sufficient. So we feel constrained, and we are in a bad place if somebody in the family gets sick." Liliana Goldín shows how diverse strategies pursued by rural Guatemalan households shape economic ideologies and the realm of what is possible and desirable. In our sample, coffee producers construct their aspirations in the difficult circumstances in which they find themselves. In this context of limited opportunities, most farmers see coffee as a beneficial (even potentially lucrative) addition to household economic strategies. Importantly, desires are constrained by what is seen as possible, the realm of what is achievable and conceivable, conceptual "limit points" that define aspirational horizons.[29]

Most of the farmers we talked to find the ideals of a neoliberal meritocracy appealing—a system that promises to duly reward their efforts.[30] They also realize that behind what poses as market freedom there is a history and enduring structure of marginalization. They would like more direct connections with the market; they realize they do not fully understand the desires at the far end of the value chain, but they would like to have closer connections to importers, roasters, and consumers. Farmers appreciate coffee and see it as an important source of cash income to supplement (or in some cases replace) their subsistence crops. They take pride in their ability to grow it well and in Guatemala's international reputation for producing quality coffees. Coffee does not have the sacred implications of maize, but it is nonetheless meaningful as well as instrumental.

MAYA VALUES WORLDS AND SECOND
WAVE MARKETS

A confluence of factors led to the emergence of the Second Wave coffee market in Guatemala. The shift in the international trade toward high-quality, regionally differentiated specialty coffees created a new demand for beans grown at higher altitudes than that of most traditional Guatemalan fincas. Anacafé began promoting regional designations of origin based on the ecological, agricultural, and botanical factors that contribute to "the cup." These changes opened new opportunities for smallholding Maya farmers, but the farmers' own aspirations and values oriented how they chose to engage with the new markets. Farmers determine how to approach the possibilities and risks, how benefits are locally distributed, who does the work, and what sorts of worth are created. We find efforts to maintain continuity with subsistence milpa agriculture; to localize labor and harvest in communities; and to navigate growth, financing, cooperative membership, marketing, and cultivation options to not only meet risk preferences but also pursue ideals of a better life. Thus new producers acquire new land at a regular, but patient, pace; plan ahead for how to respond to inevitable price fluctuations; celebrate the harvest with their neighbors; reconsider what cooperatives can and should be; and open new relationships with the international market.

In our surveys smallholders overwhelmingly report that coffee is a positive addition to their income-earning strategies. They are under no illusions that this new market is a panacea for all their problems, but they see it as an important source of income and potential growth. Crucially, it also allows them to maintain control over their land and means of production and to keep up elements of an agrarian lifestyle important to their identity. Sarah Lyon, in her study of new smallholding coffee producers in the Guatemalan town of San Juan La Laguna, reports that locals refer to the new coffee production as "'the bomb' that exploded in the community, bringing income that enabled families to end their seasonal migration to lowland plantations, build cement-block houses, and educate their children." Lyon points out the power inequities and flaws in fair trade practices and the complexities and contradictions of cooperative organization, but she also finds that coffee is valued by most growers as an important tool to help them realize the futures they envision.[31] Likewise, the small producers we interviewed view the coffee market as neither good nor bad but as a tool, a technology, a means to achieve other ends, a vehicle for their desires. This is not to say that the coffee trade is just; even in the fair trade segment there are structural inequities and inconsistencies that disadvantage small producers.[32]

The producers in our sample talk about coffee using language that is congruent with the capabilities approach to development. As one middle-aged producer commented, "Growing coffee hasn't allowed me to have all in my life that I wanted, but it moves me in that direction, and that is something." They value the income-generating potential of coffee, but this is a means to larger ends, such as educating their children, buying more land, a degree of financial security. Coffee is an imperfect vehicle for economic development, but it allows producers to retain control over their means of production, and to have a degree of control over their future. Indeed, they believe that it is not a lack of ability or agency that holds them back but rather a lack of opportunity. Said one young famer, "If we had the opportunity we could be more successful, but we don't have the opportunity."

Second Wave coffee is intimately linked to the value worlds of the smallholding farmers we interviewed. While coffee production does not directly provide sustenance, it does fit into the familiar moral conventions around farming. The farmers we interviewed mostly viewed the coffee market as a mechanism, an apparatus for mobilizing available resources toward desired ends. These ends do not generally extend to the sorts of major structural changes needed for Guatemala's long-term and sustainable human development. Rather, the coffee market is a means to achieve *algo más* given the actual context of limited opportunity and material resources. Farmers' value worlds frame and motivate the ways they engage the coffee market toward their own ends—an instrumental moralization of the market at once similar and distant from the values ascribed by northern consumers to their provenanced and fair trade gourmet coffee. The Second Wave market provides a path for upward mobility for small producers, but those best able to take advantage of the new opportunities are not the poorest. Those with a higher level of education, with some existing landholdings, and with other sources of income are best positioned to reap the benefits of specialty coffee production. While specialty coffee has been a boon for many Maya communities, the Third Wave trend, discussed in the next chapter, also puts the majority of Maya farmers at a disadvantage.

Figure 23. Coffee farmer.

CHAPTER SIX

Cooperation, Competition, and Cultural Capital in Third Wave Markets

While late nineteenth-century coffee commercialization in Guatemala was built on the forced exploitation of seasonal labor, the Second Wave quality turn starting in the 1990s led to a modest economic boom in many highland Maya communities that, because of their altitude, produced the sought-after Strictly Hard Beans (SHBs). The greater potential rewards from specialty coffee production were accompanied by greater risks, as the tenets of market capitalism would predict. In this case, however, fair trade price supports, administered through cooperatives, minimized the financial threat of market fluctuations. This encouraged risk-averse smallholding farmers to make the years-long commitment that growing coffee entails. In this new market cooperatives played a crucial role in aggregating smallholder production and providing wet milling and technical assistance. These factors converged to give this class of smallholding coffee farmers an unprecedented, if still modest, degree of market power, spurring the optimism and aspirations discussed in the previous chapter.

By the 2010s the Third Wave market was the fastest-growing and most lucrative sector of the coffee trade. Accelerating the Second Wave movement toward quality and distinctiveness, Third Wave roasters focus on high-altitude beans, unusual varietals, and single-estate lots. It would be reasonable to assume that Third Wave demand, with its heightened focus on the particulars of terroir and relationships with specific producers, would strengthen the position of Guatemalan smallholders. In fact, despite growing coffees that score highly on the hundred-point SCA scale, most Maya farmers lack the social and cultural capital to access the more symbolic and narratively driven high-end markets. Further, farmers' need and desire for cooperative forms of organizing, which aggregate the harvests from many small farms, do not mesh with Third Wave preferences for "single-estate" lots tied to the biographies of individual growers. Finally, as the Third Wave market matures, there has been a growing focus on roasting techniques and brewing technologies, adding more value at the consumer end of the circuit. These factors disadvantage smallholding Maya producers and threaten the economic power experienced in the height of the Second Wave boom.

·   ·   ·

Sebastian Canil grows Strictly Hard Bean arabicas on the steep slopes of his fields in the department of Quetzaltenango in Guatemala's western highlands. A K'iche' Maya man in his early fifties, Canil belongs to a vibrant cooperative and is an enthusiastic champion of the virtues of cooperative organization. More than once the cooperative has saved him and his neighbors from going broke. Their fair trade certification means that even during periodic market falls members are assured a minimum price. The cooperative also runs a wet mill, crucial equipment for the time-sensitive processing of washed arabicas, and yet a capital investment beyond the means of most smallholders.

While he appreciates all that the cooperative has done for him, Canil says he cannot turn down the occasional offer from one of the itinerant intermediaries (*coyotes*) to buy part of his harvest for significantly more money than the cooperative pays. He says, "There is a coyote who comes around here and pays top dollar, but he only wants really high quality. He sent his son to look at my land. They don't just want to see the coffee, they want to see where it is grown, make sure it is all Bourbon and that the Bourbon is separate from the other varietals." This is a difficult decision for Canil, one that tears at his allegiances. He does well, but not so well that he can forgo an extra thirty or forty cents per pound. "We still don't make very much," he states. "The buyers set the price and tell us what it is."

Guatemala's emergence as a major player in the Third Wave market is due in part to its unique geographic and climatic endowments: the country's volcanic slopes and varied microclimates create a range of subtly distinct flavor profiles.[1] Guatemala's outsized prominence in the world of high-end coffee also results from Anacafé's decision to "follow the market" and promote regional terroirs in areas dominated by smallholders. Guatemalan single-estate beans now command extraordinary prices based on small differences in cupping scores. These prices are largely justified in terms of quality as defined by the material and sensual properties of a particular lot, but they are also based on symbolic and narrative values as they are translated from farm to coffee shop. Consumers are paying not only for a quality cup of coffee but also for a sentiment, a felt connection to the producer, a symbolic value that is hard to quantify precisely. In turn, the Maya farmers in highland Guatemala working through cooperatives sell not only their coffee but also the stories that add the distinctive symbolic and affective elements sought after by importers and roasters. In this sense, the fruit of their labor serves to satisfy both corporeal need and imaginative desires. Yet Maya coffee farmers mostly lack the social and cultural capital needed to participate directly in high-end markets. They may control terroir in the gritty materiality of dirt and land, and thus the ability to produce beans of a certain quality, but the real economic power lies with those who define the symbolic values of "quality."

Like Canil, a majority of smallholding Maya coffee farmers in Guatemala belong to a producer cooperative, and most of the rest would like to. In addition to providing financing, wet milling, and market access to members, the cooperative as a form of organizing resonates with traditional social norms around consensus, reciprocity, and fairness found in many Maya communities. This does not mean that cooperatives are necessarily spaces of harmony; in fact, as Sarah Lyon points out, they are often arenas for political tensions and personal politics, where individual interests and collective aspirations are worked out in gritty specifics.[2] Reaching a consensus is often socially and morally complicated. Still, farmers value the cooperative as a form of insurance, both economic and social, and as a meaningful site of community building. This works well in the Second Wave market, but the highest-value Third Wave coffees mostly come from single, named producers. Mixing beans from different lots lowers the cupping score, and there is symbolic value placed on the vicarious connection to a particular farmer. This Third Wave emphasis on single-origin beans from individual producers threatens to undermine the cooperative preferences expressed by smallholders and moves the market toward a winner-take-all structure in which small differences in quality make huge differences in the prices commanded by a select few top producers. While only a small fraction of smallholding farmers produce coffees that meet Third Wave quality standards, their defections—selling to a coyote instead of the cooperative—threaten not only the economics but also the social solidarity of cooperative organization.

Thus, at one end of this coffee value chain we find smallholding farmers seeking some degree of economic security, and at the other end U.S. consumers hunting ever-more particular and unique sensory experiences. Such fluid assemblages of economic interests and cultural desires constitute distinct value worlds—sometimes converging, sometimes colliding, and always requiring accommodation. The coffee value chain results from the interaction of different value worlds around the material object—with potentially big economic gains extracted by translating goods and ideas across value worlds. In the statistics of global commerce, values are distilled into the numerical metrics of dollars and euros and yuan. But for the people who pick coffee beans by hand, filling basket after basket in the hope of eking out the barest of existences, it is about much more than the numbers can tell us.³ In these contexts, neoliberal market mechanisms often produce morally ambiguous effects.⁴

CULTURAL CAPITAL, QUALITY METRICS, AND ECONOMIC GAIN

Many of the Maya smallholders we interviewed control the material means of production to grow high-quality coffee (washed arabicas scoring above eighty-five on the SCA scale): they have the altitude, the microclimate, the varietals, and the knowledge (tacit as well as explicit). The importance of "authenticity" and direct relationships in the value creation of Third Wave coffee would seem to work in their favor, yet most lack the cultural capital and social connections that the more successful Third Wave producers have to convert their material endowments into economic gain. The inequality of power here is not the traditional differential access to productive capital; rather, it is in the ability to translate material and symbolic qualities across different value worlds.

Third Wave assumptions about producers are usually embedded in narratives of individual meritocratic rewards, with those farmers who produce the highest-quality beans being lavishly rewarded. In turn, we find growers imagining the desires of the consumers for whom their harvest is destined. The smallholding farmers we interviewed broadly buy into the neoliberal promise of hard work being justly rewarded; they would be happy to participate in a meritocracy, as they are used to playing with the cards stacked against them so severely as to crush hope. Growing coffee is backbreaking work, and Maya farmers mostly live in very modest circumstances, with limited resources and opportunities. They are acutely aware of the perils of dependency on fickle global markets. Yet controlling, even partially, the means of production allows farmers to access markets opportunistically and not just by obligation. Their investment in terroir seems to give them some degree of power, but the means of symbolic production are just as important in late capitalist markets, and these are largely controlled by tastemakers at the consumption end of the value chain.

The Alliance for Coffee Excellence runs the annual Cup of Excellence competition in Guatemala. In 2020 thirty coffees passed the preliminary round to enter the national competition; the top-ranked lot was auctioned for more than US $175 per pound, the second place earned $37.90 a pound, and the lowest came in at $15. At the time, the New York C price was under $1.10 per pound. Looking at the results of Cup of Excellence competitions, the absence of Maya farmers is striking, especially given the areas of the country where the top lots originate. During our fieldwork we had interviewed many smallholding farmers whose lands were very similar to, and sometimes adjacent to, larger (that is, medium-sized) *fincas* whose coffees were commanding high premiums, yet the Maya farmers did not appear to be participating in this lucrative segment of the market.

To investigate this, in 2015 Bart Victor and I worked with students Will McCollum and Mac Muir to document the importance of objective quality metrics in high-end Guatemalan coffees. We identified several Cup of Excellence–certified farms in Huehuetenango, a region known for exceptionally high-quality coffees, and mapped out these farms and the surrounding smallholder plots. The Cup of Excellence farms were all owned by non-Indigenous farmers, a number of whom were college educated and familiar with the U.S. market. In contrast, the smallholders were mostly Maya, with low levels of education and literacy. Many of the smallholders supplemented their income by working seasonally as day labor on the neighboring Cup of Excellence plantations.

Based on opportunistic sampling, Will and Mac went around and bought green coffee from fifteen smallholders on lands that lay between two Cup of Excellence farms; the smallholder and Cup of Excellence farms were at roughly the same altitude and had similar microclimatic conditions (map 7 shows part of the sample area). Comparing prices, we found that the medium-size, non-Maya-owned Cup of Excellence farms receive a significant premium for their beans, averaging $4 a

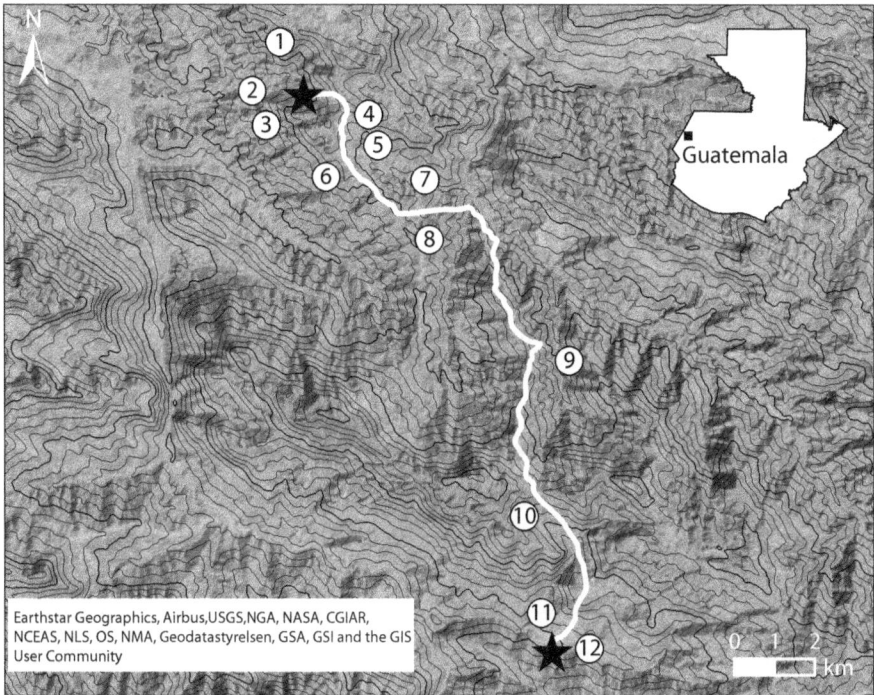

Map 7. Cup of Excellence (starred) and smallholding (numbered) coffee producers sampled.

pound, several times normal prices paid at the farm. (Demand significantly exceeded supply in the Third Wave market in 2015, keeping prices high.) At the same time, neighboring Maya smallholders were selling theirs for an average of only $1.25 a pound.

We had the sampled coffees roasted and blind graded by Anacafé's professional cuppers. Over 75 percent of them were specialty-grade coffees, scoring eighty and above, and almost 50 percent scored above eighty-five, placing them in the category of Third Wave coffee. One forty-three-year-old farmer, for example, produced twenty-two bags of Bourbon from her plots; the sample we purchased from her was cupped at eighty-six points by Anacafé's master cupper. Based on the objective quality criteria for the trade, this smallholder's coffee is worth several times what she is receiving for it—and the difference in price would represent a life-changing sum if she could access the market.[5] Part of the lower farmgate price for smallholders is due to higher transaction costs involved in buying small lots from many producers, but this can only account for a portion of the price differential we found.

Coffees produced by the Cup of Excellence–certified farms justify their premiums on their material quality, but the objective quality alone is insufficient; garnering significant premiums also requires the savvy to tell a good story that consumers want to hear and the connections to be able to tell that story to importers and roasters. The data from our survey suggests that the farmgate price depends more on the size of the farm and the social capital of the farmer than on blind cupping scores. Smallholding producers have experienced a boom, but they are excluded from the highest-value parts of the market because they lack the language abilities, market knowledge, and social capital that could provide access to channels of distribution. In this market, the real economic power rests with the ability to define the terms of symbolic value and to translate those symbolic values across the commodity chain.

Looking at sales prices of award-winning coffees in Central America, Bradley Wilson and his colleagues found that the size of a farm had a strong positive correlation with Cup of Excellence score and price.[6] This class of larger medium-sized farms (averaging just over ninety-two hectares) have more space and productive capital to experiment with different varietals and growing conditions—but they also have the cosmopolitan cultural capital to craft their narratives to speak to distant consumers' social and moral value worlds. Nobert Wilson and his colleagues have shown that such symbolic attributes add the biggest portion to Cup of Excellence premiums.[7]

Most smallholding Maya farmers lack the social capital and scale of production to tap into the most lucrative segments of the Third Wave coffee market, even if their cupping scores merit it. Many have only basic Spanish-language proficiency, and almost none speak any English. They are highly invested in local systems of social capital, with an ethos of social solidarity and communitarian moral values, but they have limited conceptions of the sorts of values U.S. consumers might desire. In our sample we found farmers to be overwhelmingly positive about market changes that rewarded quality and promised greater access to direct trade relationships—an optimism tempered by the realism of farmers who constantly face the risks of weather and pests as well as finicky markets. These farmers mostly realized the importance of "quality," but for most that was predicated on the judgments of intermediaries who assess quality through cosmetic appearance. While there is strong interest in knowing more about the people who drink their coffee, most growers' understanding of consumers is vague at best. In our surveys 59 percent of farmers reported that they did not know where their coffee went after they sold it to their cooperative or to a middleman. Almost 32 percent reported having "some knowledge," but that was generally just piecemeal impressions filtered through the cooperative.

The biggest beneficiaries of the specialty coffee boom in Guatemala have been the middle-sized producers, the smaller of the big producers. These tend to be non-Indigenous-owned farms that have been in business for generations and whose owners have inherited and built up the social capital needed to present an attractive image of production and quality to the Third Wave market.[8] These farmers tend to be better educated, often with some university education, speak at least a little English, and to be early adopters of the internet and cell phones and other technologies of commerce. They grow very high-quality coffee, but just as important they have the social capital that allows them to engage the export market and translate across value regimes. That is to say that success also depends on the social and cultural capital needed to translate material and symbolic values across arenas of valuation.[9] For the sorts of cultural and social capital that come into play in Third Wave narratives, the non-Maya local and regional elites are better positioned to translate a palatable authenticity, something authentic enough.

Let us return to Marx's observation about what happens when exchange value (price) becomes unhinged from an item's material utility, allowing for the extraction of surplus economic value. He was focused on the ways that social labor can be hidden in the process of capitalist production, but his perspective is helpful in thinking about the role of symbolic values in late capitalist markets, including that of Third Wave coffee. In what Boltanski and Esquerre term "enrichment economies," cultural and moral narratives are called upon to distinguish items from run-of-the-mill commodities and to justify high prices.[10] In these formations, symbolic values matter as much as material utility in maximizing financial gains, feeding into an identity-based consumerism that can make it easier for marketers to subvert good intentions.[11] Third Wave coffee premiums are usually justified by some combination of: 1) conventional measures of quality, such as the SCA's hundred-point scale, 2) values of artisanal commitment, authenticity, and dedication to craft, and 3) narrative connections with farmers, presumably likewise committed to the pursuit of quality. In the Third Wave market moral concerns intertwine with a valorization of artisanal quality, imagining not only the physical labor but also the skill and devotion that went into production. Such narrative de-alienation acts to singularize— de-commodify—items, which shifts power to those producers able to grow high-quality coffee and present it with an aura of authenticity. Paradoxically, it is non-Maya farmers who have the social and cultural capital to better understand the northern market who are able to project such authenticity.[12]

The Third Wave focus on terroir should be good for farmers who own their land, and Maya farmers generally highly value control over their land, for both deeply held cultural reasons and as economic security. But terroir is about more than the material and ecological; it is constructed through social conventions shot through with political and economic power.[13] A profitable understanding of the symbolic aspects valued in the Third Wave market is developing among the most savvy and successful Maya producers. Raymundo is a sixty-four-year-old

Jakaltek speaker from the Huehuetenango region of Guatemala, an area that has seen an economic boom over the last decade due to coffee, remittances, and drug smuggling (a sizable percentage of the cocaine that enters the United States comes through Huehuetenango). He says that he sells his coffee to German buyers who are looking for "real quality." Recognizing the importance of narrative and authenticity, he continues by saying, "You have to be earnest and sincere when talking about your coffee to these buyers." In the end, he says, "They still have all the power; they come in and tell us what the price for coffee is, like it or not."

COOPERATIVES AND FAIR TRADE

Cooperatives played a crucial role in Second Wave expansion, aggregating the small producers most active in the high-altitude regions of Guatemala. The majority of new entrant smallholder producers work through a cooperative and depend on cooperative technical support and financial assistance. Cooperative membership was sometimes a fatal association during the country's prolonged civil war in the 1970s and 1980s. In this period the vehement anti-communist stance of the U.S.-backed military viewed peasant cooperatives as suspect. By the late 1990s cooperatives and associations were again openly flourishing in coffee-producing areas. Mariel Aguilar-Støen shows the crucial role coffee cooperatives play in the context of liberalization, price drops, and the rise in international remittances to fund coffee expansion.[14]

Fair trade certifications were a boon for cooperatives entering the Second Wave market; until 2012, when Fair Trade USA broke from Fair Trade International (FLO), all Fair Trade–certified coffees had to be produced by a cooperative. (Capitalized, Fair Trade refers to the FLO brand name, while the lowercase "fair trade" refers to a broader coalition of parallel programs.) Still, the evidence is mixed on the real impact of fair trade on farmer livelihoods. Studies of fair trade coffee production in Mexico and Central America have shown that although certification reduces producer vulnerabilities, it also carries a high cost that can hinder capital accumulation. Christopher Bacon found that in Nicaragua the real value of fair trade prices fell 41 percent between 1988 and 2008.[15] Nonetheless, many of the Guatemala smallholders we interviewed claimed that fair trade premiums kept them afloat in the price crises of the 1990s and early 2000s, when coffee prices fell well below production costs. The impact of fair trade was in mindset and motivation as much as economic enrichment. One middle-aged Maya coffee farmer from a hamlet outside the town of Olopa told us that "fair trade is what really got us going. It provided the base for us to build on, guaranteeing a minimum price; it motivated us to build up what we have today."

In the global commodity market the basic price metric for coffee is a hundredweight of green beans, and these are usually traded in container loads of 37,500 pounds. Even "micro-lots" can be thousands of pounds of green beans. Since it takes about six pounds of ripe cherry to produce one pound of green coffee, a container load requires 240,000 or so pounds of cherry. The enormous amount of manual labor required can be a competitive advantage for small producers, who often use available familial labor. Even still, a container load is a lot of coffee to pick, and it is almost impossible to achieve relying solely on family labor; cooperatives are an effective mechanism for aggregating such small-scale production. Such periods of high labor inputs, as well as the capital investment required for wet mills, make cooperatives especially attractive to smallholding coffee farmers. For many Guatemalan smallholders it is also the alternatives that push them toward cooperatives: most are ambivalent at best about coyotes, and many see them as leeching off the hard work of those whose get their hands dirty working the earth.

In this context cooperatives are crucial for smallholding farmers. Consolidating harvests, cooperatives are able to trade in volumes attractive to exporters. Cooperatives allow for a division of labor in which those who speak fluent Spanish and are more familiar with the social expectations of the market can deal with buyers and exporters. Finally, coffee is a notoriously volatile market, with prices fluctuating significantly (figure 24), and yet it takes several years to bring new

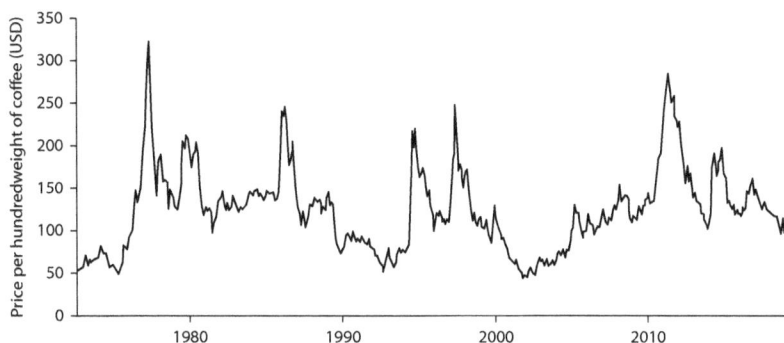

Figure 24. New York C price for coffee futures.

production online. Cooperatives are able to provide some buffer against market swings, which is especially important to the smallest producers.

More than 73 percent of our sampled respondents belong to a cooperative. The farmers in our sample have no illusions about the limitations of cooperatives, but they see them as crucial to both production and marketing. Beyond that, one often-overlooked reason for cooperative membership is that it is meaningful; there is a social and affective aspect to such collective commitment as well as a rational, calculating side. It provides a community and a sense of belonging, and, as Sarah Lyon observes, it builds on long-standing Maya community organizations of rotating public service obligations (*cargos*). Bradley Wilson shows that cooperative farmers in Nicaragua "participate in Fair Trade networks in spite of low household incomes and cycles of indebtedness because of the ability of the producer organization to maintain a sense of solidarity linking coffee contracts to a longer agrarian struggle."[16]

While only about 10 percent of coffees in the United States are certified under some ethical labeling regime (e.g., Fair Trade, Rainforest, UTZ), these programs, and especially Fair Trade, have played an important role in the rise of smallholding farms in Guatemala. The idea of fair trade coffee goes back to a 1970s collaboration between SOS Holland and the Guatemala national organization of coffee cooperatives to produce the brand "Indio-Kaffee," which supported the cooperative movement. Fair trade certification began in 1988 (in the Netherlands with Max Havelaar brand coffee). It then spread to Germany and the United States, and in 1997 the different national programs came together to form the Fairtrade Labelling Organizations (FLO, now Fairtrade International). The FLO's guiding principles dictate that they buy only from smallholder producer cooperatives; in return they pay a premium to ensure a floor price and well as provide credit and multiyear contracts.[17] Fair Trade–certified coffee sales have grown exponentially since the late 1990s, although they still only account for a small percentage the total global market. Large buyers such as Starbucks have come up with their own ethical sourcing guidelines, inspired by but apart from Fair Trade proper. Other groups, such as Cooperative Coffees, have developed "fairer than Fair Trade" alternatives.[18]

A number of studies have documented the shortcomings and complicated impact of fair trade coffee production on producers' lives and livelihoods. Mark Moberg and Sarah Lyon point to the fundamental "paradox of seeking justice through markets," themselves mechanisms of inequality. Gavin Fridell and others have argued that fair trade serves as a technique to foreshorten more radical change, and, in fact, reflects the encroachment of a neoliberal market mentality into the ethical world of solidarity. Sarah Lyon concurs, arguing that fair trade does not "fundamentally challenge the contemporary neoliberal organization of the international market." Bradley Wilson reports on the problems of farmers growing fair trade coffee, who are plagued by continual indebtedness and never able to get ahead despite the promises of higher incomes. And Daniel Jaffee shows that while fair trade farmers in Oaxaca do better than their conventional peers, this is largely because of the safety net function (when the market goes down, they lose less money).[19]

Nonetheless, the farmers in our sample overwhelmingly saw the benefits of cooperative organization as outweighing the drawbacks. Jaffee observes that no one is getting rich from fair trade coffee, but those producers who invest coffee income in other pursuits may be able to pull themselves out of poverty. He reminds us that these coffee producers do the math—they know, more or less, the risks and benefits involved, and they make their decisions accordingly. They realize their livelihoods are limited by structural conditions, but they still have to act within those constraints. One farmer in his mid-fifties that we interviewed recounted the importance of Fair Trade programs during price drops. But, he reports, when prices kept going up, Fair Trade would not pay more: "That was a problem for the cooperative because the people said to themselves, 'Well, I will go where I get paid the most.' And people dropped out of the cooperative. But with prices lower again, they will come back."

THE THIRD WAVE OF CHANGE IN THE GLOBAL COFFEE MARKET

The Second Wave movement set a higher bar for quality and introduced millions around the world to coffee that was a higher grade than the standard commodity form. The Second Wave marketed distinctiveness in flavor profiles and places of origin (Kenya AA, Guatemala Antigua), rejecting the anonymizing commodification of the First Wave market. As the Second Wave market grew globally, many of its singularizing distinctions themselves became commodified (Fair Trade, SHB washed arabica, and so on), if differentiated from bulk arabica and Robusta. Anyone producing coffee of sufficient quality can sell in this market, which benefits medium-sized producers as well as cooperatives—as these are small enough for robust quality control and yet large enough to dependably supply container loads of green beans.

The Third Wave market generally eschews cooperatives in favor of sourcing from "single estates" and particular farmers. This supports narratives of terroir and authenticity, as well as claims of increasingly exotic flavor profiles. In place of the social premium of Fair Trade, the Third Wave market pays a quality premium that can be very lucrative for certain farmers. The Third Wave style of direct trade promises to shift even more power to smallholding producers—at least those who grow the highest-quality beans—but it is problematic for the collective and, for complicated and morally entangled reasons, it often puts individual producers in a difficult position, having to choose between community and individual gain.

Third Wave coffees carry the connotation, if not explicit claim, of solidarity through "relationship sourcing" and the extensive biographical narratives that accompany many beans.[20] Yet this imagined solidarity is felt very differently on the ground in coffee-producing regions such as highland Guatemala, where new markets for quality pose a threat to a hard-won and widely popular cooperative system for smallholders. Our data show that in 2014 smallholding producers had only a vague idea of the final consumption market for their coffee. Most of the farmers in our sample joined in the Second Wave because it was a familiar agricultural endeavor with a booming market. They are aware that the market changed in the 1990s in ways that created a dramatic new opportunity for them. Still, only 17 percent of our sample are familiar with "specialty coffee" as such. They have little or no idea about roasters and baristas, cold brew and K-Cups, and Third Wave coffee shop culture.

The hefty premiums these beans command mean that the farmers who grow them are well compensated, often earning many multiples of standard farmgate prices (e.g., $4 per pound versus $1.25). But these tend toward winner-take-all markets, with marginal differences in cupping quality and social capital resulting in exponentially larger earnings. Between the First and Second Wave there was a modest but significant increase in price for farmers. There was some variation, and a system of recognized national premiums, but also a baseline for quality washed SHBs. Yet, in the Third Wave, we see dramatic variations in willingness to pay large premiums for relatively small differences in quality and imagined or real scarcities. This reflects a move away from a quality commodity market to a market much more focused on the singular and particular. Pricing is much more difficult, and variable, with singular items such as unique batches of micro-lot coffee beans.

The number of smallholding producers selling into the Third Wave market is small, and this exclusive high-end market will likely always be dwarfed by the demand for specialty and commodity coffee. However, for the fortunate producers able to grow high-quality coffee and connect with the Third Wave market, the rewards are significant and hold an outsized role in local popular imagination.

TOUGH CHOICES AND UNEVEN REWARDS

As the Third Wave changes the lives of coffee farmers in Guatemala, the results are variably spread, concentrated on certain individuals and not whole communities. On the consumer side, preferences shift quickly, but for producers this is a multiyear project that goes from planting to harvest. The Second Wave market's reliance on cooperatives and the Third Wave's focus on provenance and direct trade are two different models of economic engagement for farmers, distinct in both ideology and logistics. On the one hand, there is the route of solidarity (among producers and between producers and consumers). Cooperatives have been very good at minimizing risks, and smallholding agriculturalists justifiably tend toward risk aversion. In place of cushioning the downsides, the Third Wave micro-lot market opens the possibility of greater upsides, handsomely rewarding individual farmers who produce beans with unique cupping profiles. This neoliberal route of meritocratic rewards for quality and individual excellence can be very attractive to hardworking farmers even as it erodes community solidarity in ways disadvantageous to those same farmers.[21]

The tension between these two approaches is lived and felt by smallholding Maya producers. It is more than just rational calculation of how to maximize returns (if that is also a significant consideration); there are moral obligations to the cooperative and the community that farmers must navigate. Many farmers feel stuck between the moral economy of the cooperative, in which they believe, and the immediate (and potentially life-changing) profits from selling their highest-quality beans on the Third Wave market.[22] For cooperative members, selling to coyotes usually means defecting from at least part of one's obligation to the cooperative. This is not an easy decision, but it is also the case that these farmers are in difficult economic circumstances, doing what they see is needed to survive and hopefully get ahead. Of our sample 50 percent report selling primarily to a cooperative or association, 41 percent to a coyote, and 9 percent to both a cooperative and coyotes. A majority report that the price floor provided by cooperatives is valuable. Some cooperatives in high-demand regions estimate the defection rate to be close to 50 percent. When prices are high, farmers of specialty coffee have long diverted harvest from cooperatives to sell to coyotes, but this is exacerbated by extraordinarily high prices offered in the Third Wave market.

Smallholding farmers join cooperatives for a range of reasons, from risk management to the creation of community and the pursuit of collective ambitions about the world in which they would like to live. Take, for example, Ignacio, a fifty-eight-year-old Maya farmer from the Lake Atitlán region of Guatemala who has been growing coffee almost his whole life. He speaks Spanish well enough although he grew up speaking Tz'utujil Mayan and only completed first grade in the public elementary school. He is literate to the extent that he can sign his name and read the numbers of a sales sheet. Ignacio's father grew maize and beans, and they subsisted mainly on what they grew. Like many families, his father also had a number of coffee trees to supply the household and sell a little surplus in the local market. At some point his father expanded the coffee plantings, and Ignacio expanded it further just as the market was taking off. While his material circumstances would still seem exceedingly modest to most of the people who drink his coffee, he has done spectacularly well by local standards. He made enough money to send his kids to school; he can hardly contain his pride when he says that both finished high school and became professionals, one a bookkeeper and the other a teacher.

At the time of our 2014 survey of smallholding coffee farmers in Guatemala, the market was booming, and we found an overwhelming majority held positive views about the coffee market and its impact on household finances. "Coffee is the future" is a phrase we heard repeatedly as producers expressed their commitment to the crop. This is not idle speculation, but farmers literally betting the farm and their family's livelihood on the future direction of the global market. They are bullish: more than 74 percent predicted that the market would at least stay at current levels in the coming years, and 44.8 percent expected prices and farmer incomes to continue to increase.

The benefits of the coffee boom on Maya communities are widely recognized among our sample. Don Antonio, an older Kaqchikel Maya farmer from San Martín Jilotepeque, says that today there is less emigration and that "the level of poverty has dropped very dramatically—men who used to be day laborers now have their own land they plant." Eduardo, a young farmer with a growing family, reports that coffee has provided a huge economic benefit to his family: "Now I have a cinderblock house, and I am planning on expanding it."

The farmers we talked to are also deeply committed to coffee in a way that goes beyond the purely economic. Rolando, a survivor of the civil war violence and member of a cooperative that occupies land redistributed from an old finca to internal refugees of the war, stresses their deep commitment to coffee, even with all that they have been through: "We will stay with coffee; we are used to struggle. First there was the fall in prices—they had never been so low. Then we were hit by Hurricane Mitch, then Stan, then Agatha. Then came an earthquake. Then the coffee rust. But here we are still, and we are moving ahead." Augustín, a forty-two-year-old Q'eqchi' Maya farmer with a second-grade education, reports, "I will never abandon coffee, even in tough years like the last one."

There is clearly a realization of the importance of "quality." Almost everybody we spoke with, from the head of Anacafé to remote farmers, mentioned the central importance of quality. In our sample 73.7 percent reported that improving quality is the most important market imperative going forward. For most this means better cultivation habits and a clean harvest, as well as warding off the coffee rust fungus. Only 5 percent saw the push toward quality as also involving the search for exotic varietals. All the same, there is little depth of knowledge among farmers of the market destination of the coffee they produce: 47.6 percent reported having no knowledge of the coffee market beyond the cooperative or coyote; most of the rest reported "some knowledge," but this is usually a vague idea that it goes to the United States and Europe (with a few of the most knowledgeable farmers mentioning Japan as well).

Most of the coffee farmers we spoke with want more direct connections with the market, but they also do not understand the market well. Intermediaries are seen as somewhat suspect, but also as the necessary agents of outside connections. The farmers themselves often take pride in their coffee and their ability to grow it well, seeing virtue in earning a living from the land. All the same, while farmers drink the coffee they produce in their own fashion, they have not learned the sensory norms of cupping, and they have only a vague notion of the final consumers. This is a particular sort of alienation, and it disadvantages farmers without the social capital to translate values from field to cup.

Don Antonio, the older Kaqchikel farmer who has been in coffee for almost twenty years, says that "coyotes pay more than the cooperative" and he does "not trust that the cooperative always has our interests in first place." He feels that he owes it to his family to get the best price he can for the harvest, and so he sells to the coyotes, but not without a tinge of regret. As someone proud of his coffee and ambitious in his plans for expansion, he hopes to make connections beyond the coyotes to exporters and roasters. He says, "You need to make it into direct trade, a personal relationship, to make real money." In choosing between selling to the cooperative or a coyote, Don Antonio concludes, "Either way you won't get rich, just hopefully a little less poor."

Eduardo, a coffee cooperative member in Huehuetenango, reports selling some of his crop to coyotes rather than the cooperative. "They just mix it in with all the rest," he complains about the cooperative, "and my quality doesn't make a difference." In contrast, selling to high-end intermediaries hunting for quality is very demanding: "They come inspect the fields, make sure the right varietals are planted, and check on altitude; they monitor the whole process." He appreciates being at the production end of the relationship narrative that may accompany his micro-lots.

Chajul is an Ixil Maya community in an area hit especially hard by the violence of the early 1980s. In the aftermath of a brutal counterinsurgency campaign in which any hint of cooperative organization was considered communist subversion, the community of Chajul came together to build one of the largest and most successful coffee cooperatives in Guatemala, with more than 1400 members. Cooperatives are never without some level of discord, but by most measures the one in Chajul has especially broad support in the community. It is often held up as an example of what a cooperative can do in terms of community development. Even with this level of support, cooperative members report a constant battle with defections. One member, Arcadio, says that while fair trade guarantees a floor price, "when the price goes higher, we have to scramble to keep people selling to the association. People don't understand that they have to sell when the market is up too. They just want to earn more and more. Many are not loyal to the cooperative; they go and sell to the coyote to get the higher price." The reality of the situation is that "what most people do, when the prices go way up, is sell some to the coyote and some to the association."

QUALITY VERSUS COOPERATION

As high-end markets around the globe turn to artisanal and increasingly de-commodified goods of positional value, rewards are not evenly distributed. For the big winners, success comes not just from terroir and harvesting techniques but also from their ability to translate goods and ideas across various value worlds. The greatest proportion of value added comes from consumer tastemakers who help establish symbolic quality conventions. This requires the social and cultural capital to translate material and symbolic values across arenas of valuation. Paige West shows how importers distinguish particular coffees from the others on offer in terms of cup profile ("good acidity," "chocolaty and nutty"), and at the same time how they must be prepared to "make an alternative seem commensurable" in case a substitute is needed. One Hamburg importer describes the art of uniquely differentiating lots (e.g., Papua New Guinea's distinct fruity flavor from the bit of fermentation that happens getting beans from remote highland plots to wet mills) while also having to have backups with similar characteristics (e.g., "this Panamanian has a similar profile ... "). They work hard to singularize the product, but they must also leave the flexibility to substitute another coffee when needed, undermining the producer's market power. As William Roseberry observed with Second Wave coffees, the post-Fordist approach to coffee sourcing disadvantages labor in new ways, as styles of coffee can be moved around the world, chasing low prices, just like outsourced manufacturing.[23] In addition, smallholding farmers are not the consumers of their production—this is a disarticulated market, to borrow a phrase from Alain de Janvry[24]—and lack the social and cultural capital to position themselves in the Third Wave quality market. This results in a situation where control over the material means of production is no longer crucial to accumulation. What matters as much in this context is control over the means of symbolic production.

·   ·   ·

With the boom in Third Wave coffee, which is more concerned with cupping profiles than cooperative arrangements, farmers fortunate enough to be located on the best coffee lands are increasingly being lured away from cooperatives. Intermediaries with an eye for quality try to pick off the best producers, enticing them to defect from their cooperative commitments for significantly higher prices.[25] In this way the Third Wave market threatens the raising-all-boats structure of the Second Wave and poses a danger to the cooperative structure that most farmers see as key to protecting their position in the market. Fair trade certifications provided a buffer against market fluctuations for small-holders in the Second Wave tide, but they also tie farmers to a model that is breaking down in the market turn to quality. Third Wave coffees bring much higher incomes to some farmers, but in doing so they help erode the power of cooperatives (which farmers nonetheless say they support). The market is always chasing something new, but this shifts risks back onto smallholders who have to invest three, four, and some-times even five years ahead of a first harvest for a new flavor profile.

Consumers of Third Wave coffees, when they consider it, probably assume that the high prices they pay translate into support for farmers. Some farmers—those who produce high-grade coffees and who have the social capital to translate its value into the market—are highly rewarded. But, in the process, they also threaten structures of mutuality in pro-ducer communities. Farmers overwhelmingly support cooperatives, but most also are not in a position to turn down better financial offers. This is a moral as much as an economic issue—it is a case where economic advantage and social values come into conflict. The decisions farmers have to make about whom to sell to reflect the tension of competing value regimes: the quality market pays higher premiums but erodes the power of cooperatives, which farmers say that they value. There is also a new distribution of risks, with risk pushed down the value chain so that small-holders take on more.

As part of the broader neoliberalization of the global economy, risk is pushed as far down the supply chain as possible.[26] In terms of coffee, it is farmers who assume most of the risk. Farming is always a risky business, but it becomes exacerbated in high-end markets that are constantly changing, constantly chasing the new and rare. This risk for farmers is real and complicated: will coffee aficionados in Portland or Nashville want what I grow? This risk is in addition to the assumed risks of disease, drought, and other crop-devastating possibilities. These farmers are living in circumstances in which the continual challenge is preservation. The risk of failure is real, and potentially catastrophic. Still, as Tania Li argues, the "will to improve" is deeply motivating, especially when it is linked to meritocratic ideals of the market as neutral arbiter.

The collision of value regimes located in the consuming and producing worlds has long been a defining feature of global capitalism, but we are now seeing how increased turbulence in the moral preferences of consumers rebounds back to producers in unintended ways. The small size of the Third Wave market means that its economic impact is limited in scope, and the few winners, if they are rural Maya people in Guatemala, are still vulnerable to dislocation due to discrimination, corruption, and the labyrinthine complexity of the system. The capacity of Maya smallholding growers to translate their material and cultural endowments into the symbolic value worlds of consumer markets is limited. It turns out, then, that poor Maya farmers are systematically marginalized in subtle and counterintuitive ways by new, seemingly more direct, market relations.

Conclusion

This research began with an intriguing story about the role of specialty coffee in Maya communities. Little did I know where pursuing it would lead. Such is the nature of the ethnographic endeavor: in unravelling the complexities of lived experience, and taking seriously the hopes and concerns of those we study, we follow the imbroglios where they take us. Having worked in Maya communities throughout most of my career, I began with a strong preconception of the role of coffee in Guatemala's political economy. The conservative coffee oligarchy seemed to represent much that is wrong in this highly unequal and ethnically stratified country, while Maya workers described coffee *fincas* as places of hardship, deprivation, and racist abuse. Guatemala's coffee economy seemed to reinforce an all-too-familiar tale of colonial legacies: a landed, European elite supplying the world market with a high-volume, low-cost commodity on the backs of Indigenous laborers. This is all true, but it turned out to be only part of the story.

As the previous chapters detail, the Second Wave consumer trend toward high-quality, high-altitude coffee resulted in a dramatic shift in Guatemalan production, with tens of thousands of Maya smallholders beginning to cultivate on their own lands for the specialty market. Talking to these farmers, I realized that while they grew coffee primarily for the income, the values it represented in their lives went far beyond the economic. The crop fit into local worlds of valuation, both material and moral, conceptually linked to cosmological cycles of agricultural regeneration and tied to a range of culturally informed aspirations and fears that guided market decisions. The additional income from specialty coffee expanded horizons and accelerated change, but these changes were grounded in local value worlds. Bill Hempstead's claim about the economic boom in many rural communities was borne out by the data, but here again, the story turned out to be more complicated than it first looked.

Committed to a particular Austrian-inspired ideological notion of freedom and free markets, leaders of the coffee industry in Guatemala supported the specialty coffee boom, promoting regional designations of geographic origin and unique cupping profiles. By the 2000s Guatemala had emerged as a center of Third Wave production, the source of some of the world's most rarified coffees. Their eye-popping premiums are justified within the Third Wave value world by a focus on "quality," both material and symbolic. Roasters and aficionados earnestly search out quality, relishing in the lengths they will go to discover it. Yet, in the act of seeking out quality—and debating what that means—these actors also create understandings of quality in a back and forth with the material and organoleptic properties of beans.[1] And the ability to define what is quality is where real power resides in this system. Many Third Wave professionals and enthusiasts see themselves involved in a de-colonizing project, de-commodifying, at least in part, production that has long been associated with violent exploitation and colonial expropriations. Alas, while they may control the material asset of land and its associated terroir, most smallholding Maya farmers lack access to the cultural capital and means of symbolic production, excluding them from the narrative enrichment crucial for Third Wave premiums.

Tracing the values that attach to coffee at different points along the commodity circuit provides a lens for understanding the complex interrelatedness of politics and economics, social structures and cultural desires, plant biology and ideological commitments, seeing these all as mutually constitutive. On the one hand, coffee is big business, an often brutally unsentimental industry. At the same time, it is laden with all sorts of valuations and moralizations—upscale coffee is marketed with a warm glow around the value chain, stressing its origins, the benefits for farmers, and their connection to the consumer. Following the beans, we can see the fibers that connect the aspirational values of Maya farmers and the ideological commitments of Guatemalan oligarchs to the quality conventions of Third Wave coffee, all within the framework of neoliberal trade and neocolonial structural inequalities built into Guatemalan society and the world system.

Over the course of this research I began to see it as a project about values as much as about coffee. Understanding the coffee trade requires that we grapple with how values—in the plural, economic and otherwise—affect individuals' decisions, how they shape (and are shaped by) social norms and institutions.[2] The lesson here extends far beyond the case of Guatemalan coffee. Values frame the way we look at the world— the way things are and ideals about the ways things should be—and motivate actions. In addition to self-interest and economic maximization, people are motivated by a complex balance of shifting values that are irreducible to hard metrics. That is not to say that a desire for material gains is inconsequential, just that it is not the only guiding principle in decisions. This is true of "them" (whoever they may be, from Guatemalan oligarchs to Maya farmers) as well as of us. The study of values is important not to advocate for "good" values or decry "bad" values, but to understand the role they play in linking social, political, and economic lives. The lens of value worlds shows how moral, social, symbolic qualities intertwine with the material trade in coffee to constitute a value chain.

Fluid and ever-negotiated in practice, value worlds provide guiding principles, shared measures of worth that can be referred to for justification within a particular discourse community.[3] Much of the art and practice of living revolves around balancing and translating between multiple and overlapping value worlds. These operate at different scales and levels of coherence, deriving meaning from being shared even while they are open to situational and idiosyncratic interpretation. David Graeber sees such spheres as "imaginary totalities," each making totalizing claims, and that "the ultimate stakes of political life tend to lie precisely in negotiating how these values and arenas will ultimately relate to one another."[4] Gaps between value worlds create opportunities for arbitrage and accumulation, as in translating one sort of value (say, social) into another (such as market).[5] In this, value worlds are shot through with power relations, and hierarchies can become solidified in durable conventions, norms, and institutions. André Theimann and Christof Lammer term this process "infrastructuring value," a way of organizing and channeling the flows of ideas, goods, and money along certain pathways to facilitate and create value worlds.[6]

At the same time, values are not just criteria to be applied when making a judgment; rather, they provide a starting point for improvisational practice enacted in specific thoughts, words, and deeds. Value worlds provide an orientation around a desired ideal, a Foucauldian *dispositif*, a particular framing of the world that orients knowledge and informs implicit and explicit value judgments. In this way value worlds intersect with both the personal and the structural,[7] and we may understand much of social, economic, and political life as a choreography of values.[8]

Lives take place at the intersection of numerous value worlds, and the action is in their interaction, when we have to translate moral values into economic decisions, or make trade-offs between religious values and political choices, striving for that delicate balance between things held dear.[9] Such is the art of living that Aristotle describes as practical wisdom (*phronesis*), built up through the daily practice of balancing values and virtues, and that Maya cosmologies extol as producing metaphysical equilibrium.[10] In the Western tradition, judgment brings together many heterogeneous and variably weighted criteria to compare incommensurate objects—an artful practice informed by social norms and life experiences.[11] Calculative devices and quantitative measures reduce the burden of making sometimes difficult value judgments by delegating them to seemingly objective and rational metrics. Therein lies their allure, what drives the expansion of market logics into ever more areas of life. This involves calculations of the "optimal" allocation of resources (including mental energy and emotional labor) to maximize gains and efficiencies.[12] But to see the system as a system, we have to look beyond individual choice to larger political-economic contexts, including structural forms of neocolonial inequalities and the constellation of values that clusters around neoliberal politics and capitalist markets. It turns out that even domains of valuation grounded in quantifiable metrics are built on intangible and symbolic values.

SPECIALTY COFFEE AND HOPES FOR SOMETHING BETTER

Looking at the impact of the rise of specialty coffee production in Maya communities, we can see the ways value worlds converge and collide. Coffee in Guatemala has been long associated with a largely German oligarchical class and its often brutal conservatism. Starting in the 1960s, an anti-communist and pro–free market worldview inspired by Austrian economics took hold among key members of the coffee oligarchy. "Follow the market" was the mantra Bart Victor and I heard over and over in interviews with coffee industry leaders in Guatemala, so much so that it became a running joke. Of course, Hayek and von Mises were writing in a very different context, that of a post–World War II solidification of the Soviet bloc and the rise of social democratic welfare states in Western Europe. But for many of the coffee elite, this antisocialist, laissez-faire approach translated neatly to the Cold War context of Guatemala. It justified support for Guatemala's genocidal military campaigns against Marxist revolutionaries and Indigenous communities more broadly. It also led to Anacafé's opposition to the market controls of the International Coffee Agreement. The ICA was emblematic of the post–World War II consensus to manage trade and to aid developing economies in pursuit of international stability—even if the concern with increasing equity between the Global South and the Global North did little to lessen the stark inequalities within countries such as Guatemala.

"Following the market" provided an important ideological justification for Anacafé's turn toward regional distinctions and support of smallholders. In effect, a value-driven commitment to the neoliberal principles of Austrian economics led Guatemala's coffee oligarchy to cede market share to new smallholders, as the sought-after Strictly Hard Bean coffees were grown in the Maya-majority highlands. This created a boom in a number of historically impoverished and marginalized communities, as Maya farmers entered the market on a tide of steadily increasing demand and prices. For these farmers, coffee allows them to maintain important cultural ties to the land, feeding into cosmological cycles of regeneration while also making some extra money. Although they are working lands far off the beaten path, they are well aware of their connectedness to the global economy. Most have cell phones, and many have smartphones; Facebook and WhatsApp are the preferred forms of communication, especially among the younger people. Their aspirational horizons are broader than in the past; they yearn for something better, something more (*algo más*) for themselves and their families. They see in coffee a way to maintain traditional economic, social, and moral values around earning a living from the soil and controlling one's means of production. Coffee represents not just cash but also symbolizes hopes and dreams for the future. Their material investment in the future is, perhaps tragically, linked to distant narratives of consumer values.

"The tradition of all dead generations weighs like a nightmare on the brains of the living," Marx writes in *The Eighteenth Brumaire;* thus, he continues, while we may all make our own futures we do not make them just as we please or under circumstances of our choosing. For this reason we tend to look to the past to explain the present, to show how things got the way they are. Yet privileging the past can lead us to forget that people in the present are not only trying to re-create yesterday but also have an eye toward tomorrow and next year and the lives of their children and grandchildren. Arjun Appadurai calls on us to view imagination and aspiration as fundamental drivers of individuals' engagement with global flows.[13] For farmers, coffee is seen not as a way to get rich, but as a significant source of income that can keep a family out of absolute poverty. It is a cash crop, a commodity lacking the spiritual importance of maize-and-beans *milpa* agriculture. At the same time, coffee connects to a sense of communitarian obligation and cooperation that intersects with the agricultural cycle. The familial and cooperative labor employed by smallholders is deeply embedded in local social relations and norms of reciprocity. In contrast, most view seasonal plantation labor and a form of dependency, wrought with the hardships of being separated from one's family that they want to avoid if at all possible.

The high-end coffee market, insulated from the dizzying swings of the New York C price, is based not only on material conditions of terroir, but also on the ability to translate those qualities into symbolic Third Wave value worlds. Third Wave roasters and baristas along with the SCA and its corporate and academic partners promote "better" coffee—meaning both a higher quality and a more just supply chain built on relationships. They respect authenticity, rarity, and craft. They tell stories about the coffee they sell and how it was produced and roasted. In valuing craftsmanship, artisanal devotion, and the unalienated fruits of production, there is an implicit assumption that this can counter inequities characteristic of the commodity trade.[14] But consumer preferences for high-quality artisanal production can exacerbate inequalities and result in winner-take-all markets.[15] Third Wave coffee presents a case where the consumer quest for excellence, quality, and artisanal sensibilities results in some big winners but many more losers, at least some of whom produce coffee that scores just as highly in blind cuppings.

While Third Wave professionals and enthusiasts develop the vocabulary and metrics of quality, coffee farmers in places like Guatemala are developing their own understandings of quality and the market. Farmers appreciate coffee, seeing it as an important source of cash income to supplement (or in some cases replace) their subsistence crops. They take pride in their ability to grow it well and Guatemala's international reputation for production quality coffees. Building on long-standing Maya and agrarian traditions, most see a virtue in earning a living from the land and producing something of quality.

Nonetheless, with tastemakers in the Global North constantly looking for new and increasingly exotic flavors, farmers in tropical coffee-growing regions of the world find themselves at an impossible disadvantage in making decisions for planting and harvests four to five years down the road. Third Wave trends toward the singular and the unique threaten cooperative structures by pulling away the highest-quality producers. In this way the Third Wave concern with "quality in the cup" elides appeals to social justice in the conditions of production: it is a postjustice infatuation with artisanry and authenticity that assumes expensive coffee will be produced under ethical conditions.

Farmers seek to hold on to (and expand) their landholdings while tastemakers and consumers chase ever more unique flavors and stories. The retail de-commodification of coffee—in terms of the specialty market for micro-lots, the importance of provenance, and the connection with farmers—has shifted some power to smallholding producers who are fortunate enough to control land at the right altitudes and microclimates. While many Maya farmers have benefited from the specialty coffee boom, they are largely excluded from the highest-value segments of the Third Wave market because they lack the social capital to translate their material endowments into the symbolism of consumer value worlds. In this way, the Third Wave coffee market reflects the sort of late-capitalist formations in which the greatest economic rewards come not through control of physical production but from setting the terms for cultural narratives of worth.

MATERIAL AND SYMBOLIC VALUES

In the beginning, there was use value. Or so the usual narrative goes. It is assumed that the material utility of the thing-as-such gave it value. In *Capital,* Marx distinguished a socially embedded use value from exchange value, a relative worth, such as price, defined in comparison to other goods. He argued that when exchange value becomes untethered from human labor and use value, people begin to fetishize commodities, which take on fantastical proportions in the imagination, exerting a seductive pull over desires. Deirdre McCloskey's rejoinder to Marx's material determinism is that, actually, in the beginning, there was the Word. That is to say, ideas make the material world useful, literally defining what useful is; a stick can only become a spear when predicated by an idea.[16] The imagination is as important as material circumstances.

One way to create value is with machinery: to make things, to control the material means of production. Another way is with ideas: inventing the machines or controlling the means of *symbolic* production. With high-end coffee, crucial to extracting maximum economic value is constructing a narrative that can entice customers to pay extra for symbolic, moral, and imaginative values in addition to material utility. Third Wave purveyors justify high margins by invoking stories of geographic origins and artisanal authenticity as well as the science of sensory analysis. For producers to be successful in this context requires the social and cultural capital to influence value narratives, to participate in discussions around quality. This disadvantages smallholding Indigenous farmers—even though they are endowed with sought-after terroir and rich cultural legacies.

Power once rested with control over the means of production, as Marx noted and as was well understood by capitalists from early water loom operators churning out textiles to Henry Ford and his attempts at vertical integration. In twenty-first-century capitalism—with its unprecedented shift toward production and consumption of intangible, nonmaterial assets and objects—accumulation happens not so much through control over the material means of production but through influencing narratives and symbolic meanings. Today the assembly, if not all aspects of production, of consumer material goods is largely carried out in lower- and middle-income countries. As postindustrial economies have focused investment in the service and information sectors, manufacturing and industrial and agricultural production shifted to the Global South.[17] Taiwan-based Foxconn has done very well in assembling iPhones and other products in Shenzhen, China, but the device's "designed in California" label nods to the intellectual property and branding that extracts the most surplus value. The same is true of Third Wave coffee: the greatest share of profits goes to those at the consumer end who shape cultural narratives around quality and intangible values. Luis Samper and colleagues illustrate this in their analysis of the share of value distributed in 2014 between producing and consuming countries in First Wave ("Mainstream"), Second Wave ("Differentiated"), and Third Wave ("Relational") coffees (figure 25).[18]

Luc Boltanski and Arnaud Esquerre observe that in the current phase of late capitalism, two primary market worlds operate simultaneously, one based on material production, the other based on symbolic and affective forms of "enrichment."[19] Twenty-first-century global capitalism is expanding largely by turning things once seen as unique into new sorts of commodities (witness the rise of intellectual property rights, the branding of personas, the market for human organs) and turning former commodities into more singular goods, such as with coffee. There is a long tradition of privileging economic worth over symbolic values, with the symbolic often viewed as a distraction or obfuscation of material conditions. But as these markets show, the two are mutually constitutive.[20] In fact, much of what we call the knowledge economy is really a symbolic economy, selling an idea or a connection to de-alienated production, including authenticity, artisanship, a sense of a social as well as economic relationship. Take non-fungible tokens (NFTs), a unique blockchain provenance that one can purchase to certify the singular original for a digital good. This is not so much

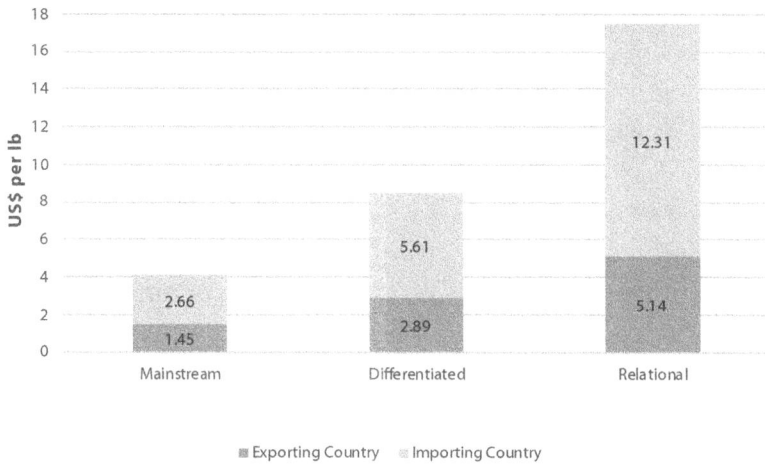

Figure 25. Value distribution in 2014 between coffee market segments.

buying a thing—a digital original can be endlessly and exactly reproduced—but rather, Sophie Haigney writes, "buying the concept of owning a thing—which feels like the logical endpoint of a society obsessed with property rights, and finding new ways to buy and sell almost anything."[21]

The shift toward symbolic and intangible goods is reflected not only in consumer markets, but also in the types of capital investment being made. Intangible assets cannot be easily touched or counted, and their worth is largely positional. Intangibles operate quite differently than "real" capital (that is, productive material assets): they are easily scalable, nonrival goods that can be reused without decay.[22] *The Economist* writes that intangible assets are nebulous: "Complex supply chains or a set of distribution channels, neither of which is easily replicable, are intangible assets. So are the skills of a company's workforce. In some cases the most valuable asset of all is a company's culture: a set of routines, priorities and commitments that have been internalized by a workforce. It can't always be written down. You cannot easily enter a number for it onto a spreadsheet. But it can be of huge value all the same."[23] Jonathan Friedman observes that growth in fictitious capital (such as symbolic value and intangible assets) occurs at a faster rate than "real" capital (meaning materially productive capital), opening a gap he terms the "postmodern space of investment" partially unlinked from the constraints of material production.[24] Research done by Carol Corrado and colleagues shows that starting in the mid-1990s, overall nonfarm business investment in intangible assets (brand value, intellectual property, software, data, algorithms, etc.) exceeded those of tangible assets (machinery, tools, computers, financial capital, etc.).[25] We may read Corrado's chart of investments in tangible versus intangible assets as an empirical representation of Friedman's theoretical model (figures 26 and 27).

All of the "laws" and rules of thumb about the market called upon by coffee traders are predicated on a particular political and social order that produces "rational" subjects to pursue certain ends and work out the "correct" solutions to cost/benefit analyses. Traders often talk about the market as an intentional and purposeful agent, a moral arbiter that rewards or punishes actors and actions through changes in price.[26] At the same time, there are other values at play beyond rational economic maximization. It is important to acknowledge the gritty reality of farming, which can be easy to romanticize from afar, and the ways coffee is wrapped up in the lives of those who harvest and pack and ship and roast and brew it. Growing coffee is hard, calloused-hand work, an endeavor fraught with risks of all sorts, from fungal scourges to fickle consumer tastes. On the ground, on the steep slopes of coffee farms in Huehuetenango, the abstractions of global trade and value worlds are grounded in the harsh materiality of labor and the hopes, dreams, fears, and desires of those who toil.

Coffee presents an ideal subject for studying the interplay of economic value and other sorts of value worlds. It stands as a symbol of the best and the worst of global trade and north/south relations—from the harsh realities of much plantation labor to the bright promise of Fair Trade. Such values are ascribed not only by affluent Northern consumers, but also by the mostly poor and rural producers in places like Guatemala. Coffee has a particularly rich biography, built from histories of relations good and bad,

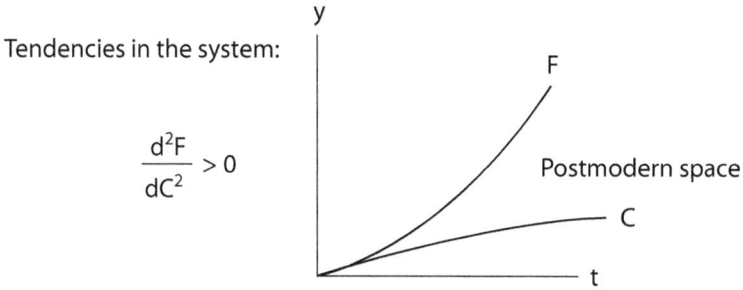

Tendencies in the system:

$$\frac{d^2F}{dC^2} > 0$$

F: fictitious capital
C: real capital
y: total capital
t: time

Figure 26. Growth curves for real versus fictive capital, adapted from Jonathan Friedman (1994).

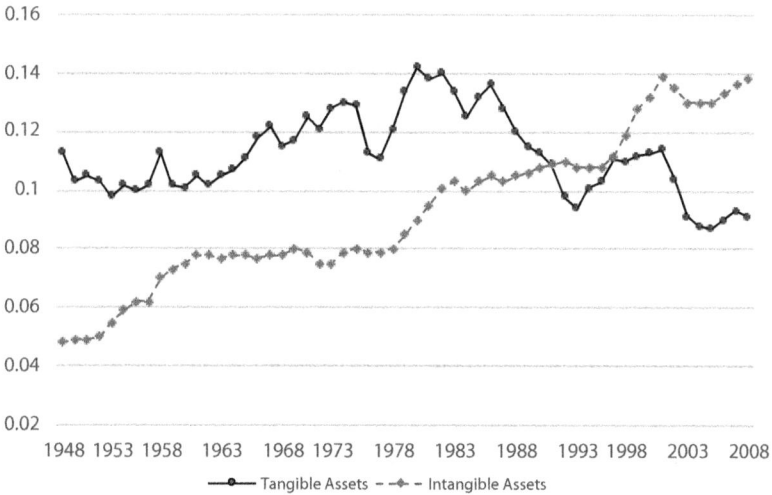

Figure 27. Investment in tangible and intangible assets, adapted from Carol Corrado (2009).

illustrating how people—individuals and communities—in different parts of the world interact with global flows of goods and ideas.[27] Today coffee stands for both the best and the worst of global commodity chains, a posterchild for economic dependency and a model of market-based solutions for smallholding farmers.

While this book focuses on the case of Third Wave coffee, the dynamics described reflect broader trends. Economic market power has come to rest more and more with intangible assets and control over means of symbolic production, exacerbating inequalities within and between countries in ways that reflect a colonial matrix of power. Anna Tsing describes capitalism as a "translation machine," and the Third Wave coffee market illustrates how late capitalist forms of accumulation result from arbitraging worth across material and symbolic value worlds.[28] In today's high-end coffee market, farmer narratives and attention to the particularities of terroir make up a significant part of the value proposition. What we find are multiple value worlds linked to the same commodity chain: the dual imaginations of Third Wave aficionados imagining distant producers and the Maya farmers in Huehuetenango imagining the drinkers of their coffee while seeking a better life for their own families in difficult circumstances. There is a lot of room for misunderstandings here, but also a glimpse at how economic value is created by translating across seemingly incommensurate domains of worth. A market driven by esoteric tastes and a continual search for something new and unusual systematically disadvantages Maya smallholders, who lack cultural knowledge of Third Wave markets and the social capital to act on that knowledge.

VALUES IN THE POST-ENLIGHTENMENT WORLD

Difference is what makes trade possible and desirable. There are the sterile, if often lucrative, differences in exchange value—buying cheap and selling dear—that fill mercantilist ledgers and fuel turn-of-the-millennium global trade. While the precision of accounting suggests otherwise, any dealmaker will tell you that trade is more art than rational scientific practice, and there can be great financial gains to be made in translating meanings as well as transporting goods across different domains of valuation. Savvy traders well understand the power and worth of the social and symbolic—and the ways capital accumulates through translating values across symbolic and material realms. The production and trade of Guatemalan specialty coffee brings together numerous arenas of valuation (moral, social, political, economic, biological, agricultural) to form a commodity chain that is about more than just beans and dollars. Still, the intangible and symbolic qualities of high-end coffee can be converted into economic gain by tastemakers with the right cultural capital and a bit of luck.

The Enlightenment project of categorizing and measuring the world has produced great wealth and technological innovation, but we have begun to see the limits of breaking the world up into discrete domains of life and study (psychology, physiology, ecology, economy, religion, politics, art, culture, business, biology, and so on, each with its own conventions and truth conditions). Bounded fields of study allow us to plumb depths of knowledge, but they also foreshorten our understanding of the world's interconnectedness. The closer we look at coffee, the blurrier the boundaries between botany and politics, philosophy and economics, identity and consumption become.

We cannot separate caffeine's effects on neurochemistry from its enthusiastic uptake in cultures around the world; those aspects, in turn, are not distinct from the cruelties of slave labor or current consumer trends toward the exotic and artisanal. When traders at the International Commodity Exchange in New York place a contract to buy a container of washed arabica from Guatemala, they are mapping value-laden categories onto the world, creating a reality that shapes the lives of all those along the circuit. What coffee *is* and what coffee *means* are not inherent to the object but stem from the interaction between human value worlds and the material and biological traits of the plant.[29] Coffee is enmeshed in a web of relations that ultimately ties it to many aspects of existence, and to focus on any one element misses the mutually constitutive nature of the system. This is not simply to argue that everything is connected—which is true—but that the particulars of the connections matter.

When the New York C price falls dramatically, migration from Maya communities in the coffee-growing regions of Guatemala spikes. The economic shock forces farmers to reevaluate their life projects, and, in the context of limited possibilities, many see the dangerous journey to the United States as the best alternative. In such ways crises bring values into sharp relief, making people explicitly consider what is more important and what is less important in their lives. While personal tragedies make one rethink individual priorities, large-scale crises force us to do the hard work of reconsidering our collective values.

As I finish this book in the summer of 2021, we are in the midst of a global pandemic. While caused by the SARS-CoV-2 virus, the pandemic is much more than a medical challenge: its devastation results from political decisions, economic structures, and social networks as much as from microbial causes.[30] Much of the debate around COVID-19 has concerned differences of values, judgments of what is "essential" and "fair," and the meanings and implications of "freedom" and "equity." The different positions expressed reflect qualitatively different value worlds, and our political system's inability to translate and reconcile them has resulted in higher transmission and mortality rates.

We can train our tastes to be calibrated through cupping courses, and we can assign almost absurdly precise numerical ratings to what is ultimately a subjective experience of drinking a cup of coffee. Yet behind the numbers always lurks a value judgment where the real power rests. We have seen how this works in the realm of high-end coffee, but the lesson applies more broadly to the ways tough moral and political decisions are disavowed onto the market and its neat calculus of risks and rewards.[31] With the neoliberal turn in the 1980s, public policy equations became ever more dependent on quantifiable measures built around rational-actor assumptions. Relying on econometric algorithms, probabilities, and cost/benefit analyses to make policy judgments imparts a sense of objectivity and precision, leaving little room for nonquantifiable values.[32] In this context, economic maximization can overwhelm other values, making it difficult to tackle big challenges that require coordinated responses.[33]

Numerical data tell us a lot, but they do not tell the whole story, and relying on them can lead us to discount the importance of that which cannot be counted. Data is not wisdom, and balancing different sorts of value worlds requires judgment and not just calculation. But nonquantifiable values can be difficult to work into systems based on quantifiable metrics. What we need is a post-Enlightenment approach to political economy that recognizes the interrelatedness of domains of life and the qualitatively different value worlds in which they are enmeshed.[34] Toward that end, we might return to humanistic, narrative approaches to decision making that address political and moral issues as such, and not just as technical problems of humans failing to conform to rational expectations.[35]

ACKNOWLEDGMENTS

This research was conceived of and carried out with my friend and colleague Bart Victor. Bart's ideas and incisive framings permeate this book, and I owe him a greater debt than I am able to pay here.

Kedron Thomas's insightful and critical reading of the whole manuscript helped me rethink key aspects of the argument. Sarah Lyon, Monica DeHart, Michiel Baud, Bob Klitgaard, Siyuan Wang, Soni Akshay, and an anonymous reviewer also read the whole manuscript and provided generous and detailed comments that I have tried to incorporate. A special thanks also to Kate Marshall of University of California Press, who helped frame and shape the manuscript from its early days.

I have had productive discussions and correspondence on the topics presented here with Mareike Sattler, Emily Yates-Doerr, Peter Mancina, James Carrier, Dan Reichman, T. S. Harvey, Kees Koonings, Avery Dickins de Girón, George Lovell, Ashley Carse, Betsy Carter, Hanes Motsinger, Bruce Barry, Peter Martin, David Napier, Noa Berger, Sara Marquart, Dan Cornfield, Jon Shayne, Ingrid Wuerth, Josh May, Joseph Mella, James Foster, André Theimann, Christof Lammer, and Karoline Krenn—and their insights inform the arguments I make.

Generous feedback and ideas came from Tom Perrault, Karl Zimmerer, Kendra McSweeny, Marygold Walsh-Dilley, and the other participants in the UNM Greenleaf Symposium; and from Clarence Gao, Carmella Quintos, Jared Baumann, Lily Hauptman, and others from my honor's seminar on coffee. Jennifer Bostwick-Owens, Bruce Barry, and Judie Maxwell constituted the dinner table focus group for title possibilities.

This book was largely written during stays at the Max-Planck-Institut für Gesellschaftsforschung (MPIfG) in Köln and at the Centre for Latin American Research and Documentation (CEDLA) in Amsterdam. Special thanks to Jens Beckert, Lisa Suckert, Moisés Kopper, and Matías Dewey at the MPIfG for productive conversations and useful feedback. At CEDLA, Michiel Baud, Barbara Hogenboom, and Kees Koonings helped make Amsterdam my second home for a while.

The smallholder surveys in Guatemala were developed and conducted with Linda Asturias de Barrios, Tatiana Paz, Aracely Martínez, Carlos Pérez-Brito, Luis Velásquez, Ixchel Espantzay, and Pakal B'alam. Special thanks to Will McCollum, Mac Muir, and the Project Pyramid teams for the coffee price research reported on in chapter 6. At Anacafé, invaluable assistance was provided by Bill Hempstead and Blanca Castro.

Many coffee professionals have generously shared their time and expertise with me. A special thanks goes to Aaron Duckworth, Nick Scott, Michael Ripps, Tom Einsenbraun, Peter Giuliano, Bob Bernstein, Elika Liftee, and Chris Ayers.

Thanks to Mitch Denburg and CIRMA for providing archival photos. Jean-Marie Simon generously provided the photographs of coffee workers in 1981 found in chapter 3. Natalie N. Robbins drew the map in chapter 6. Thanks to her and Steve Wernke, the director of the Vanderbilt Spatial Analysis Research Laboratory. Grace Freeman generously arranged the use of images from the SCA in the introduction and chapter 1. Elder Daniel Dubón López permitted use of illustrations from Anacafé. Maps were drawn by Don Larson and his colleagues at Mapping Specialists. Fernando E. Vega generously provided a photograph of the botanical drawing of *C. arabica* from Diderot's 1751 *Encyclopédie*. Thompson Owen of Sweet Maria's Coffee took the frontispiece photo for chapter 5. Christian Bunn of the Alliance of Bioversity International and the International Center for Tropical Agriculture facilitated adapting some of his data, and Luis Samper encouraged the adaptation of his value distribution chart in the conclusion. Tatiana Paz Lemus redrew several charts, and Siyuan Wang created the spider graph and word cloud in chapter 1. Thank also to the efforts of Enrique Ochoa-Kaup at University of California Press and to Sharron Wood for her expert copyediting.

Sections in chapters 1, 4, 5, and 6 were adapted from Fischer and Victor (2014), Fischer (2021), and Fischer, Victor, and Asturias de Barrios (2020).

NOTES

NOTES TO THE INTRODUCTION

1. This description comes from my interviews with Liftee, watching his Nashville presentation, and reading Chris Ryan's (2020) profile in *Barista* magazine.

2. See Sabine Parrish's (2020) and Noa Berger's (n.d.) thick descriptions of competitive coffee making. Parrish writes that such competitions "exist partly as a means to legitimate the idea of the specialty barista as a serious profession, and partly to position specialty coffee in an industry whose practitioners are highly skilled; coffee competitions normalize a refined product that requires professional labor to a customer base that pays significantly more on average for a cup of standard drip coffee" (2020: 79). These are examples of what Arjun Appadurai (2013) terms "tournaments of value," and what Michel Callon (Callon, Méadel, and Rabeharisoa 2002) and Sarah Besky (2020) term "qualification tests" or "experiments."

3. In her study of the tea trade, *Tasting Qualities,* Sarah Besky writes that the pursuit of quality is often portrayed as "a way of liberating select consumers, conscientious retailers, and even some laborers from the entrenched systems of provision in which they find themselves" (2020: 178).

4. Callon, Méadel, and Rabeharisoa describe quality as emerging from an ongoing practice of qualification that "aims to establish a constellation of characteristics, stabilized at least for a while, which are attached to the product and transform it temporarily to a tradeable good in the market" (2002: 199).

5. In *Gastropolitics and the Specter of Race: Stories of Capital, Culture, and Coloniality in Peru,* María Elena García (2021) describes how the well-intentioned, socially conscientious chefs leading a movement in Peruvian haute cuisine are products of, and help reproduce, racialized coloniality of power.

6. Paige West's *From Modern Production to Imagined Primitive: The Social World of Coffee from Papua New Guinea* shows how the creation of symbolic values is obscured by a double commodity fetishism: "We forget that the value of the commodity fetish also derives from its place in a hierarchy of value ... [and] that it is people that make that hierarchy of value" (2012: 250). Similarly, Heather Paxson (2013) shows the ways artisanal cheese makers sell not only their product but also the social and moral values associated with craft production; Benoît Daviron and Stefano Ponte (2005) trace the value chain of African coffee to show how symbolic and experiential qualities are used to justify retail prices in Europe; see also Boltanski and Esquerre (2016) on "enrichment economies."

7. From this perspective, we may understand value as produced not only by material wants but also by subjective desires fueled by symbolic qualities and imaginative ideals of what is good. The definition cited comes from Beckert's (2016: 195) wide-ranging study of the ways imagined futures underwrite capitalist dynamics. Imaginative value is based on a subjective, symbolic, and socially constructed understanding of "the good," as well as on longing for how things should be. That implies hope, what Michael Jackson calls the "sense that one may become other or more than one presently is or was fated to be" (2011: xi). Brad Weiss (2003) shows that coffee embodies potential, what can be, for Haya producers in Tanzania. The Haya use coffee as a medium to store various sorts of value, and to make commensurate different sorts of values. The welfare of farmers is linked, materially and symbolically, with the health of their coffee trees, and coffee consumption is used to create relationships and reinforce the hierarchies of kingly authority. At the same time, coffee is not considered "real" food. As a commodity it connects the Haya to the larger world; its meanings are at once intensely local and inherently global. In a compelling essay, Galina Kallio (2020) argues that value emerges from pursuit of the good.

8. The period is what some term "late capitalism," which raises the question of what comes next, and when. "Late capitalism" first appeared in German in the early twentieth century; later, Ernest Mandel used it to describe the period of post–World War II economic growth and widespread prosperity; Fredric Jameson (1991) invoked it to characterize late twentieth-century capitalism; and it has gained popular usage in the 2000s (see Lowrey 2017). See Lash and Urry (1987) on "the end of organized capitalism," and Jonathan Fried-

man (1994) on the "post-dependency phase" of world capitalism. These authors link this phase of capitalism (whatever it may be called) to the condition of postmodernity.

9. See David Harvey (1989) on post-Fordism. Fordism (a term coined by Antonio Gramsci) denotes the mass-production model Ford employed to change the automobile industry—breaking down the assembly process into its smallest components and assigning each to a worker who would do the same repetitive task over and over again. In Marxist terms, this greatly increased worker alienation, not only from their means of production but also from the fruits of their labors. Great strides in improving the human condition have been made through the efficiencies of Fordist mass production techniques— and this is really the promise of liberal capitalism: greater efficiencies mean that more people can buy more stuff, raising everyone's standard of living. Indeed, as prices for mass-produced products fall because of increased efficiencies, they become within the reach of greater and greater numbers of people down the economic ladder. This happened with sugar in England around the turn of the nineteenth century: a product at first enjoyed only by the aristocracy and wealthy merchants gradually entered the diet of commoners (along with tea). Next came textiles, then cars, then all sorts of consumer devices. More stuff for everybody: This is the basis of free market optimism. Such mass-produced affluence seemed to buy off the American worker for much of the twentieth century.

10. Karpik (2010), Callon and Muniesa (2005), Gudeman (2008), Chibnik (2011).

11. Callon, Millo, and Muniesa (2007) observe that in such an "economy of qualities" the worth of an item changes as it crosses market domains, with particular attributes alternately highlighted or deemphasized to make a product more or less singular (see also Callon, Méadel, Rabeharisoa 2002); Besky notes that these qualifications are not unilaterally decided by producers or traders. Rather, they are subject to experiments, qualification tests in which buyers and other actors judge not just the quality of the product but also the underlying justification. These are risky events for individuals, but, as Besky writes, "No one actor—no one form of expertise—maintains the system" (2020: 14).

12. In the view of Baudrillard (1981, 1998), we ceased to define ourselves through production and began to see ourselves primarily as consumers—and this is a very ephemeral basis for identity. And because of this we are no longer satisfied with mass-produced affluence, which is not enough to define us as the individuals we see ourselves as being. As a consequence, in this late capitalist, post-Fordist age, we want to de-alienate our consumption. Despite rising

standards of living, we are more alienated than ever, and we yearn to get out of our McMansion fortresses and connect with something more real, more authentic. If we are to define ourselves through what we consume, then we must have great variety. These is no more of Henry Ford's "any color you want as long as its black" mentality; we need literally hundreds of breakfast cereals and thousands of colors, the more metaphoric their names the better.

13. Gibbings (2020: 9) notes that this experience in the northern highlands differs from that in the western highlands.

14. Heather Paxson writes that terroir is a palimpsest whose "appeal lies precisely in its ideological flexibility; it can be translated to frame various relations between place and production" (2013: 211). Elizabeth Carter (2018) highlights the political power struggles behind the establishment of Burgundy terroir, showing that such markets of distinction are politically—as well as economically and socially—constructed.

15. Graeber (2013).

16. The region also has a significant trade in lower-quality coffees. Rebecca Galemba (2017) describes the active smuggling operations on the Hue-huetenango/Mexico border; these are largely separate from the drug trade and involve the smuggling of workaday coffee and consumer goods. Galemba's work vividly illustrates the permeability between the realms of the licit and illicit, and how commodities flow in and out of these domains. See also Aguilar-Støen (2019) on cooperatives and migration from the region.

17. See, for example, Besky (2014) on tea; Meneley (2014) on olive oil; Weiss (2016) on heirloom pigs; Terrio (2000) and Martin and Sampeck (2015) on chocolate; Diaz-Bone (2013) on wine; and Brulotte (2019) on mezcal.

18. On the increasing importance of symbolic and intangible qualities in the global political economy, see Beckert (2016), Storper (2001), Carrier and Miller (1998), Friedman (1994), Haskel and Westlake (2017).

19. Benoît Daviron and Stefano Ponte (2005) show how the production of symbolic and experiential qualities results in the greatest share of value extraction in specialty coffee, with the concentration of convention-setting power at the consumption end of the chain. They divide that coffee trade into three spheres of value creation: the material (based on intrinsic attributes of the product), the symbolic (qualities that cannot be measured by the human senses), and the affective (as expressed through in-person service). Their analysis is based on remarkable documentation of the value added in several specific coffee commodity chains (e.g., Tanzania to U.S. specialty coffee shops).

20. Roseberry (1996); see also Doane (2010), West (2012), Reichman (2018).

21. In 2005, specialty coffee shop chains surpassed independent coffee-houses in market share; by 2016, chains made up 65 percent of specialty coffee outlets (Samper, Giovannucci, and Vieira 2017: 45).

22. Doane (2010: 235).

23. In chapter 6 I look more closely at Fair Trade and certification regimes; see Bacon (2005, 2010), Jaffee (2007), Lyon, Ailshire, and Sehon (2014), Méndez et al. (2010), Moberg and Lyon (2010).

24. West (2012); cf. Hernández Castillo and Nigh (1998) on how the specialty coffee market's push toward organic agriculture converged with Mam Maya identity politics in Chiapas, Mexico.

25. The Germans call pure coffee *Bohnenkaffee* (bean coffee) to distinguish it from varieties mixed with chicory or other substitutes.

26. Jeff Pratt's (2007) "Food Values" shows how such value keywords often get conflated (e.g., "local" is "authentic") by the affluent consumers who support these markets. See also Richard Wilk's (2006) exploration of the tensions between authenticity and globalization in local cuisines. Theodossopoulos (2013) offers a productive view of authenticity's many valences—including critiques of naive understandings and the contradictions of such critiques—concluding that we should allow for multiple and simultaneous authenticities.

27. Clarence Gao encouraged me to stress that the three waves are more like market segments than time periods; in the United States, as of 2022, First, Second, and Third Wave coffees are all widely available, each targeting a different market segment. See Roseberry (1996) and West (2012) on coffee marketers' demographic categories; see Tucker (2010), Manzo (2015), and Morris (2019) on the emergence of these waves.

28. See Robert Klitgaard (1991) on the role of information and relationships in the construction of quality and standards.

29. See Molly Doane (2010) on relationship coffee; on virtual proximity, see Forster, Quiñones-Ruiz, and Penker (2019); on bypassing certification bureaucracy, see Motsinger (2018).

30. This builds broadly on the observation of David Harvey (1989) and others on post-Fordist flexible accumulation; specifically, I draw on the work of William Roseberry (1996), Paige West (2012), and Daniel Reichman (2018) and their analyses of the contradictions of high-end coffee markets trying to scale up based on particularities rather than Fordist homogeneity; Sarah Lyon's (2011) analysis of how Maya values and community norms engaged with the rising coffee market; and Benoît Daviron and Stefano Ponte's (2005) detailed

study of the conventions behind symbolic and affective forms of adding value in specialty coffee.

31. See https://www.newyorker.com/culture/culture-desk/the-rise-of-coffee-connoisseur-culture for a short video introduction to a coffee trade show and competition.

32. This is rapidly changing, and the SCA has made a concerted effort to increase diversity. Today there are a growing number of women and people of color becoming roasters, baristas, and coffee shop owners.

33. Cojtí (1991, 1994); see also Achille Mbembe's (2001) *On the Postcolony.*

34. Indigenous women also face serious gender discrimination; see Espant-zay Serech (2018).

35. On the violence and its impact in Maya communities, see Simon (1988), Smith (1990), Carmack (1988), Manz (2004); on the aftermath of the war, see Little and Smith (2009), Nelson (2009), Burrell (2013), O'Neill (2009).

36. Tzul Tzul (2018); Tzul Tzul shows the complexity of power relationships in such collective forms of governing while also rejecting romantic and utopian views of Indigenous communities.

37. See Carol Smith (1984) on the historical context of Maya economic strategies; Goldín (2009) on contemporary strategies. See also Way (2021) on how rural Guatemala is changing.

38. Much like coffee-fueled eighteenth-century physiocratic philosophers in France, as Stephen Gudeman and Alberto Rivera (1990) argue in their study of household economics in Colombia.

39. Monica DeHart (2010) shows a very different way ethnicity and entrepreneurialism intersect in postwar Guatemala.

40. Sarah Lyon (2011) shows the complicated impact of this economic boom on a Maya community and its coffee cooperative; see also Fischer and Victor (2014).

41. This, and a number of other helpful observations, came out of a presentation at the Greenleaf Symposium at University of New Mexico organized by Marygold Walsh-Dilley.

42. From a capabilities approach to development, the ability to envision and pursue goals that people themselves value (agency) and real opportunities to achieve these goals (including material resources and opportunity structures) are key (Sen 1999, Nussbaum 2011). From this perspective, the specialty coffee boom in Guatemala looks like a success. As we will see, however, aspirations also exceed available opportunity structures, leading to a condition of "frustrated freedom" (Victor et al. 2013)

43. Berlant (2011); Victor et al. (2013).

44. This built on my previous work with smallholding export farmers in the Guatemalan highlands, looking at the ways their desires for a better future intersect with national politics and international markets (Fischer and Benson 2006).

45. See Fischer and Victor (2014), Fischer, Victor, and Asturias de Barrios (2020).

46. See Wilson (2013) on the tensions in the moral economy of coffee cooperatives; see DeHart (2010) and Copeland (2011) on conflicts between prosocial community values and neoliberal market forces in the Guatemalan context.

47. I use the familiar term "commodity chain" here to denote the material trade of beans grown in the Global South and largely consumed in the Global North, yet this material trade is also more than a one-way flow of goods; it is embedded in multiple value worlds and circuits of economic and symbolic exchange. Cook and Crang (1996), Cook (2004), Topik (2009), and others argue that "chain" fails to capture the permeability and fluidity of these networks. Cook and Crang (1996) prefer "commodity circuits," focusing on circulation rather than a linear progression from one end point to another. While the "global commodity chain" approach has focused on connecting consumer choices to conditions of production, Cook and Crang's approach shifts attention to how goods and meanings are displaced from site to site and embedded in different cultural contexts with different meanings and values. In this view, consumers actively and creatively inhabit the commodity circuit; they are not mere pawns of manipulative commercial interests (see also Carrier 1997, Miller 1998, Lash and Urry 1987, Friedman 1994). Arjun Appadurai (1986) envisions these as nonlinear commodity paths, with significant diversions and transitions to other contexts. Some prefer the term "value streams" to indicate this fluidity. I will vary usage in this book to avoid repetition but will always be indexing the idea of porous, dynamic, and interconnected networks of relations based around the trade of a particular item—coffee, in our case.

48. See Beckert (2019) on "markets from meaning." Philosophers, economists, and social theorists have long grappled with the question of how value, whether discovered or produced, comes to be. The physiocrats saw value as ultimately stemming from the fruits of the earth; Adam Smith and Karl Marx agreed, with a few caveats, that value derived from labor; and Carl Menger's theory of marginal utility revolutionized economics with a view of value as deriving from the subjective desires of consumer demand. In this, Menger's

approach converges with critical social theory. Here I am thinking of Georg Simmel's (2004 [1900]) description of when a subjective sense of value comes to be understood as intrinsic to the thing or idea, and subsequent work that shows the ways symbolic consumption is tied to identity construction and the ways desires meld into needs in such a way as to fuel production. Menger's (1950 [1871]) *Principles of Economics* observes that after people satisfy their material needs they start to desire other goods and have to make subjective evaluations of worth based on relational values. See also John Kenneth Galbraith (1958) on the production of subjective desire and Jean Baudrillard (1998) on the semiotic and positional values that emerge in symbolic economies. Jens Beckert (2016) observes, "In an economic system that depends on the willingness of consumers to desire more and newer products, human fiction-ability creates a demand for products that are independent of the differences the product makes in the physical world." See the excellent discussion of value by Christof Lammer and André Thiemann (n.d.).

49. See Tsing (2015: 133); Ashley Carse (2014) cites a number of studies that show how capitalist economies and moral economies are intertwined around the tension of making the incommensurate commensurate (e.g., Reichmann 2013, Fisher 2013). Mezzadra and Neilson (2019) focus on the ways material and symbolic extraction gets translated across circuits of valorization. Paxson (2021) shows how value is created in the artisanal cheese trade "through skillful logistical and semiotic practices," which include modalities of time and timing and microbes and fermentation. Looking at global tuna, Theodore Bestor (2001, 2004) emphasizes connecting/translating across temporal differences: it is not simply that activities take place at different times, but rather that each node is structured, existentially, in different times that impact how actors envision the temporality and scale of their activity.

50. Andrew Sayer defines values as "sedimented valuations," that is, attitudes that "merge into emotional dispositions and inform the evaluations we make of particular things, as part of our conceptual and affective apparatus. They are more abstract than the particular concrete evaluations from which they derive and which they in turn influence" (2011: 25–26). See also Zigon (2008) on "embodied dispositions."

51. Amartya Sen (2002) defines commitment as doing something for the common good or for another individual that is counter to one's own material self-interest. Michiel Baud (2020) unpacks the idea of *confianza* in Latin America, an ideal of relational trust linked to pro-social norms of solidarity. Confianza is crucial to the coffee trade, providing the trust needed for handshake

deals and the cultivations of relationships in "relationship coffee." Confianza names and formalizes a sort of moral relationship that is at once local and personal and yet linked to a largely recognized value world. Baud's argument points the way to integrating such moral value into political and social values and actions.

52. Inspired by Ayn Rand as much as Adam Smith, a view of humans as driven primarily by self-interest and the accompanying belief in the power of markets to best provision the common good have had enormous influence in public discourse and policy. While recognizing the importance of what she terms "P" variables (such as property, profit, and predation), Deirdre McCloskey (2006) points out that seeing humans solely as rational maximizers ignores an equally important source of motivations, "S" variables (including the social, the sacred, and the symbolic). She argues that economic utility—indeed, human behavior—results from a balance of P and S variables. We see this with coffee growers, traders, roasters, and consumers, all of whom are motivated by a range of social, cultural, political, and other values beyond the quantitative calculations of economic self-interest.

53. Economic cost/benefit approaches are seemingly able to integrate different value worlds. Stephen Gudeman (2008) argues that trade nurtures "calculative reason," but that can give only an incomplete picture. Bruno Latour (2013: 445) writes that economic models are equipped "with devices, abacuses, benchmarks, instruments, arrangements, models, in short, VALUE METERS, to help the actors get their bearing in an ever increasing number of linkages and thus obtain ALLOCATION KEYS acceptable to the various parties." But these models rest on a number of dubious assumptions about human nature, and this book argues that markets cannot be understood solely in terms of economic measures of worth. We need models that incorporate other sorts of moral and social values that shape behavior so that, as Latour concludes, "We may benefit from an ontological pluralism that will allow us to populate the cosmos in a somewhat richer way, and thus allow us to begin to compare worlds, to weigh them, on a more equitable basis" (2013: 23).

54. Fourcade (2016); see also Fourcade and Healy (2007), Lamont (2012), Beckert and Aspers (2011), Krenn (2017).

55. Bourdieu (1977, 1984) writes of "dispositions." These are learned, but often in subtle ways that "come without saying because they go without saying" (1977: 167) Some involve more disciplined training (as with rational argumentation) and others are more subtly internalized (as with a "natural" sense of taste or style).

56. People do not simply apply the metrics of a received value regime; rather, they actively and creatively interpret and adapt broad (often vague) ideals of the good (see Kallio 2020), compromising between the sometimes competing pulls of different value worlds. Spaces of improvisation, value worlds are dialectically constructed through practice. Some are more rigid than others, but all have their own dynamic logics based on intuitive dispositions or codified tradition. See my argument for "cultural logics" in Fischer (2001).

57. Webb Keane adds that a lot of social life is about making "ethical affordances" to others (2016: 31). Rainer Diaz-Bone (2015) points out that a plurality of justifications can almost always be called upon by a single actor in a given circumstance, and that actors question and contest conventions (see also Ponte 2016). David Stark (2009) has studied the productive friction created by work environments that simultaneously invoke different evaluative orders for workers. He notes that there is creative friction in the spaces where evaluative domains come together, but that the dissonance can also be destructive.

58. Cf. MacIntyre (1984) on tradition; Boltanski and Thévenot (2006) on justification.

59. On the ontological turn in anthropology, see Holbraad and Pedersen (2017), Kohn (2013), Holbraad, Pedersen, and Viveiros de Castro (2014), Descola (2013), Viveiros de Castro (2014). Such a perspective opens the possibility of engaging epistemologies outside of the dualism of the Western metaphysical tradition, often more open to the fluid relationships between human and nonhuman, material and symbolic, and other realms of life. At the same time, Julie Gibbings (2020) points out that the ontological perspective also reifies the Western/non-Western division. On interconnectedness, see also Wagner (1975), Deleuze and Guattari (1987), Ingold (2016).

60. Graeber (2013) observes that in any society or community there are many such domains of valuation, each totalizing in its own sphere, operating simultaneously. Paul Kockelman presents a study of ontologies of value around a conservation and development program in a Maya community. He argues that such domains of valuation are "simultaneously a locus of causation, representation, reflexivity, and accountability" (2016, 69) in which many frames of "ontological reflexivity" operate simultaneously in the act of evaluating the world as it presents itself; see also White (2000) on "weak ontologies." Kockelman offers the concept of "portability" to refer to translating values across domains and making evaluative standards commensurate. See also Harvey (2013). David Pedersen (2008) proposes a relational model of value that

sees the worth of a particular object (a specific instantiation) as resulting from its link to a broad, conceptual value regime, and the potential it embodies.

61. Boltanski and Thévenot (2006), Appadurai (1986), Weber (1978). Boltanski and Thévenot also refer to "worlds" as the spaces where the values of a "polity" are worked out.

62. Dewey (1939). Bruno Latour observes that much of the tension and opacity around different modes of existence results "from the fact that the veracity of one mode is judged in terms of the conditions of veridiction of a different mode" (2013: 18). Some value worlds can overwhelm other value worlds, as neoliberal valuation regimes have done in much public discourse. Kevin Lewis O'Neill (2009) shows how a particular form of "Christian citizenship" in neoliberal Guatemala shifts moral responsibility away from structural factors and onto individuals. See Mitchell (2005), Dean (2019), Carrier and Miller (1998) on the power of economics in creating its own world. See also Karpik's (2010) analysis of singular items.

63. Robbins draws on the work of Louis Dumont (1994) and his view of "ideologies" guided by a paramount value. See Robbins 2007a, 2007b, 2012. Jarrett Zigon (2009) highlights the always contingent and often conflictual processes through which institutional and individual moral values get worked out; he sees values not as obligatory codes but as spaces of conjuncture. See also Web Keane (2016), Andrew Sayer (2000, 2011).

64. Philip Balsiger (2019) defines "moralized markets" as fields of heterogeneous interests in which ideological purists reject market logics. Lisa Suckert (2018a) presents a compelling case in which value worlds collide in the German organic milk market. As a "moralizing market," organic producers must appeal to their base by stressing moral (and narrative) integrity. But the economic side of the equation values growth. The conflict occurs because "economic growth can lead to a structural loss of moral integrity, while adherence to ecological orientation hinders commercial potential" (499). Suckert shows how successful producers are able to use the inherent ambiguity of translating across multiple sets of values to mitigate this potential structural opposition. Kedron Thomas (2016) presents a case in which moral values around sharing come into tension with formal intellectual property rights in the market for pirated clothes in a Guatemalan Maya community. Maya weavers have a long tradition of innovating designs, with moral norms around borrowing and sharing patterns. In the community where Thomas worked, a booming business emerged in weaving knit shirts using pirated international brand names. In fact, as Thomas shows, the designs are not mere copies but rather hybridized

versions designed to appeal to local tastes. The use of logos is understood in a local value world of design openness and not under the international law governing intellectual property. From the consumer side, Anne Andersen (2011) looks at Danish shoppers, finding food consumption as a site of conflict between different sorts of moralities (e.g., economic thrift versus environmental concerns). In her study of matsutake mushrooms, Anna Tsing concludes that amassing wealth in the current capitalist world system is not just about rationalizing labor but rather based on "acts of translation across varied social and political spaces" (2015: 62). Bennett (2018) looks at the moral complications of ethical consumerism in the cannabis market. For more on ethical consumerism, see Meneley (2018), Dubuisson-Quellier (2013), Carrier and Luetchford (2012).

65. Their work has inspired a growing body of research in "convention theory" that looks at shared (and contested) understandings and mutual expectations that provide a framework for interpreting the values of objects and behavior. For an overview of convention theory, see Diaz-Bone (2015), Ponte (2016). For useful extensions, see Storper and Salais (1997) and Carter (2018). Not so much rigid frameworks as evaluative logics worked out in practice and dialogue, conventions provide a socially valid (if still contestable) justification for determinations of value within a given sphere. This line of theory shares much in common with Bourdieu's emphasis on improvisation, cognitive templates, and the tension between agency and structure; see Suckert (2018b).

66. This approach also hews to the sort of "polyphony" that T. S. Harvey (2013) presents in his study of views toward health in a K'iche' Maya community. He shows how K'iche' "wellness seekers" navigate and balance different domains of knowledge, from biomedicine to traditional beliefs.

67. See Gudeman (2008), Chibnick (2011), Wilk (1996), Fischer (2014b).

68. Rudi Colloredo-Mansfeld (1999) writes that "by speaking of values rather than 'models' or 'schemas,' I draw attention to the moral nature of the principles structuring economic activity. As matters of morality, they go to the very core of the self and constitution of society." Indeed, the concept of "values" also indexes the shared qualities of "culture" while accounting for the variably distributed nature of cultural values—see Rodseth (1998), Brumann (1999)—and the dynamic ways cultural elements flow across time and space; see Appadurai (1996).

69. Of course, we too are embedded in our own value worlds and moral projects. We must take care that romantic notions of Maya communities or

idealized views of suffering do not distract us from taking seriously their moral projects, their desires as well as needs. My intention here is empirical description and theoretical analysis rather than normative prescription. All the same, my bias is with the marginalized, and I take seriously what they say about their hopes and dreams and fears and anxieties, and the complicated ways these come together in real lives.

70. Latour (1993: 3).

71. In this book, "we" is used to refer to "we humans" or, depending on the context, the sort of humans who read books like this one.

72. Montejo (2021); see also Raxche' (1992). On Gladys Tzul Tzul, see the interview with her by Oswaldo J. Hernández at https://upsidedownworld.org/archives/guatemala/confronting-the-narrative-gladys-tzul-on-indigenous-governance-and-state-authority-in-guatemala/. As Walter Mignolo (2011) describes it, the decoloniality perspective does not respect disciplinary borders. It offers options—not alternatives, which would presuppose modernity as a reference point—from outside the modernity/coloniality episteme.

73. The core Enlightenment distinction between rationality and emotion is not so stark as once imagined. In her study of quality in the tea trade, Sarah Besky (2020: 14) observes that "sensation and affect matter not just when it comes to consumption, but throughout the production and circulation of everyday things." Even the border between the individual and other organisms is not as clear-cut as once thought: our "self" includes large populations of microbes.

74. I situate this in the tradition of both Boasian anthropology and Latourian science and technology studies. Lars Rodseth shows how Latour's method shares with Boasian anthropology "an ontologically 'reckless' approach that traces the interwoven pathways of humans and nonhumans" (2015: 865).

NOTES TO CHAPTER 1

1. As of 2021, London also has a vibrant Third Wave scene, and awareness and consumption are on the rise across Western Europe, China, and Brazil. Sabine Parrish (2021) looks at specialty coffee *apaixonados* in São Paulo, examining the complicated class position of these urban and urbane enthusiasts in relation to geographically proximate rural producers and to the cosmopolitan landscape of craft roasters across Europe and the United States.

2. Peter Giuliano estimates that all of specialty coffee (Second and Third Wave combined) likely make up around 27 percent of the global market.

3. In 2017, Nestlé acquired a majority stake in Third Wave pioneer Blue Bottle; in 2019, Coca-Cola bought Costa Coffee, the second largest coffee shop chain in the world specializing, like Starbucks, in mass-market specialty coffees. And JAB Holding Company has been buying up coffee companies at a furious pace. JAB, a privately held German firm headquartered in Luxembourg, traces its roots to an early nineteenth-century chemical venture between a Reimann ancestor and Johann Adam Benckiser (whose initials live on in the company name). Now controlled by the Reimann family, JAB is a food and consumer goods conglomerate—a company of which you may have never heard but that you have likely patronized. They own Panera, Bruegger's, Krispy Kreme, Keurig Green Mountain, Dr Pepper Snapple, and many other consumer brands, including Gucci. The Reimanns have generally eschewed the spotlight, although recent revelations about Albert Reimann's Nazi collaborations have led the company to open its archives. The *New York Times* reveals that Reimann, who died in 1984, was a fervent support of Aryan race theory and yet maintained a decades-long extramarital relationship with Emilie Landecker, whose Jewish father was murdered in a Nazi death camp in 1942. Reimann had no children with his wife, but in the 1960s he adopted the three children he fathered with Landecker. Two of them today control almost 50 percent of JAB. The Reimanns have opened up about their complicated history with National Socialism, pledging their foundation's resources to education about the Holocaust. (See Katrin Bennhold, "Nazis Killed Her Father, Then She Fell in Love With One," *New York Times,* 14 June 2019.)

After a decade-long buying spree, JAB now owns a number of staple First Wave brands, such as Jacobs and Douwe Egberts, Second Wave stalwarts such as Peet's and Caribou, and Third Wave pioneers such as Intelligentsia and Stumptown. While the brand landscape and ownerships have changed, U.S. and European companies maintain control of the high value–add segment of the market closest to consumers while producers large and small are left to compete on price and quality. Control over the means of distribution and symbolic production turn out to be more important than farmers' control over the material means of production.

4. Terrio (2000) shows how artisanal chocolatiers went about educating French consumers about quality—teaching them to like and appreciate dark chocolate—so that they could accrue the symbolic capital to discern valued attributes.

5. On moralized markets see Suckert (2018b), Balsiger (2019), Dubuisson-Quellier (2013), Carrier and Luetchford (2012), Fischer (2014a,2014b).

6. West (2012: 65). This marketing of poverty and native authenticity as a part of the coffee experience results in what Cook and Crang (1996) call the "double commodity fetish" of foodstuffs, an ignorance of the origin and conditions of production combined with "lores" about these origins.

7. Lyon (2011), Lyon, Ailshire, and Sehon (2014).

8. On alternative food networks, see Pratt (2007); on singularizing markets, see Karpik (2010); on the varied meanings of consumption, see Meneley (2018); on individual foods and drinks, see Brulotte (2019), Ocejo (2014), Meneley (2014), Paxson (2013), Terrio (2000); see also Pratt (2007), Karpik (2010).

9. Boltanski and Esquerre (2016), Callon, Millo, and Muniesa (2007).

10. Data on the Third Wave coffee market in the United States comes from ethnographic interviews conducted between 2012 and 2020 with dozens of importers, roasters, baristas, coffee association leaders, and scientists working in the field; from attending the SCA annual meetings, coffee competitions, and other trade shows; and from extended participant observation at several Third Wave coffee shops in Nashville, Tennessee.

11. The specialty market trades at higher values than the "New York C price" (the market standard for washed arabicas), but for many the two remain conceptually linked. Peter Roberts at Emory's business school has been tracking specialty coffee prices as part of his Transparent Trade Coffee project, and in 2018 he started releasing an annual "Specialty Coffee Transaction Guide" with green coffee prices at the point of export broken down by quality category. See the 2020 guide at https://www.transactionguide.coffee/en/2020. As Roberts observes, despite rational expectations, the specialty market is still linked in traders' minds to the New York C price—a reminder of the power of ideas in the market. Daviron and Ponte (2005) identify a market paradox of coffee in the transition from First Wave to specialty coffee: even when the bulk commodity market is down, prices at the high end stay level or even rise. For Third Wave coffees, sold as unique micro-lots, pricing opacity is part of the design.

12. See Schenker and Rothgeb (2017) on roasting science and techniques.

13. Besky (2020: 178).

14. Badiou (2013); see also MacIntyre (1984) on "projects" and "practices," and Richard Sennett's (2008) study of skilled work that requires years of training and practice and focuses on the intrinsic rewards that come with such practices.

15. Weissman (2008).

16. See the excellent study by Sarah Besky (2020) on documenting and producing quality in the commodity tea market.

17. Paxson (2013).

18. There are a few dozen import houses in the United States (and several more in London, Amsterdam, Hamburg, and a few other key sites) that do at least some trade in Third Wave coffees. They will work with exporters in producer countries to identify desired lots and try and matchmake these with roasters. Larger coffee shops and small chains often try to establish direct ties to farmers, even making trips to visit farms. But only the largest of these can manage to directly import, and the majority make their direct ties through or alongside an importer. At all scales, the coffee trade is not that different than it was a hundred years ago, built on relationships along the commodity chain. Even a player as big as Starbucks still sends buyers to trudge around the Guatemalan countryside, maintaining ties to growers under contract and seeking out new supplies.

19. Doane (2010).

20. Forster, Quiñones-Ruiz, and Penker (2019); Daviron and Ponte also point out that symbolic values created by roasters and retailers seek to close the "spatial, cognitive, and institutional distances" (2005: 226) between grower and consumer. Sonia Bookman (2013) shows how the global narratives of specialty coffee can feed into a "cosmopolitan cool" identity among consumers, and Steinberg, Taylor, and Moran-Taylor (2014) show how idealized images of the Maya are used in the marketing of Guatemalan coffees.

21. Samper, Giovannucci, and Vieira (2020: 52).

22. Motsinger (2018); West (2012: 25, 213).

23. Thanks to Ole Mouritsen for his insights. See Harold McGee (2020) on smell; Mouritsen and Styrbæk (2017) on mouthfeel; and Thomas, Puget, Valentin, and Songer (2017) on sensory evaluation in coffee.

24. Karen Wistoft and Lars Qvortrup (2019) present a model in which there are three systems of taste—the physiological, the mental, and the social—that can be divided into seven dimensions—sensed taste, moral taste, healthy taste, religious taste, trendy taste, pleasant taste, loving taste. These dimensions overlap with what I term value worlds, but Wistoft and Qvortrup focus on how these dimensions shape perceived sensory experiences (e.g., a moral dimension making an item taste better) and the didactic possibilities.

25. See Evans and Lorimer (2021) on what they term "taste-shaping-nature," the recognition that taste is (at least in part) shaped by nature, but also that our tastes shape nature in the way we select for certain flavors.

26. See Ponte and Gibbon (2005), Diaz-Bone (2013), Beckert, Rössel, and Schenk (2014), Carter (2018).

27. Until 2017 the association was the "SCAA," but "of America" was dropped from the title and the group merged with the Specialty Coffee Association of Europe.

28. Lingle (1984), Lingle and Menon (2017: 184).

29. World Coffee Research (2016).

30. To get a visual sense of the scene, see this *New Yorker* video of a coffee exposition and competition that I attended in Nashville, Tennessee: https://www.newyorker.com/culture/culture-desk/the-rise-of-coffee-connoisseur-culture.

31. Much like the tea tasters described by Sarah Besky (2020).

32. See Sage (2016).

33. See Bradley Wilson et al. (2012). Some think that altitude is fetishized. I have visited enough farms to know that precise altitude distinctions often do not mean much on the ground, filling bags. Nonetheless, the theory is that coffee is stressed more at high altitudes, and this produces more complex sugars and more pronounced spicy or fruity elements.

34. See Wilson (2014), Traore, Wilson, and Fields (2018), Wilson and Wilson (2014).

35. The word cloud comes from the dataset made available by Traore, Wilson, and Fields (2018).

36. Holland, Kjeldsen, and Kerndrup (2016) show determinations of coffee quality to be an ongoing process, negotiated and discussed across actors; they conclude that "doing quality" takes place across the value chain without a fixed object. Beckert, Rössel, and Schenk (2014) show how valuing difference is learned, and often arbitrary, in the wine market. They show that price differences in wines are mostly unrelated to production costs and to blind tasting evaluations. For example, winemakers seek to distance themselves from the industrial realities of production and present an image of artisanal craftsmanship. Both coffee and wine markets have moved toward de-commodification and singularization (Kopytoff [1986], Karpik [2010]), and toward the lucrative long tail of artisanal rarity and away from the cookie-cutter trade in commodities. Croijmans and Majid (2016) show that wine experts are more consistent in their evaluations than coffee experts, and that this is not just a matter of perception training but also linguistic usage.

37. Boaventura et al. (2018), Manzo (2010, 2015).

38. West (2012: 204). Roseberry (1996) observed with respect to Second Wave coffees that the post-Fordist approach to coffee sourcing disadvantages labor in new ways, as styles of coffee can be moved around the world, chasing low prices, just like outsourced manufacturing.

39. Besky (2020: 179).

40. Graeber (2013), Galbraith (1958), Baudrillard (1981); see also Daviron and Ponte (2005) (2011), Beckert (2016), Haskel and Westlake (2017).

NOTES TO CHAPTER 2

1. Michel-Rolph Trouillot writes that "North Atlantic universals" make totalizing claims of neutrality but are, in fact, "loaded with aesthetic and stylistic sensibilities, religious and philosophical persuasions, cultural assumptions ranging from what it means to be a human being to the proper relationship between humans and the natural world, [and] ideological choices ranging from the nature of the political to its possibilities of transformation" (2003: 35).

2. See Deborah Thomas (2019). This decolonizing move in social theory uses different names to describe the ongoing legacies of colonialism. Demetrio Cojtí (1991, 1994) terms it neocolonialism; Achille Mbembe (2001) calls it the postcolony; and Silvia Cusicanqui (2010, 2012) prefers "internal colonialism." Aníbal Quijano (2008) uses the term "coloniality" to denote how race and labor came together in the colonial period to set up a structure that persists to the present. Walter Mignolo (1995, 2011) promotes the convention of "modernity/coloniality" as a shorthand for the power matrix that emerged from Western European starting during the Renaissance, and whose universalizing pretensions have since been widely accepted around the world. In this way, coloniality is seen not as a byproduct of modernity but co-constitutive of it. It is a totalizing epistemological framework and a system of power relations based on racialization, exclusion, and oppression that includes colonization of the mind as well as physical enforcement. See Moraña, Dussel, and Jáuregui (2008) for an excellent survey of coloniality theory.

3. On the complexities and problematics of Linnaean legacies, see Marks (2007) and Moran-Thomas (2019: 192–93). From this perspective, the story of coffee in Guatemala branches off in two directions. One part of the story starts with Linnaean taxonomies and scientific botany, which led to the practice of selective breeding, the discovery of genetics, and the development of engineered cultivars of *C. arabica;* another begins with Linnaeus's racialized categories of human subspecies, giving rise to eugenic theories and policies and ultimately to the sort of pseudoscientific racism common in Guatemala today.

4. See Geoffrey C. Bowker and Susan Leigh Star's (1999) *Sorting Things Out: Classification and Its Consequences* on how classification schemes operate, with a

particular focus on the International Classification of Disease. They begin their book with the following description:

> Our lives are henged round with systems of classification, limned by standard formats, prescriptions, and objects. Enter a modern home and you are surrounded by standards and categories spanning the color of paint on the walls and in the fabric of the furniture, the types of wires strung to appliances, the codes in the building permits allowing the kitchen sink to be properly plumbed and the walls to be adequately fireproofed. Ignore these forms at your peril as a building owner, be sued by irate tenants; as an inspector, risk malpractice suits denying your proper application of the ideal to the case at hand; as a parent, risk toxic paint threatening your children.
>
> To classify is human. Not all classifications take formal shape or are standardized in commercial and bureaucratic products. We all spend large parts of our days doing classification work, often tacitly, and we make up and use a range of ad hoc classifications to do so. We sort dirty dishes from clean, white laundry from colorfast, important email to be answered from junk. We match the size and type of our car tires to the amount of pressure they should accept. Our desktops are a mute testimony to a kind of muddled folk classification: papers that must be read by yesterday, but that have been there since last year; old professional journals that really should be read and even in fact may someday be, but that have been there since last year; assorted grant applications, tax forms, various work-related surveys and forms waiting to be filled out for everything from parking spaces to immunizations.

Emily Yates-Doerr and colleagues provide a compelling analysis of how problems get framed and addressed in nutrition and public health through the use of anthropometrics (Yates-Doerr 2015, Yates-Doerr and García-Meza 2020, García-Meza and Yates-Doerr 2020). On how states developed through and depend on certain sorts of categorizations and metrics, see James Scott's (1998) *Seeing Like a State*. And on how markets are likewise co-constituted through classifications, see the articles in Krenn (2017).

5. See Karpik (2010) on judgment devices; see Callon and Muniesa (2005), Callon, Millo, and Muniesa (2007) on "calculative devices." Use of the term "device" builds on Foucault's concept of *dispositif*, sometimes translated as apparatus. Muniesa, Millo, and Callon (2007) borrow from Deleuze in viewing the dispositif as an entanglement between subject and object.

6. Episode 695 ("Everyone's a Critic") of *This American Life* gives compelling examples of "people squirming in a world where everything is rated and reviewed." https://www.thisamericanlife.org/695/everyones-a-critic.

7. Fourcade (2016) shows how scores and rankings are used to produce nominal classification schemes associated with judgments of worth, and Fourcade and Healy (2017) observe that "contemporary market institutions, in particular, are inveterate classifiers. They count, rank, measure, tag and score on various

metrics of varying degrees of sophistication, automation, and opacity." See also Krüger and Reinhart and the other contributions in the edited collection by Karoline Krenn (2017).

8. Arjun Appadurai (2013). See also Deborah Stone (2020). Reducing lives to numbers also erases the particularities that make a life meaningful, the lived experience enmeshed in webs of social relations. People are more than descriptive categories: patients are more than just patients; victims are more than just victims; the Maya are more than just their ethnicity. I am thinking here also of the work of João Biehl (2013), Paul Farmer (2003), Diane Nelson (2015), Michael Jackson (2011), and others who complicate neat categories of Others by stressing the singularity and nonequivalence of individual experiences, especially suffering.

9. See Mignolo (2011), Quijano (2008) on the "coloniality of power"; see Sabine Parrish (2021) on modernity/coloniality and coffee in Brazil.

10. Such assemblages consist of material and symbolic agents converging into interconnected networks that traverse traditional scales of analysis (the personal, the local, the global) and disciplinary borders. See Monica DeHart's (2021) productive usage of "assemblages" and Collier and Ong's (2005) influential collection (cf. Deleuze and Guattari 1987). Such assemblages may be understood as a sort of "hybrid collectif" (Callon and Law 1995, De León 2015); collectif (Latour 1993, 2005); or "meshwork of lines" (Ingold 2016). The hybrid collective concept embraces the multiple and fluid ways networks and domains become interconnected through practice, and the conjunctures, both intentional and serendipitous, that arise.

11. *C. arabica* actually emerged from a speciation event between Robusta and *Coffea eugenioides* sometime between ten and twenty thousand years ago (Scalabrin et al. 2020).

12. Today, broadly speaking, East Africa and Central and South America grow arabicas and West Africa and Southeast Asia grow Robusta. But there are also many exceptions; Brazil, for example, is the world's second largest producer of Robusta (as well as the world's largest exporter of arabica). The world's largest producers, Brazil, Vietnam, and Indonesia, largely supply a lower-end mass market.

13. See Bunn et al. (2015) for models of how coffee-growing areas are predicted to change in coming decades due to climate change.

14. See Taya Brown's talk at the 2019 Re:co symposium, part of the SCA's Coffee Expo: https://scanews.coffee/video/taya-brown-on-supporting-smallholder-entry-into-the-specialty-coffee-market-reco-symposium-2019/.

15. Koehler (2017).

16. My understanding of coffee history builds on Morris (2019), Topik (2009), Pendergrast (2010), Koehler (2017), Clifford and Wilson (1985), Luttinger and Dicum (2006). Topik argues that it was Middle Eastern, not European, cafés that first created "public space" as such (2009: 91). See also Markman 2011 on the rise of the Arabic coffee house.

17. This history and the following paragraphs call on Markman (2011), Morris (2019), Topik (2003), Pendergrast (2010).

18. Koehler (2017).

19. See Carpenter (2015); for a useful and concise summary of this research, see https://chem.ku.edu/sites/chem.ku.edu/files/docs/CHEM190/caffeine.pdf.

20. The discovery and exploration of the chemistry of caffeine also led to research aimed at reducing its unwanted effects. The first decaffeination process was developed in 1903 by German merchant Ludwig Roselius; he used repeated application of solvents to remove between 80 and 99 percent of coffee's caffeine content. See Fischer et al. (2019), Topik (2009).

21. In fact, coffee is made up of a complex mix of bioactive chemicals and compounds beyond caffeine that have significant impacts on health. Research over the last two decades has shown the importance of chlorogenic and caffeic acids found in coffee in lowering drinkers' risk of liver, breast, lung, and prostate cancers as well as Alzheimer's disease and type 2 diabetes. Based on data from more than 400,000 individuals, a 2012 study in the *New England Journal of Medicine* found that "coffee consumption was inversely associated with total and cause-specific mortality." Based on the preponderance of evidence, in 2015 the U.S. Food and Drug Administration changed its dietary guidelines to recommend up to five cups of coffee per day. See Fischer et al. (2019) for a summary of this research. The meta-analysis of the study is from Freedman et al. (2012). Over the last two decades there has been a growing body of research looking at other components of coffee and their impact on human physiology. Much of this work began at the Vanderbilt Institute of Coffee Studies (ICS) in the late 1990s. Led by psychiatrist and addiction specialist Peter Martin, the ICS seeded initial work that has grown into a large body of empirical studies that have fundamentally changed how we see coffee from a health perspective.

22. See Roland Barthes' version of Michelet's history (Michelet and Barthes 1992).

23. Habermas (1996). My historical overview draws from Pendergrast (2010), Topik (2009), Markman (2011), Lipp (2017).

24. It is easy to overestimate the diversity of these spaces, and in fact participation was limited to those with the financial resources and leisure time to spend in coffeehouses. All the same, the idea of a democratic space, and its imperfect practice, stimulated Enlightenment visions.

25. While many recognized coffee as a positive alternative to alcohol, there were also moral backlashes. In 1674 a group of women in London protested the rise in coffee consumption among men, calling it a "drying and enfeebling liquor" that distracted their men and made them impotent. In Leipzig, as elsewhere, coffeehouses also had a more questionable reputation. They were regarded by opponents as "breeding places for immorality and light-heartedness." Leipzig's efforts to clean up the coffeehouses were successful, and by the time Johann Sebastian Bach wrote his famous "Coffee Cantata" in the early 1730s, there were eight licensed coffeehouses there, "where people of all rank," including women, could enjoy the beverage and partake in conversation and musical entertainment. Indeed, secular music would not have come about without a lively coffeehouse culture. Performing in a coffeehouse allowed musicians and composers of the time to experiment with new musical styles and form. Most musicians had to work within the parameters of Church and Crown: the coffeehouse offered ensembles an opportunity to perform and afforded musicians the opportunity to experiment with more cutting-edge styles.

26. Topik (2003: 28) notes that Bourbon, Java, and Mocha coffees traded in the early days were all "theoretically" related to the original Yemeni varietals (see also Daviron and Ponte 2005: 69). The terminology can be confusing; the Typicas in early world trade would have been classed as "Mocha" because of the port, but there is also an heirloom varietal named "Mocha" much admired by Third Wave aficionados.

27. Koehler (2017) documents that in 1696 a VOC ship first took coffee seeds from India to Java for planting; the harvest from the resulting plants first reached Amsterdam in 1706.

28. The Dutch ran a significant portion of their slave trade through their East Indies colonies, although it seems that only a small percentage of the slaves were sent to work on coffee plantations.

29. See Lipp (2017), Pendergrast (2010). Michiel Baud (1988, 1991) presents a fascinating, and contrasting, case of smallholding peasant production of tobacco in what is today the Dominican Republic.

30. Parrish (2021).

31. See Morris (2019), Pendergrast (2010), Topik (2003), Luttinger and Dicum (2006), Tucker (2010).

32. Alexander von Humboldt became an international star as he sought to measure the earth's highest mountains and longest rivers.

33. An alternative slogan might be "Efficiency, Profitability, and Objectivity," which Bruno Latour (2013) identifies as the "three sisters of modernity." These take on moral valences in economic value worlds that revolve around cost/benefit analyses. As Max Weber (1978) explained, judging economic behavior and public policy from this perspective equates the question of whether something is good or bad with whether it is efficient or inefficient. Efficiency is championed as the ultimate moral practice—producing the most goods for the most people with the least effort. While this can be highly democratizing, it also facilitates the concentration of economic power, which heightens inequalities.

34. See Eakin (1997).

35. Reichman (2018).

36. Even with the growing market, Brazil's efficiency led to a global glut in supply in the 1880s, and then to a cycle of booms and busts throughout the first half of the twentieth century.

37. Jesuits first brought coffee to Guatemala around 1750, but it did not become an important crop until a century later. See Koehler (2017).

38. A number of processing techniques that involve the controlled fermentation of beans are used in the production of Third Wave coffees. "Honey" coffee is partially natural dried and then washed; "black honey" coffee is only infrequently turned as it is drying, allowing it to rot in a particular way. There is also growing experimentation with anaerobic techniques developed for wine.

39. Reichman (2018).

40. On perceptions of rust among Costa Rican farmers and the differences between "looking" and "seeing," see Hugøy and Ødegaard (2021).

41. I recommend Peter Giuliano's video lecture with a brilliant explication of varietals and their links to colonial expansion (https://youtu.be/uRNci2lywmg).

42. Sarah Besky observes that quality then becomes "about how products take on value as commodities and the role of experts in keeping that value consistent, or, put another way, making that value appear consistent and commensurable with that of other things" (2020: 13).

43. Mintz (1985).

44. Gasparin, M. (1850).

45. See Anna Tsing (2004) on the ways frictions are elided and produced in late capitalist formations.

46. Marx (1990 [1867]: 1.4.8). Igor Kopytoff, Arjun Appadurai, and others have shown how goods transition in and out of commodity status, assigned worth through other-than-economic value regimes as they become part of people's lives. See Appadurai (1996), Kopytoff (1986), Miller (1998), Weiss (2003) on how items can move in and out of commodity status.

47. When studies or commercials speak of a cup of coffee, generally they are referring to a standard six-ounce cup. Most coffee makers are marked in six-ounce increments, a holdover from an era when that was considered a generous portion.

48. See https://www.theice.com/products/15/Coffee-C-Futures. ICE contracts stipulate future delivery in March, May, July, September, and December. Note that coffee harvests often span two calendar years so coffee harvests are referred as the 2001/2002 year, the 1916/1917 year, etc.

49. Rosa Luxemburg, Immanuel Wallerstein, André Gunther Frank, Fernando Henrique Cardoso, and others argue that capital-intensive technological innovations and other feedback mechanisms baked into the world system of trade from its early days acted to restrict capital accumulation to core regions of Western Europe and North America while fostering underdevelopment in the periphery to ensure a continued cheap supply of goods and labor. See Luxemburg (1913), Frank (1967), Cardoso and Faletto (1967), Wallerstein (1974, 1979). For an insightful update, see Wallerstein (2004).

50. Critics conclude, as Panhuysen and Pierrot observe, that in the coffee trade, "Coffee profits are made in industrialized countries, at the expense of environmental and social problems in the coffee producing countries" (2018: 3).

51. See Daviron and Ponte (2005).

52. In the 1950s and 1960s the market was dominated by just a few big roasters: General Foods (Maxwell House), Standard Brands, Proctor and Gamble (Folgers), Hills Brothers, and A&P made up 40 percent of the market. And this consolidation increased: by the early 1970s General Mills had 33 percent of the market and Proctor and Gamble had 20 percent. Then, in the early 1990s, after more consolidations, what Robert Rice terms "industrial coffees" were dominated by Philip Morris's Kraft (which owned Maxwell House and Jacobs, among other brands), Proctor and Gamble (led by their Folgers brand), Sara Lee (Douwe Egberts), Nestlé, and Tchibo (from Germany). These buyers held enormous and concentrated power in the market, controlling 60 percent of the world market and 73 percent of the U.S. market. See Rice (2003), Topik (2003), Martinez-Torres (2006: 30), Pendergrast (2010). After another wave of consolidations in the 2000s, ten large roasters now account for 35 percent of the mar-

ket, led by Nestlé and JAB and followed by Lavazza, Smuckers (with their Folgers brand), and Starbucks, in that order. See Panhuysen and Pierrot (2018).

53. In this scheme, defects are visible, such as color, the presence of stones or sticks, parchment remaining on beans, etc. See http://www.coffeeresearch .org/coffee/scaaclass.htm.

54. Peter Roberts and colleagues at the Emory business school have developed a "Specialty Coffee Transaction Guide" (https://www.transactionguide. coffee/en/2020) to increase transparency in specialty coffee pricing. Given the smaller lots and particular selling points, specialty coffee pricing has been largely opaque, with the only common reference being the New York C price, which bears little relation to the specialty market. With data from dozens of buyers and importers, Roberts has been able to track ranges and averages for the specialty market year over year. In the 2019/2020 season, specialty coffee contracts averaged $2.60 a pound, with the seventy-fifth percentile averaging $3.50 a pound. Over the period, the C price average was $1.10 a pound.

55. Jon Shayne (2014) recounts an apocryphal story of an apprentice sardine trader taking a break one day at the exchange. Sitting on the boxes of wares, he decided to open a tin and try the product. He quickly spit the fish out, declaring it to be disgusting. His mentor shook his head and explained, "Those aren't eating sardines, those are trading sardines." Shayne uses this tale to illuminate the gap between the reality the market creates and the reality it represents.

NOTES TO CHAPTER 3

1. See Casaús Arzú (1992), Grandin (2000), Nelson (1999, 2015), Hale (2006). In the social science of Guatemala, the term *ladino* denotes Spanish-speaking, non-Indigenous Guatemalans. The majority of ladinos are, like most Maya, rural agriculturalists of very modest circumstances. Guatemala's urban and rural middle classes are overwhelmingly ladino, as are the institutions of governance and commerce. An easy shorthand is to call the Guatemalan oligarchic elite ladinos, but in fact they themselves are careful to make a distinction between their "more pure" European ancestry—be it Spanish or German or English—and the mestizo mix of ladinos.

2. Cojtí (1991, 1994, 1997). What Cojtí characterizes as a neocolonial state, Shannon Speed (2019) terms a "settler-capitalist state."

3. Walter Mignolo writes that the colonial matrix of power is composed of two sides, "one constantly named and celebrated (progress, development,

growth) and the other silenced or named as problems to be solved by the former (poverty, misery, inequalities, injustices, corruption, commodification, and dispensability of human life)" (2011: xviii).

4. See Achille Mbembe's (2001) *On the Postcolony;* he goes on to show how the postcolony formations replicate the colonial patron-client relationships (through government contracts and phantom jobs, for example) and the transformation of public goods into private gain. His description fits Guatemala equally well.

5. From Julie Gibbings's richly sourced article "Mestizaje in the Age of Fascism: German and Q'eqchi' Maya Interracial Unions in Alta Verapaz, Guatemala" (2016: 223). As I was doing final revisions of this manuscript, I read Gibbings's (2020) *Our Time Is Now: Race and Modernity in Postcolonial Guatemala,* a compelling analysis that brings an ontological approach to history to document the different modes of existence between the German oligarchs and Guatemalan elite and Maya communities.

6. Tzul Tzul (2018).

7. Gibbings (2020: 6).

8. See Hale (2006) on neoliberal multiculturalism. Deborah Thomas (2019: 3) observes that "modern, liberal democratic political arrangements have been designed to hide these ontological processes" that link extractive labor regimes with racialized definitions of humanity and citizenship.

9. This information, and my understanding of Dieseldorff, come from Penny (2017), Wagner (1991), Grandin (2004), Náñez Falcón (1970), and Cambranes (1985).

10. This quote and the description of Krupp come from Fenner (2013: 35).

11. On Brazil's positivistic tradition, see Eakin (1997); on the ways scientific botany was used to promote capitalist coffee production, see Reichman (2018).

12. Latour (2013) notes that in such "modes of existence" there are inevitably contradictions left unresolved as there is still heterogeneity, fluidity, and spaces of conflict and creativity. Historically, we can only know the broad outlines of such modes of existence, and what we can glean from the records left behind often paints a one-dimensional portrait. But, by bringing together various forms of inquiry and critical analysis, a more complex story can emerge.

13. Here I rely on the excellent historical accounts by McCreery (1994) and Woodward (1990).

14. My understanding of the history of coffee in Guatemala starts with foundational works by Regina Wagner (2001, 2003), Lovell (2014), and Cambranes (1985), from which these dates and figures come.

15. Figures cited come from Wagner (2003), Cambranes (1985); other sources for this section include Lovell (1994), Woodward (1990: 50), McCreery (1994, 2003), Gudmundson and Lindo-Fuentes (1995), Hempstead (2006); on the concentration of political power among the Guatemalan coffee oligarchy, see Williams (1994), Paige (1997).

16. See Williams (1994), Paige (1997), Cambranes (1985). Sedgewick (2020) provides a vivid portrait of the situation in El Salvador, focusing on the Hill family.

17. See the detailed historical account behind this assertion in Lutz and Lovell (1990).

18. Regina Wagner describes this in a tone reminiscent of the times: liberal reforms "freed up the acquisition of lands for the establishment of private property, and helped provide a stable and dependable workforce for farming" (2003: 87).

19. See McCreery (2003), Wagner (2003), Berth (2014); on the Alta Verapaz population, see Grandin (2004: 24).

20. McCreery (2003).

21. Cambranes (1985: 245).

22. See Cambranes (1985), McCreery (1994, 2003).

23. See Cambranes (1985), Grandin (2004).

24. Quote from McCreery (2003: 199); the list of uprisings is from Grandin (2004). See also Gibbings (2020).

25. Gibbings (2020: 63–65).

26. Grandin (2004: 26).

27. See H. Glenn Penny's (2017) nuanced portrayal of Dieseldorff and other Germans in Guatemala.

28. Cited in Berth (2014: 133).

29. Penny (2017: 7).

30. See Arden King's (1974) history of Alta Verapaz and the documentary film *Los Civilizadores: Alemanes en Guatemala*.

31. This paragraph and the next are based on Grandin (2004) and Gibbings (2020).

32. Cited in Cambranes (1985: 163).

33. Fenner (2013: 37).

34. The legacy of this early quality turn lives on in the standard blends of Jacobs, Douwe Egberts, and other European First Wave brands, which have a level of conventional quality a notch above the U.S. standard.

35. Cambranes (1985), Wagner (1991, 2003), Berth (2014).

36. Michiel Baud (1988) presents a similar connection to the homeland in a very different context in his study of German merchants trading in Dominican tobacco.

37. Penny (2017), Gibbings (2016).

38. Christiane Berth (2014) illustrates the tension between German perspectives seeing the Guatemalan countryside as, on the one hand, an awe-inspiring "wild tropics" and, on the other hand, a space to be conquered and made economically productive. Julie Gibbings (2016) shows how such views also underwrote German views on taking Q'eqchi' women as consorts and wives (and plantation rape culture). See also the interviews in the documentary film *Los Civilizadores.*

39. Berth (2014), Wagner (1991), Penny (2017); cf. Cambranes (1985), McCreery (1994), Grandin (2004).

40. Wagner (1991), Grandin (2000), Berth (2014).

41. Gibbings (2016).

42. Casaús Arzú (1992).

43. Grandin (2004), Gibbings (2016), Williams (1994). The figure on the 1936 vote comes from the movie *Los Civilizadores*

44. See David Carey's (2001) history of the era based on a remarkable collection of Maya oral histories.

45. Grandin (2004), Wilkinson (2004).

46. McCreery (2003), Wilkinson (2004), Grandin (2004).

47. See Payeras (1983), Lovell (2001), Carmack (1988), Manz (2004).

48. Grandin (2004), Richards (1985), Simon (1988), Smith (1991).

49. Income citation from Programa de las Naciones Unidas para el Desarrollo (2016: 41); on the coffee elite and inequality, see Paige (1997).

50. Kevin Sieff, "The Migration Problem Is a Coffee Problem," *Washington Post,* 11 June 2019; see LAPOP's public opinion data on reasons for considering migration at https://www.vanderbilt.edu/lapop/. Aguilar-Støen (2019) writes that in 2018 remittances from migrants abroad made up 11.3 percent of Guatemala's GDP; 38 percent of the population received an average of $379 per month (more than the agricultural minimum wage). See Patrica Foxen's (2007) account of how remittances bind transnational Maya communities, and David Stoll (2012) on how microcredit has fueled migration.

51. Kedron Thomas, Kevin Lewis O'Neill, and Thomas Offit (2011) detail the link between the rise of neoliberal forms of governance and the postwar violence in Guatemala.

52. Even under democracy, Guatemalan voters are fond of authoritarian figures. Former dictator Efraín Ríos Montt was elected to congress, and Otto Pérez Molina, former military leader during the war, was elected president, as was Alejandro Giammattei, a former director of Guatemala's notorious prison system who was charged and briefly jailed (before being acquitted) for extrajudicial executions.

53. Given the institutional instability in Guatemala after the peace accords, the country did a remarkable thing in 2006: working with the United Nations, the country established the International Commission against Impunity (popularly known by its Spanish acronym, CICIG, the Comisión Internacional contra la Impunidad), an independent investigatory body staffed with international lawyers experienced in organized crime (many from Colombia and Italy), to investigate and help prosecutors assemble cases in instances of drug trafficking or high-level corruption. In an early win, CICIG was able to assemble a case against former president Alfonso Portillo for embezzlement and money laundering; he was convicted and served time in both Guatemala and the United States. The first head of CICIG resigned in frustration with having to work through the Guatemalan attorney general (a man later forced from office over his ties to drug traffickers), leading the United Nations to appoint Colombian jurist Iván Velásquez to the lead role. Velásquez proved to be a savvy and media-friendly leader for CICIG, and his efforts were immeasurably aided by the appointment of Thelma Aldana as attorney general. Aldana embraced the fight against corruption; to call her actions fearless is not hyperbole, for they were the sort of things that often get people killed in Guatemala. The collaboration between Velásquez and Aldana made CICIG one of the country's most trusted institutions, admired for its independence and willingness to go after powerful people who would normally enjoy impunity.

In 2012 Otto Pérez Molina, a retired colonel who had led military operations in Nebaj, one of the hardest-hit zones during the height of the civil war, was elected president, running on a "mano dura" platform for the right-wing populist party. According to Francisco Goldman, Pérez Molina was involved in the murder of Archbishop Juan Gerardi in 1998. In his book *The Art of Political Murder,* Goldman, an astute student of Guatemala and a compelling storyteller, unravels the chain of events that led to Gerardi's death. The archbishop had just released a monumental report on the findings of the Church's Commission for the Recovery of Historical Memory; that report was highly critical of the military and its human rights abuses during the war. Goldman's investigation places Pérez Molina, along with Colonel Byron Lima, at the scene the night of the crime. Lima was later convicted of his role in the murder. Such is the state of Guatemalan justice that he went on to run a successful drug network and clothing venture out of prison. His jailhouse assembly lines made T-shirts for Pérez Molina's Partido Patriota, and he was known to leave prison almost at will, traveling in a caravan of SUVs with tinted windows. Coincidentally—or not, which is the way the intrigue of Guatemalan politics works—soon Pérez Molina was elected president and Lima was assassinated, execution style, in his jail cell by unknown perpetrators. Still, there was some optimism in Guatemala at the time of his election that, although he certainly had blood on his hands, Pérez Molina was an efficient technocrat with few ties to the oligarchy who could bring order to an increasingly chaotic Guatemala.

In 2015 Velásquez and Aldana announced investigations in a corruption scandal that came to be known as La Linea. This was a massive operation that collected payments (as much as one million dollars per week) in return for bypassing customs and tariffs; importers would call a number (*la linea*) to set up the details and arrange payment. It turned out that the investigation had been going on for a year, and there were ample recordings of phone calls (some ninety thousand, plus additional texts and emails). Those recordings implicated Guatemalan vice president Roxana Baldetti (referred to as *la jefa* and *la número dos*) and her private secretary. Baldetti, a former beauty queen and television reporter, was known for an extravagant lifestyle, which including owning helicopters and lavish estates. In May 2015 she resigned in the face of massive street protests and was subsequently arrested. While awaiting trial on the La Linea charges, she was convicted in 2018 for a scheme that paid an Israeli accomplice eighteen million dollars to use a secret formula to clean a highly polluted lake just outside Guatemala City. The "magic water" formula, as it came to be known, was in fact nothing more than a mixture of chlorine and salts.

The street protests against government corruption grew in size over the course of 2015, as people found a public voice to vent their frustration with corruption and system seen as stacked against them. The protests brought together students, the middle class, Maya organizations, and a wide swath of Guatemalan society. Having started with a Facebook post, the protests grew to more than 100,000 people by August, when crowds gathered in Guatemala's central plaza on the weekends. As more and more evidence emerged, it became clear that Pérez Molina himself (*el número uno* and *el mero mero* on the tapes) was directly involved. He resigned in September 2015, was arrested, and currently awaits trial in a Guatemalan prison. It is estimated that Pérez Molina and Baldetti reaped close to forty million dollars in illicit gains.

In 2019, the Guatemalan government de-authorized CICIG and barred its head, Iván Velásquz, from the country.

54. LAPOP, https://www.vanderbilt.edu/lapop/guatemala.php.

55. See the agenda laid out in Raxche' (1992) and the overview by Montejo (2005). I have written on the pan-Maya movement elsewhere (Fischer and Brown 1996, Fischer 2001) as has Kay Warren (2002); see also DeHart (2010) on ethnic entrepreneurship.

56. See Warren (2002), Smith (2009).

57. See the report by Verité (2012); figures are from the 2010/11 harvest year.

58. Verité (2012); see also Ruiz (2011).

59. Like a Badiouian "event" (Badiou 2013).

60. Penny (2017: 11).

61. Scott (1985).

NOTES TO CHAPTER 4

1. See Hempstead and Chajon (2016).

2. The information here on CACIF, and below on Manuel Ayau, comes from an excellent unpublished manuscript by Tatiana Paz Lemus (n.d.), "Neoliberalism in Guatemala."

3. Quoted in Harvey (2005: 20).

4. Carl Menger (1950 [1871]) defined utility in terms of the subjective evaluations and preferences of consumers, a very anthropological approach. In economics, great emphasis has been placed on revealed preferences, that is, what people actually choose in their market decisions. This glosses over the fact that the *revealed preferences* of what people "really" want are framed in particular ways by the market; *stated preferences*—what people say they desire, including unrealistic aspirations—also reflect what people really want. See Fischer (2014a).

5. Here I draw on Tatiana Paz Lemus's unpublished manuscript cited above.

6. Dickins de Girón (2011).

7. Following a devastating 1899 market bust, Brazil led efforts to keep coffee prices stable. In the early 1900s they introduced a "valorization" scheme, with the government buying surplus production; see Pendergrast (2010). Eventually, Brazil had so much coffee on its hands that they began burning it: by 1942 a total of seventy-eight million bags had been destroyed; see Luttinger

and Dicum (2006). Colombia's Federación Nacional de Cafeteros (FNC), established in the 1920s, took a different approach, working to brand Colombian coffee to command a quality premium. In 1960 the FNC began their Juan Valdez campaign, and over the coming decades "Café de Colombia" came to be associated with quality.

8. A version of the ICA was resurrected, but it does not seek to enforce quotas.

9. Martinez-Torres (2006) observes that after the breakup of the ICA, a quality-based pricing system emerged that recognized "Colombian milds," "other milds," "non-washed arabicas," and "Robustas" as standard categories. See Johnson (2010) on the ICA and Guatemala.

10. This was the corruption scandal uncovered by CICIG that brought down President Otto Pérez Molina, Vice-President Roxana Baldetti, and a host of other officials.

11. See Glacia (2018) in *Nomada* and O'Grady (2018) in the *Wall Street Journal*.

12. See Rice (2003), Martinez-Torres (2006), Renard (1999).

13. Lyon (2011), ITC (2002).

14. Full disclosure: López's son is currently a graduate student of mine.

NOTES TO CHAPTER 5

1. The *cuerda* is a regionally variable unit of land measurement ranging from 50 × 50 *varas* to 20 × 20 varas, with a vara commonly measured as 0.84 meters. In this instance the cuerda is 40 × 40 varas, or a little more than 1000 square meters.

2. See Sarah Grant (2021) on how risks get shifted to smallholders in Vietnam, and how that risk is actually experienced and acted upon.

3. See Sen (1999), Nussbaum (2011), Alkire (2002), Alkire and Foster (2011), Foster (2011). A capabilities approach emphasizes the importance of individual freedom and agency, upending traditional top-down perspectives on international development. Human development, it is argued, should seek to build capabilities as well as provide opportunities and resources so that individuals have the freedom to build the sort of life that they want.

4. See Li's (2007) analysis of such choice in the context of neoliberal self-cultivation; and Laidlaw (2014) on the limits of freedom in terms of economic and moral choices.

5. For a discussion of desires and neoliberal economic structures, see Fischer and Benson (2006). Looking at Indonesian cacao farmers, Tania Li (2007) shows

how the neoliberal aspirations of "a will to improve" get channeled in particular directions, making smallholders into agents of their own marginalization.

6. In 2011 we conducted eighty-two in-depth interviews, including life histories, with smallholding coffee farmers to help understand their perspective on the changing market and to inform our own research questions. The interviewees were selected from panels of new entrant (within the last twenty years) smallholders (farming fewer than five hectares of coffee). In 2014 we conducted a survey of 315 smallholder households in ten communities. The preliminary sample started with the selection of nine coffee-producing departments; within these, we selected ten municipalities based on their production of SHB coffees. To reach a sample size {{gt}}300 we randomly selected forty producer households in each community, and after accounting for those who opted not to participate, we ended up with a final sample size of 315 households. The survey included 111 questions and took an average of 2.5 hours to complete. Interviews were conducted by five teams of two interviewers each; interviewers were all either native Spanish or Mayan language speakers.

7. We classify smallholders as those farmers with fewer than 2.2 hectares of coffee; in our sample the average landholding in coffee production was one *manzana,* a regionally variable measure roughly equivalent to 0.7 hectares.

8. There is a fundamental paradox of fair trade, which is that it seeks to reform markets toward social justice ends but it also depends on those same markets; see Jaffee (2007), Bacon (2010), Bacon et al. (2014), Sick (2008), Moberg and Lyon (2010), Smith (2010), Raynolds and Bennett (2015). On the complicated effects of the price crisis on small producers, see Murray, Raynolds, and Taylor (2006), Gliessman (2008), Sick (1999), Smith (2009).

9. See Mariel Aguilar-Støen's (2019) study of the link between remittances and coffee cooperative development.

10. See Edelman (1999), Kearney (1996), Netting (1993).

11. Fischer (2001).

12. Following are descriptive statistics of our 2014 survey of 315 Guatemalan smallholder farmers.

Respondent gender	75% male	25% female
Ethnicity	82% Maya	18% ladino
Language	64% bilingual	36% Spanish only
Religion	59% Catholic	31% Protestant
Average household size	5.8 members	
Mean years of education	females: 4.8	males: 2.9
Average age	females: 48	males: 42

13. See Stoll (1982), Garrard-Burnett (1998).

14. Hendrickson (1995).

15. Thomas (2016).

16. J. T. Way (2021) shows how the tradition rural/urban divide between Guatemala City and the rest of the country has broken down as small cities and large towns in the western highlands participate in global flows of ideas and goods.

17. Milpa agriculture and nutrition is remarkable. Maize is a very nitrogen-hungry plant, and beans planted at their base naturally release nitrogen into the soil. Dried maize kernels have to undergo nixtamalization, which involves soaking the maize with the highly alkaloid lime to break down the hulls. Maize processed this way, combined with black beans, can provide all the amino acids essential to one's diet.

18. Montejo (2021); see also Fischer (2001), Woodfill (2019), Stanzione (2003).

19. Many rural Maya communities have parallel structures of government and Indigenous authorities; Indigenous mayors (*alcaldes indígenas*) and officials can organize group labor, allocate communal lands, and order traditional punishments.

20. Montejo (2021); see also Raxche' (1992) and Tzul Tzul (2018).

21. See Callon and Law (1995), who build on Latour to describe the hybrid collectif as "Relations. Links. Interpenetrations. Processes. Of any kind" (Callon and Law 1995: 486); see also De León (2015). In the context of Maya health and wellness, T. S. Harvey (2013) shows how Indigenous "patients" often refuse the categories to which the biomedical system assigns them (including that of "patient") while constructing an epistemological stance at the confluence of different systems of knowledge.

22. See J. T. Way (2021) on the cosmopolitanization of areas of Guatemala long considered the hinterlands.

23. As told by Manuel Tahay, and documented in an unpublished manuscript by Mareike Sattler, Jim Mondloch, and Manuel Tahay (story 77).

24. Bogin et al. (2002).

25. Holmes (2013).

26. But see Ernst Bloch's (1995) *The Principle of Hope*, Henrietta Moore's (2011) view of the role of hope in her theory of "ethical imagination" (cf. Appadurai's [2013] "ethics of possibility"), and Miyazaki's (2004, 2006) analysis of hope as it informs knowledge creation.

27. Robbins (2013: 457). A concern with the good, and the hope it implies, could be a starting point for Mark Goodale's vision of "a radically reconfigured

approach to knowledge, one in a conceptual space that draws from aspects of both poles of the classic fact-value spectrum without positioning itself anywhere between them" (2009: 187). See also Sherry Ortner (2016), who points out anthropology's abiding focus (over the last three decades or so) on suffering and the dark side of life at the margins of the neoliberal global economy. This has been important work, but at its best, ethnography presents lived experience in its full complexity, the good, the bad, and especially the many shades of gray.

28. See Fischer and Benson (2006).

29. Goldín (2009); see also Little (2004) on varied strategies; on limit points, see Fischer and Benson (2006).

30. Based on her fieldwork in Indonesia, Tania Li (2014) observes that for many smallholding farmers the attraction of a "fair market," one where rewards are based on hard work, is compelling.

31. Lyon (2011: 6). Hernández Castillo and Nigh (1998) and Martinez-Torres (2006) have shown how, in certain circumstances, small farmers can effectively mobilize social and cultural capital to competitive advantage in the specialty organic coffee market. Daniel Reichman (2008: 3) similarly reports that "Honduran farmers do not see the coffee trade as fundamentally unjust or exploitative."

32. On Fair Trade see Raynolds and Bennett (2015), Lyon (2007), and Jaffee (2007), and the discussion in chapter 6.

NOTES TO CHAPTER 6

1. Third Wave beans make up the fastest-growing segment of the coffee market today, although they are still just a small fraction of the overall supply (probably less than 3 percent).

2. See Sarah Lyon's (2011) rich ethnographic account of a Guatemalan coffee cooperative as embedded in the local politics of a Maya community.

3. On bare existence, see Agamben (1998), Taussig (1986); on the power of singularity, see Nelson (2015).

4. Nicholas Copeland (2011) shows how neoliberal approaches to development can result in pessimism, a weakened sense of community, and political disengagement. See also Copeland (2019), Granovskey-Larsen (2013), DeHart (2010), Fischer and Benson (2006).

5. I am using "objective" here as it is commonly used in the trade. Of course, even the most seemingly objective metrics are based on social conventions (do you use imperial or metric?).

6. Wilson et al. (2012).

7. See Wilson (2014), Traore, Wilson, and Fields (2018), Wilson and Wilson (2014).

8. The Japanese, South Korean, and Chinese markets are rapidly growing, but producer orientations and imaginations are still primarily oriented toward the United States, and to a lesser extent Germany and the rest of Europe.

9. See Reichman 2011 on social capital and cultural capital in the context of coffee production and marketing.

10. Boltanski and Esquerre (2016); see also Callon, Méadel, and Rabeharisoa (2002) and Beckert (2016).

11. Carrier (2008), Carrier and Luetchford (2012); see also Moberg (2014), Wilson (2013).

12. Peter Roberts at Emory University has developed an innovative curriculum to help smallholders craft a narrative for the specialty market. The SCA has also instituted a Coffee Corps to help train smallholders and transfer knowledge, and Sweet Maria's, Cooperative Coffees, and others have made efforts to address this gap.

13. See Besky (2014), Carter (2018), Meneley (2018).

14. Aguilar-Støen (2019).

15. Bacon (2010); see also Moberg and Lyon (2010), Bacon (2005), Bacon et al. (2014), Jaffee (2007), Méndez et al. (2010), Smith (2010, 2018), Raynolds and Bennett (2015).

16. Lyon and Moberg (2010), Wilson (2013: 177).

17. See Lyon, Ailshire, and Sehon (2014).

18. Elizabeth Bennett and Janina Grabs (2021) show the power of profit-sharing arrangements in promoting equitable distribution along the supply chain.

19. Lyon (2007), Moberg and Lyon (2010), Fridell (2007), Wilson (2010), Jaffee (2007), Doane (2010).

20. West (2012); see also Doane (2010) on relationship coffees and their complexities, and Smith (2010) on the tension between "elite" coffee and the cooperative model in Costa Rica.

21. See Copeland (2011), Li (2014).

22. Mariel Aguilar-Støen (2019) presents a compelling study of how conjunctures of forces come together to form and shape a Guatemalan coffee cooperative; these forces include changes in the global market (liberalization, price drops, the rise of specialty coffee); the drug trade that flows through the area; and the role of migration and remittances. She also observes that coop-

erative members struggle morally and emotionally with selling to the narco-coyote rather than the cooperative.

23. Roseberry (1996); see Daviron and Ponte (2005) on the distribution of profits along the coffee value chain; and see West (2012: 204) on the ways importers create equivalences between different coffees.

24. De Janvry (1981).

25. This is similar to the globalized artisan markets that Jason Antrosio and Rudi Colloredo-Mansfeld (2015) study; they show that the structure of these markets moves them toward winner-take-all situations, with a few artisans who have the skill and the social capital doing spectacularly well and the vast majority losing out in the competition for the best. Bradley Wilson (2010, 2013) finds a similar situation with high-end coffee production in Nicaragua.

26. Harvey (2005), Beck (1992). Alberto Alonso-Fradejas (2015) shows how flex crops replacing coffee on large fincas, such as oil palm, increase the agility of capital to chase profits while leaving workers to assume most of the risk.

NOTES TO CHAPTER 7

1. This is to say that quality conventions do not arise de novo within symbolic value worlds; they emerge from ongoing practices that intertwine the material and the social. This is a process, a coming together of different value worlds that involves material properties, social conventions, and symbolic traits.

2. It may be helpful to distinguish different sorts of values, from the semantic and semiotic to the cultural and symbolic to the moral and imaginative. Graeber (2001) reminds us of the important linguistic sense of values. Semantics, as the study of meaningful difference, offers a useful model for understanding how meaning is produced through relative and positional values in a purely symbolic system; see Baudrillard (1998). Kockelman productively combines the semiotic with the political-economic in his study of ontological differences in value systems around an ecotourism project in a Q'eqchi' Maya community in Guatemala. He portrays a dynamic system of moral worlds in constant interaction, a mutually constitutive dialectic "in which processes that create, interpret, and reveal values are concomitant with processes that capture, carry, and reify them" (2016: 3). On moral values, see also Sayer (2000, 2011), Zigon (2008, 2009).

3. Didier Fassin (2008) writes of "moral discourse communities." I see value worlds as "discourse communities" in which there is a common conversation although no singular agreement, dynamic and yet with a narrative continuity.

Here I am also thinking of the literature in convention theory, e.g., Boltanski and Thévenot (2006), Stark (2009), Diaz-Bone (2015).

4. Graeber (2013: 226); see also Graeber (2001). Similar to the concept of cultural logics (Fischer 2001), Graeber (2013: 233) writes of "tacit interior values" or "infravalues," underlying general values and relational templates that get socially realized in specific arenas. These shared evaluative stances mediate but do not determine one's particular application of values to a given context; and therein lies one's range of freedom, autonomy, and agency; cf. Laidlaw (2014). Shared cultural logics allow actors to react to novel situations and consciously and unconsciously deploy their value systems in a manner that makes cultural sense to others in their discourse community. The idea of value worlds allows for the creative improvisation of individuals and recognizes the tradeoffs they often have to make between different arenas of value.

5. Capitalism can extract value from producers' varied notions of what they desire, the differences between value worlds. If, following Deleuze and Guattari (1987), we understand humans as desiring machines that are mutually and continually constituted through interaction with larger-scale social machines, then promulgating certain values (through means of symbolic production) can orient desires in ways that feed into political-economic assemblages and power structures; see also Fischer and Benson (2006). From this perspective there is no single logic running throughout the global system of values; rather there are varied logics and lived realities that shape each other, and economic value is extracted by arbitraging these logics across value worlds.

If we think about the ways desires are constituted as future-oriented projections and projects, there is often hope intertwined in the moral framing. Hirokazu Miyazaki (2006) calls our attention to the constitutive role of hope in global capitalism, and Arjun Appadurai (2013) shows that the role of imagination and aspiration are crucial to understanding different regimes of value. See also Fischer (2014), Beckert (2016).

6. Lammer and Theimann (n.d.) in a special issue of *Ethnos;* cf. what Latour (2013) calls "modes of existence"

7. While value orientations are internalized in individual and idiosyncratic ways, they also exist outside one's head, importantly (if imperfectly) shared by others and reinforced by social norms. Not "just" of the realm of emotion and social construction, value worlds, like Durkheimian social facts, become reality.

8. Rudi Colloredo-Mansfeld (1999: 218) observes that by looking at values we are able to "draw attention to the moral nature of the principles structur-

ing economic activity. As matters of morality, they go to the very core of the self and constitution of society."

9. Value worlds have the power to create their own reality and their own "social facts," to use Emile Durkheim's phrase, yet they hold that power only insofar as people believe in them. Constructions that survive only as long as they are not recognized as such, value worlds cloak themselves in a matter-of-fact sense that their presuppositions are just the way things are.

10. Barry Schwartz and Kenneth Sharpe (2006) make a strong case for revaluing the role of phronesis, the Aristotelian virtue of practical wisdom. Practical wisdom, they argue, is not a list of rules but a state of mind, a capacity for discernment and judgment built up through social interaction and personal experience. They write, "It is distressing that modern social trends are conspiring to make wisdom ever more difficult to cultivate" by "substituting financial incentives for motivation to do the right thing" (2006: 390). They conclude that "market incentives and bureaucratic rules may be an appropriate short-term response to greedy doctors or unimaginative teachers, but in the long term, they only make doctors greedier and teachers less imaginative" (ibid).

11. Karpik (2010) writes that judgment devices are 1) representations of the world, particular framings that we delegate judgment to; 2) cognitive supports that orient knowledge and inform implicit and explicit evaluations; and 3) actors in their own right, producing certain outcomes.

12. Foucault (2010), from his 1978–79 lectures on biopolitics; his description of neoliberalism here turned out to be prescient. See also Gudeman (2008) on the allure of "calculative reason" and how it is cultivated in market relations. Algorithms enact certain types of value judgments, but they are limited by the simplicity and numerical basis of their language—those ones and zeros follow a particularly rigid logic. Algorithms have insinuated themselves into our lives, and they give us a lot, making our lives easier with suggestions and shortcuts that guide choices. They work exceedingly well in some contexts, but trying to fit the full complexity of the world into strings of code is futile ∂ and can lead to counterproductive outcomes.

13. Marx (1963 [1852]), Appadurai (2013).

14. See Richard Sennett (2008) on craftsmanship as tacit and explicit skills developed over time as part of a community of those devoted to the same task, simultaneously social and individual and encompassing bodily practices and powers of the imagination. Sennett focuses on how skilled work that requires years of training and practice provides its own intrinsic rewards as well as

instrumental ones. See also Dorinne Kondo's (1990) look at the construction of identity and craft in a Japanese chocolate factory.

15. Antrosio and Colloredo-Mansfeld (2015).

16. Marx (1990 [1867]), McCloskey (2016). And Marx might well have agreed, to an extent; recall that the second paragraph of *Capital* defines a commodity as "a thing which through its qualities satisfies human needs of whatever kind. The nature of these needs, whether they arise, for example, from the stomach, or the imagination, makes no difference" (from Ben Fowkes's masterful translation).

17. See Harvey (1989): "Given the ability to produce images as commodities more or less at will, it becomes feasible for accumulation to proceed at least in part on the basis of pure image production and marketing." See also Lash and Urry (1987), Friedman (1994), Collier and Ong (2005), Storper (2001). Contracting foreign production allows transnational corporations access to cheap labor while hedging the risk of direct capital investment in the areas of the world where wages are lowest. One example among many: in the 1960s about 95 percent of clothes sold in the United States were domestically produced, and today 98 percent of clothing is imported.

18. Samper, Giovannucci, and Vieira (2017).

19. Boltanski and Esquerre (2016).

20. Studying markets ranging from art to finance, Jens Beckert (2019) finds that rather than actors giving meaning to markets, these are "markets from meaning." Beckert looks at the role of "valuation collectives" in art and financial markets, observing that "prices emerge in such markets from a combination of intersubjectively established quality assessments, institutions and existing structural characteristics of the market" (285). See also the prescient work of Galbraith (1958), Baudrillard (1998 [1970]), and Harvey (1989).

21. Haigney (2021).

22. Jonathan Haskel and Stian Westlake (2017) argue that this is a new era of what they term "capitalism without capital"—that is, at least without capital in the traditional sense of tangible and productive assets. Now more than ever, value is created through means of symbolic production rather than from means of material production.

23. The Economist (2020).

24. See Friedman (1994) for a productive analysis of the relation of fictitious and real capital.

25. Corrado et al. (2013), Corrado, Haltiwanger, and Sichel (2005). See also Carrier and Miller (1998) on what they term "virtualism" in this sector of the

economy, as well as Harvey (1989). With use values having become intertwined with, and increasingly eclipsed by, symbolic values in determining exchange value in a wide swath of turn-of-the-millennium capitalism, it is useful to recall Pierre Bourdieu's (1977, 1984) expansive notion of the different sorts of capital, recognizing not just traditional economic and financial capital but also social, cultural, and other forms of symbolic capital. Looking at French class structure, Bourdieu shows that accumulation happens not just with money but also with forms of symbolic capital. He describes the structure of symbolic and social distinctions in terms of overlapping fields. These fields are organized in ways that differently distribute capital (in its many forms: symbolic, social, cultural, financial) and that structure the "space of possibles" open to a given individual. It matters where one went to school, how one deals with the more obscure utensils of a place setting, and if one can discuss the literary contributions of Proust. Bourdieu shows how such cultural capital and social capital in the form of networks of friends and classmates, kith and kin, get translated into economic opportunities and material gain. Thus Bourdieu's model consists of fields (of positional interaction and competition), habitus (internal structuring structures that condition practice), and capital (of various sorts, including economic and material as well as symbolic and cultural). Value worlds overlap these categories and can help illuminate the mutual constitution of these domains.

26. Caitlin Zaloom (2006) shows how the commodity traders she writes about view the market as an ethical arbiter, punishing and disciplining those who transgress.

27. Igor Kopytoff (1986) suggests that it is useful to think about the "cultural biographies of things."

28. Tsing (2015).

29. On the connections between humans and nonhumans, see Galvin (2018), García (2019), Paxson (2013), Descola (2013), Kohn (2013). In the realm of organizations and policy, see Gillian Tett's (2015) *The Silo Effect*.

30. Thanks to David Napier and Jonathan Metzl for this insight.

31. See Wolfgang Streeck (2009). The deeper problem, argues Streeck (2016), is a looming crisis of capitalism (foretold by neofeudal patterns of distribution) and a prolonged interregnum of social and political disorder.

32. Such apparatuses are usually designed to remove biases—at least individual biases—and they do that, often successfully. All the same they give a false sense of objectivity because numerical formulations often hide the larger value judgments behind them. As Appadurai and Kift (2020) argue, numbers

are empirical, but metrics give them normative meaning. They also give a
false sense of precision, not only because the numbers may be made up, as
with business plans or projects that convert uncertainty into probabilities (see
Knight [1921], Beckert [2016]), but also because of the nonquantifiable nature of
many domains of value.

33. See the book *Value(s)* by Mark Carney (2021), former governor of the
Bank of England.

34. The economic values implied in cost/benefit analyses are instrumental—
means to other ends—while other sorts of values tend to be intrinsic, worthy in
and of themselves. In her book *Value in Ethics and Economics,* philosopher Elizabeth
Anderson writes of value not as an abstract idea shared across societies, but rather
as something produced through social practice. She shows how individuals refuse
significant monetary gains to pursue values that provide the "narrative unity" of
their lives. Such narrative unity provides a larger purpose to human existence
beyond immediate self-interest, which I have elsewhere (2014a) argued is crucial
to pursuits of the good life. Deirdre McCloskey points to the importance of devotion to something (anything) with a transcendent quality. And John Ruskin, the
nineteenth-century English art critic and social theorist, himself a frequenter of
coffeehouses, wrote that what is worth working for is worth dying for, as with the
soldier, pastor, physician, lawyer: "And the duty of all of these men is, on due
occasion, to die for [their calling]. The Soldier, rather than leave his post in battle.
The Physician, rather than leave his post in plague. The Pastor, rather than teach
Falsehood. The lawyer, rather than countenance Injustice." While that may be
more dramatic than roaster Nick Scott's declaration of his commitment to coffee
in chapter 1, or the pride of Maya farmers in their crop from chapter 5, the sentiment is the same.

35. John Kay and Mervyn King (2020) make this case.

BIBLIOGRAPHY

Agamben, Giorgio. 1998. *Homo Sacer: Sovereign Power and Bare Life.* Stanford, CA: Stanford University Press.

Aguilar-Støen, Mariel. 2019. "Between a Rock and a Hard Place: Rural Transformations and Migrant Communities in Guatemala." *Canadian Journal of Development Studies / Revue canadienne d'études du développement* 1–17.

Alkire, Sabina. 2002. *Valuing Freedoms: Sen's Capability Approach and Poverty Reduction.* New York: Oxford University Press.

Alkire, Sabina, and James E. Foster. 2011. "Counting and Multidimensional Poverty Measurement." *Journal of Public Economics* 95 (7): 476–87.

Alonso-Fradejas, A. 2015. "Anything But a Story Foretold: Multiple Politics of Resistance to the Agrarian Extractivist Project in Guatemala." *Journal of Peasant Studies* 42 (3–4): 489–515.

Andersen, Anne Holst. 2011. "Organic Food and the Plural Moralities of Food Provisioning." *Journal of Rural Studies* 27 (4): 440–50.

Anderson, Elizabeth. 1993. *Value in Ethics and Economics.* Cambridge, MA: Harvard University Press.

Antrosio, Jason, and Rudi Colloredo-Mansfeld. 2015. *Fast, Easy, and in Cash: Artisan Hardship and Hope in the Global Economy.* Chicago: University of Chicago Press.

Appadurai, Arjun. 1986. "Introduction: Commodities and the Politics of Value." In *The Social Life of Things: Commodities in Cultural Perspective,* 3–63. Cambridge: Cambridge University Press.

———. 1996. *Modernity at Large: Cultural Dimensions of Globalization.* Vol. 1. Minneapolis: University of Minnesota Press.

————. 2013. *The Future as Cultural Fact: Essays on the Global Condition*. London: Verso.

Appadurai, Arjun, and Paula Kift. 2020. "Beware the Magic of Metrics." *Eurozine,* 27 June. https://www.eurozine.com/beware-the-magic-of-metrics/.

Bacon, Christopher M. 2005. "Confronting the Coffee Crisis: Can Fair Trade, Organic, and Specialty Coffees Reduce Small-Scale Farmer Vulnerability in Northern Nicaragua?" *World Development* 33 (3): 497–511.

————. 2010. "Who Decides What Is Fair in Fair Trade? The Agri-environmental Governance of Standards, Access, and Price." *Journal of Peasant Studies* 37 (1): 111–47.

Bacon, Christopher M., Ernesto Méndez, Stephen R. Gliessman, and D. Goodman. 2008. *Confronting the Coffee Crisis: Fair Trade, Sustainable Livelihoods and Ecosystems in Mexico and Central America*. Food, Energy and Environment Series. Boston, MA: MIT Press.

Bacon, Christopher M., William A. Sundstrom, María Eugenia Flores Gómez, V. Ernesto Méndez, Rica Santos, Barbara Goldoftas, and Ian Dougherty. 2014. "Explaining the 'Hungry Farmer Paradox': Smallholders and Fair Trade Cooperatives Navigate Seasonality and Change in Nicaragua's Corn and Coffee Markets." *Global Environmental Change* 25: 133–49.

Badiou, Alain. 2005. *Being and Event*. London: Continuum.

————. 2013. *Ethics: An Essay on the Understanding of Evil*. London: Verso.

Balsiger, Philip. 2019. "The Dynamics of 'Moralized Markets': A Field Perspective." *Socio-Economic Review*. doi: 10.1093/ser/mwz051.

Baud, Michiel. 1988. "German Trade in the Caribbean: The Case of Dominican Tobacco, 1844–1940." *Jahrbuch für Geschichte Lateinamerikas* 25 (1): 83–115.

————. 1991. "A Colonial Counter Economy: Tobacco Production on Espanola, 1500–1870." *Nieuwe West-Indische Gids / New West Indian Guide* 65 (1/2): 27–49.

————. 2020. *Confianza: Governance and Trust in Latin America and the Netherlands*. Amsterdam: CEDLA.

Baudrillard, Jean. 1981. *For a Critique of the Political Economy of the Sign*. St. Louis, MO: Telos Press.

————. 1998. *The Consumer Society: Myths and Structures*. London: Sage Publications.

Beck, Ulrich. 1992. *Risk Society: Towards a New Modernity*. Newbury Park, CA.: Sage Publications.

Beckert, Jens. 2016. *Imagined Futures: Fictional Expectations and Capitalist Dynamics*. Cambridge, MA: Harvard University Press.

———. 2019. "Markets from Meaning: Quality Uncertainty and the Intersubjective Construction of Value." *Cambridge Journal of Economics* 44 (2): 285–301.

Beckert, Jens, and Patrik Aspers. 2011. "Value in Markets." In *The Worth of Goods: Valuation and Pricing in the Economy,* ed. Jens Beckert and Patrik Aspers, 3–40. Oxford: Oxford University Press.

Beckert, Jens, Jörg Rössel, and Patrick Schenk. 2014. "Wine as a Cultural Product: Symbolic Capital and Price Formation in the Wine Field. In *MPIfG Discussion Paper.* Köln: Max Planck Institute for the Study of Societies 14/2.

Bennett, Elizabeth A. 2018. "Extending Ethical Consumerism Theory to Semi-Legal Sectors: Insights from Recreational Cannabis." *Agriculture and Human Values* 35 (2): 295–317.

Bennett, Elizabeth A., and Janina Grabs. 2021. "Rethinking the 'Necessary' Trade-offs of Distributing Value to Suppliers: An Analysis of the Profit-sharing Model." In *Carr Center Discussion Paper Series.* Cambridge, MA: Harvard Kennedy School Carr Center for Human Rights Policy.

Berger, Noa. n.d. "'Qualitising' Coffee: Infrastructures for 'Specialty' Production in Brazil." Unpublished manuscript.

Berlant, Lauren. 2011. *Cruel Optimism.* Durham, NC: Duke University Press.

Berth, Christiane. 2014. "Between 'Wild Tropics' and 'Civilization': Guatemalan Coffee Plantations as Seen by German Immigrants." In *Comparing Apples, Oranges, and Cotton: Environmental Histories of the Global Plantation,* ed. Frank Uekötter, 113–38. Frankfurt: Campus Verlag.

Besky, Sarah. 2014. *The Darjeeling Distinction: Labor and Justice on Fair-Trade Tea Plantations in India.* Berkeley: University of California Press.

———. 2020. *Tasting Qualities: The Past and Future of Tea.* Berkeley: University of California Press.

Bestor, Theodore C. 2001. "Supply-Side Sushi: Commodity, Market, and the Global City." *American Anthropologist* 103 (1): 76–95.

———. 2004. *Tsukiji: The Fish Market at the Center of the World.* Berkeley: University of California Press.

Biehl, João. 2013. "Patient Value." In *Cash on the Table: Markets, Values, and Moral Economies,* ed. Edward F. Fischer, 67–90. Santa Fe, NM: SAR Press.

Bloch, Ernst. 1995. *The Principle of Hope, Volume 3.* Cambridge, MA: MIT Press.

Boaventura, Patricia Silva Monteiro, Carla Caires Abdalla, Cecilia Lobo Araújo, and José Sarkis Arakelian. 2018. "Value Co-creation in the Specialty Coffee Value Chain: The Third-Wave Coffee Movement." *Revista de Administração de Empresas* 58: 254–66.

Bogin, B., P. Smith, A.{this}B. Orden, M.I. Varela Silva, and J. Loucky. 2002. "Rapid Change in Height and Body Proportions of Maya American Children." *American Journal of Human Biology* 14 (6): 753–61.

Boltanski, Luc, and Arnaud Esquerre. 2016. "The Economic Life of Things: Commodities, Collectibles, Assets." *New Left Review* 98 (March–April): 31–54.

Boltanski, Luc, and Laurent Thévenot. 2006. *On Justification: Economies of Worth.* Princeton Studies in Cultural Sociology. Princeton, NJ: Princeton University Press.

Bookman, Sonia. 2013. "Branded Cosmopolitanisms: 'Global' Coffee Brands and the Co-creation of 'Cosmopolitan Cool.'" *Cultural Sociology* 7 (1): 56–72.

Bourdieu, Pierre. 1977. *Outline of a Theory of Practice.* Cambridge, MA: Harvard University Press.

———. 1984. *Distinction: A Social Critique of the Judgment of Taste.* New York: Routledge.

———. 1998. *Acts of Resistance: Against the Tyranny of the Market.* New York: New Press.

Bowker, Geoffrey C., and Susan Leigh Star. 1999. *Sorting Things Out: Classification and Its Consequences.* Cambridge, MA: MIT Press.

Brulotte, Ronda. 2019. "A Taste for Agave: The Emerging Practice and Politics of Mezcal Connoisseurship." In *Taste, Politics, and Identity in Mexican Food,* ed. Steffan Igor Ayora-Diaz, 83–98. New York: Bloomsbury.

Brumann, Christoph. 1999. "Writing for Culture: Why a Successful Concept Should Not Be Discarded." *Current Anthropology* 40 (S1): 1–27.

Bunn, Christian, Peter Läderach, Oriana Ovalle Rivera, and Dieter Kirschke. 2015. "A Bitter Cup: Climate Change Profile of Global Production of Arabica and Robusta Coffee." *Climatic Change* 129 (1): 89–101.

Bunn, Christian, Mark Lundy, Peter Läderach, Pablo Fernández Kolb, Fabio Castro-Llanos, and Dylan Rigsby. 2019. *Climate-Smart Coffee in Guatemala.* Cali, Colombia: International Center for Tropical Agriculture.

Burrell, Jennifer L. 2013. *Maya After War: Conflict, Power, and Politics in Guatemala.* Austin: University of Texas Press.

Callon, Michel, and John Law. 1995. "Agency and the Hybrid Collectif." *South Atlantic Quarterly* 94 (2): 481–507.

Callon, Michel, Cécile Méadel, and Vololona Rabeharisoa. 2002. "The Economy of Qualities." *Economy and Society* 31 (2): 194–217.

Callon, Michel, Yuval Millo, and Fabian Muniesa, eds. 2007. *Market Devices.* Oxford: Blackwell.

Callon, Michel, and Fabian Muniesa. 2005. "Peripheral Vision: Economic Markets as Calculative Collective Devices." *Organization Studies* 26 (8): 1229–50.

Cambranes, J. C. 1985. *Coffee and Peasants in Guatemala: The Origins of the Modern Plantation Economy in Guatemala, 1853–1897.* Stockholm: Institute of Latin American Studies.

Cardoso, Fernando Henrique, and Enzo Faletto. 1967. *Dependencia y desarrollo en América Latina.* Lima: Instituto de Estudios Peruanos.

Carey, David. 2001. *Our Elders Teach Us: Maya-Kaqchikel Historical Perspectives.* Tuscaloosa: University of Alabama Press.

Carmack, Robert M., ed. 1988. *Harvest of Violence: The Maya Indians and the Guatemalan Crisis.* Norman: University of Oklahoma Press.

Carney, Mark. 2021. *Value(s): Building a Better World for All.* New York: PublicAffairs.

Carpenter, Murray. 2015. *Caffeinated: How Our Daily Habit Helps, Hurts, and Hooks Us.* New York: Penguin.

Carrier, James G. 1997. *The Meanings of the Market: The Free Market in Western Culture.* Oxford: Berghahn Books.

———. 2008. "Think Locally, Act Globally: The Political Economy of Ethical Consumption." *Research in Economic Anthropology* 28: 31–51.

Carrier, James G., and Peter Luetchford. 2012. *Ethical Consumption: Social Value and Economic Practice.* New York: Berghahn Books.

Carrier, James G., and Daniel Miller, eds. 1998. *Virtualism: A New Political Economy.* Oxford: Berghahn Books.

Carse, Ashley. 2014. "The Year 2013 in Sociocultural Anthropology: Cultures of Circulation and Anthropological Facts." *American Anthropologist* 116 (2): 390–403.

Carter, Elizabeth. 2018. "For What It's Worth: The Political Construction of Quality in French and Italian Wine Markets." *Socio-Economic Review* 16 (3): 479–98.

Casaús Arzú, Marta. 1992. *Guatemala: linaje y racismo.* San José, Costa Rica: FLACSO.

Chibnik, Michael. 2011. *Anthropology, Economics, and Choice.* Austin: University of Texas Press.

Clarence-Smith, W. G., and Steven Topik. 2003. *The Global Coffee Economy in Africa, Asia and Latin America, 1500–1989.* Cambridge: Cambridge University Press.

Clifford, Michael N., and K. C. Wilson. 1985. *Coffee: Botany, Biochemistry and Production of Beans and Beverage.* Westport, CT: AVI Publishing.

Cojtí Cuxil, Demetrio. 1991. *Configuración del pensamiento político del pueblo maya.* Quetzaltenango, Guatemala: Asociación de Escritores Mayances de Guatemala.

———. 1994. *Políticas para la reivindicación de los mayas de hoy (fundamento de los derechos específicos del pueblo maya).* Guatemala: Cholsamaj.

———. 1997. *Ri maya' moloj pa Iximulew; El movimiento maya (en guatemala).* Guatemala: Cholsamaj.

Collier, Stephen J., and Aihwa Ong. 2005. "Global Assemblages, Anthropological Problems." In *Global Assemblages: Technology, Politics, and Ethics as Anthropological Problems,* ed. Aihwa Ong and Stephen J Collier, 3–21. Malden, MA: Blackwell.

Colloredo-Mansfeld, Rudi. 1999. *The Native Leisure Class: Consumption and Cultural Creativity in the Andes.* Chicago: University of Chicago Press.

Cook, Ian. 2004. "Follow the Thing: Papaya." *Antipode* 36 (4): 642–64.

Cook, Ian, and Philip Crang. 1996. "World on a Plate: Culinary Culture, Displacement and Geographical Knowledges." *Journal of Material Culture* 1: 131–53.

Copeland, Nicholas. 2011. "'Guatemala Will Never Change': Radical Pessimism and the Politics of Personal Interest in the Western Highlands." *Journal of Latin American Studies* 43 (3): 485–515.

———. 2019. "Meeting Peasants Where They Are: Cultivating Agroecological Alternatives in Neoliberal Guatemala." *Journal of Peasant Studies* 1–22.

Corrado, Carol, John C. Haltiwanger, and Daniel E. Sichel. 2005. *Measuring Capital in the New Economy,* Studies in Income and Wealth. Chicago: University of Chicago Press.

Corrado, Carol, Jonathan Haskel, Cecilia Jona-Lasinio, and Massimiliano Iommi. 2013. "Innovation and Intangible Investment in Europe, Japan, and the United States." *Oxford Review of Economic Policy* 29 (2): 261–86.

Croijmans, Ilja, and Asifa Majid. 2016. "Not All Flavor Expertise Is Equal: The Language of Wine and Coffee Experts." *PLoS ONE* 11 (6): e0155845.

Cusicanqui, Silvia Rivera. 2010. *Ch'ixinakax utxiwa: una reflexión sobre prácticas y discursos descolonizadores.* Buenos Aires: Tinta Limón Ediciones.

———. 2012. "Ch'ixinakax utxiwa: A Reflection on the Practices and Discourses of Decolonization." *South Atlantic Quarterly* 111 (1): 95–109.

Daviron, Benoît, and Stefano Ponte. 2005. *The Coffee Paradox: Global Markets, Commodity Trade, and the Elusive Promise of Development.* London: Zed Books.

Dean, Mitchell. 2019. "What is Economic Theology? A New Governmental-Political Paradigm?" *Theory, Culture & Society* 36 (3): 3–26.

DeHart, Monica. 2010. *Ethnic Entrepreneurs: Identity and Development Politics in Latin America.* Stanford, CA: Stanford University Press.

———. 2021. *Transpacific Developments: The Politics of Multiple Chinas in Central America.* Ithaca, NY: Cornell University Press.

De Janvry, Alain. 1981. *The Agrarian Question and Reformism in Latin America.* Baltimore, MD: Johns Hopkins University Press.

De León, Jason. 2015. *The Land of Open Graves: Living and Dying on the Migrant Trail.* Berkeley: University of California Press.

Deleuze, Gilles, and Félix Guattari. 1987. *A Thousand Plateaus: Capitalism and Schizophrenia.* Minneapolis: University of Minnesota Press.

Descola, Philippe. 2013. *Beyond Nature and Culture.* Chicago: University of Chicago Press.

Dewey, John. 1939. "Theory of Valuation." In *International Encyclopedia of Unified Science.* Chicago: University of Chicago Press.

Diaz-Bone, Rainer. 2013. "Discourse Conventions in the Construction of Wine Qualities in the Wine Market." *Economic Sociology: The European Electronic Newsletter* 14 (2): 46–53.

———. 2015. *Die "Economie des conventions": Grundlagen und Entwicklungen der neuen französischen Wirtschaftssoziologie.* Wiesbaden: Springer.

———. 2016. "Convention Theory and Neoliberalism." *Journal of Cultural Economy* 9 (2): 214–20.

Dickins de Girón, Avery. 2011. "The Security Guard Industry in Guatemala: Rural Communities and Urban Violence." In *Securing the City: Neoliberalism, Space, and Insecurity in Postwar Guatemala,* ed. Kevin Lewis O'Neill and Kedron Thomas, 103–25. Durham, NC: Duke University Press.

Doane, Molly. 2010. "Relationship Coffees: Structure and Agency in the Marketplace." In *Fair Trade and Social Justice: Global Ethnographies,* ed. Sarah Lyon and Mark Moberg, 229–57. New York: New York University Press.

Dubuisson-Quellier, Sophie. 2013. *Ethical Consumption.* Halifax, Nova Scotia: Fernwood.

Dumont, Louis. 1994. *German Ideology: From France to Germany and Back.* Chicago: University of Chicago Press.

Eakin, Marshall C. 1997. *Brazil: The Once and Future Country.* New York: St. Martin's Press.

The Economist. 2020. "Diminished Value." *The Economist,* 14 November, 62–64.

Edelman, Marc. 1999. *Peasants Against Globalization: Rural Social Movements in Costa Rica.* Stanford, CA: Stanford University Press.

Espantzay Serech, Ixchel Carmelina. 2018. "Etnicidad, subalternidad, género y participación política: aspiraciones y estrategias de las mujeres Mayas del altiplano de Guatemala para acceder a espacios de poder." PhD diss., Vanderbilt University.

Evans, Joshua, and Jamie Lorimer. 2021. "Taste-Shaping-Natures." *Current Anthropology* 62 (S24): S361–S375.

Farmer, Paul. 2003. *Pathologies of Power Health, Human Rights, and the New War on the Poor.* Berkeley: University of California Press.

———. 2009. "On Suffering and Structural Violence: A View from Below." *Race/Ethnicity: Multidisciplinary Global Contexts* 3 (1): 11–28.

Fassin, Didier. 2008. "Beyond Good and Evil? Questioning the Anthropological Discomfort with Morals." *Anthropological Theory* 8 (4): 333–44.

Fenner, Justus. 2013. "Shaping the Coffee Commodity Chain: Hamburg Merchants and Consumption of Guatemalan Coffee in Germany, 1889–1929." *América Latina en la Historia Económica* 20 (3): 28–55.

Fischer, Edward F. 2001. *Cultural Logics and Global Economies: Maya Identity in Thought and Practice.* Austin: University of Texas Press.

———. 2014a. *The Good Life: Aspiration, Dignity, and the Anthropology of Wellbeing.* Stanford, CA: Stanford University Press.

———. 2014b. "Introduction: Markets and Moralities." In *Cash on the Table: Markets, Values, and Moral Economies,* ed. Edward F. Fischer, 3–18. Santa Fe, NM: School for Advanced Research Press.

———. 2021. "Quality and Inequality: Creating Value Worlds with Third Wave Coffee." *Socio-Economic Review* 19 (1): 111–31.

Fischer, Edward F., and Peter Benson. 2006. *Broccoli and Desire: Global Connections and Maya Struggles in Postwar Guatemala.* Stanford, CA: Stanford University Press.

Fischer, Edward F., and R. McKenna Brown, eds. 1996. *Maya Cultural Activism in Guatemala.* Austin: University of Texas Press.

Fischer, Edward F., and Bart Victor. 2014. "High-End Coffee and Smallholding Growers in Guatemala." *Latin American Research Review* 49 (1): 155–77.

Fischer, Edward F., Bart Victor, and Linda Asturias de Barrios. 2020. "Quality Versus Solidarity in Third Wave Coffee: Consumer Values and Producer Aspirations Among Smallholding Maya Farmers in Guatemala." *Journal of Peasant Studies* 48 (3): 640–57.

Fischer, Edward F., Bart Victor, Daniel Robinson, Adriana Farah, and Peter R. Martin. 2019. "Coffee Consumption and Health Impacts: A Brief History of

Changing Conceptions." In *Coffee: Consumption and Health Implications,* ed. Adriana Farah, 1–19. London: The Royal Society of Chemistry.

Fisher, Josh. 2013. "Fair or Balanced? The Other Side of Fair Trade in a Nicaraguan Sewing Cooperative." *Anthropological Quarterly* 86 (2): 527–57.

Forster, Hanna, Xiomara Fernanda Quiñones-Ruiz, and Marianne Penker. 2019. "Analytic Framework to Determine Proximity in Relationship Coffee Models." *Sociologia Ruralis* 60 (2): 458–81.

Foster, James E. 2011. "Freedom, Opportunity, and Well-Being." *Handbook of Social Choice and Welfare* 2: 687–728.

Foucault, Michel. 2010. *The Birth of Biopolitics, Lectures at College de France, 1978–1979.* New York: Picador.

Fourcade, Marion. 2016. "Ordinalization." *Sociological Theory* 34 (3): 175–95.

Fourcade, Marion, and Kieran Healy. 2007. "Moral Views of Market Society." *Sociology* 33 (1): 285.

———. 2017. "Categories All the Way Down." *Historical Social Research / Historische Sozialforschung* 42 (1 [159]): 286–96.

Foxen, Patricia. 2007. *In Search of Providence: Transnational Mayan Identities.* Nashville, TN: Vanderbilt University Press.

Frank, Andre Gunder. 1967. *Capitalism and Underdevelopment in Latin America: Historical Studies of Chile and Brazil.* New York: Monthly Review Press.

Frank, Robert H., Thomas D. Gilovich, and Dennis T. Regan. 1996. "Do Economists Make Bad Citizens?" *Journal of Economic Perspectives* 10 (1): 187–92.

Freedman, Neal D., Yikyung Park, Christian C. Abnet, Albert R. Hollenbeck, and Rashmi Sinha. 2012. "Association of Coffee Drinking with Total and Cause-Specific Mortality." *New England Journal of Medicine* 366 (20): 1891–1904.

Fridell, Gavin. 2007. *Fair Trade Coffee: The Prospects and Pitfalls of Market-Driven Social Justice:* University of Toronto Press.

Friedman, Jonathan. 1994. *Cultural Identity and Global Process.* Thousand Oaks, CA: Sage Publications.

Galbraith, John Kenneth. 1958. *The Affluent Society.* New York: Houghton Mifflin.

Galemba, Rebecca Berke. 2017. *Contraband Corridor: Making a Living at the Mexico—Guatemala Border.* Stanford, CA: Stanford University Press.

Galvin, Shaila Seshia. 2018. "Interspecies Relations and Agrarian Worlds." *Annual Review of Anthropology* 47 (1): 233–49.

García, María Elena. 2019. "How Guinea Pigs Work: Figurations and Gastro-Politics in Peru." In *How Nature Works,* ed. Sarah Besky and Alexander Blanchette, 131–48. Albuquerque: University of New Mexico Press.

————. 2021. *Gastropolitics and the Specter of Race: Stories of Capital, Culture, and Coloniality in Peru.* Oakland: University of California Press.

García-Meza, Rosario, and Emily Yates-Doerr. 2020. "The Social Life of Metrics." *Somatosphere.*

Garrard-Burnett, Virginia. 1998. *Protestantism in Guatemala: Living in the New Jerusalem.* Austin: University of Texas Press.

Gasparin, M. 1850. "Sur le regime alimentaire des mineurs belges; influence remarquable du café." *Bulletin Général Thérapeutique* XXXVIII, 380–83.

Geertz, Clifford. 1973. *The Interpretation of Cultures: Selected Essays.* New York: Basic Books.

Gibbings, Julie. 2016. "Mestizaje in the Age of Fascism: German and Q'eqchi' Maya Interracial Unions in Alta Verapaz, Guatemala." *German History* 34 (2): 214–36.

————. 2020. *Our Time Is Now: Race and Modernity in Postcolonial Guatemala.* Cambridge: Cambridge University Press.

Glacia, Jody. 2018. "La sentencia del caso de corrupción que mató a 51 pacientes deja tranquilos a acusados y acusadores." *Nomada.*

Gliessman, Stephen R. 2008. "Agroecological Foundations for Designing Sustainable Coffee Agroecosystems." In *Confronting the Coffee Crisis: Fair Trade, Sustainable Livelihoods and Ecosystems in Mexico and Central America,* ed. Christopher M. Bacon, V. Ernesto Méndez, Stephen R. Gliessman, David Goodman, and Jonathan A. Fox, 27–42. Cambridge, MA: MIT Press.

Goldín, Liliana R. 2009. *Global Maya: Work and Ideology in Rural Guatemala.* Tucson: University of Arizona Press.

Goldman, Francisco. 2007. *The Art of Political Murder: Who Killed the Bishop?* New York: Grove Press.

Goodale, Mark. 2009. "Between Facts and Norms: Towards an Anthropology of Ethical Practice." In *Anthropology of Moralities,* ed. Monica Heintz, 182–200. Oxford: Berghahn.

Graeber, David. 2001. *Toward an Anthropological Theory of Value: The False Coin of Our Own Dreams.* New York: Palgrave Macmillan.

————. 2013. "It Is Value That Brings Universes into Being." *HAU: Journal of Ethnographic Theory* 3 (2): 219–43.

Grandin, Greg. 2000. *The Blood of Guatemala: A History of Race and Nation.* Durham, NC: Duke University Press.

————. 2004. *The Last Colonial Massacre: Latin America in the Cold War.* Chicago: University of Chicago Press.

Granovsky-Larsen, Simon. 2013. "Between the Bullet and the Bank: Agrarian Conflict and Access to Land in Neoliberal Guatemala." *Journal of Peasant Studies* 40 (2): 325–50.

Grant, Sarah G. 2021. "Complicated Webs: Experiential Risk in the Vietnamese Coffee Industry." *PoLAR: Political and Legal Anthropology Review* n/a (n/a). doi: https://doi.org/10.1111/plar.12416.

Gudeman, Stephen. 2008. *Economy's Tension: The Dialectics of Community and Market.* Oxford: Berghahn Books.

Gudeman, Stephen, and Alberto Rivera. 1990. *Conversations in Colombia: The Domestic Economy in Life and Text.* Cambridge: Cambridge University Press.

Gudmundson, Lowell, and Héctor Lindo-Fuentes. 1995. *Central America, 1821–1871: Liberalism Before Liberal Reform.* Tuscaloosa: University of Alabama Press.

Habermas, Jürgen. 1996. *Between Facts and Norms: Contributions to a Discourse Theory of Law and Democracy.* Cambridge, MA: MIT Press.

Habersaat, Katrine Bach, Cornelia Betsch, Margie Danchin, Cass R. Sunstein, Robert Böhm, Armin Falk, Noel T. Brewer, Saad B. Omer, Martha Scherzer, Sunita Sah, Edward F. Fischer, Andrea E. Scheel, Daisy Fancourt, Shinobu Kitayama, Eve Dubé, Julie Leask, Mohan Dutta, Noni E. MacDonald, Anna Temkina, Andreas Lieberoth, Mark Jackson, Stephan Lewandowsky, Holly Seale, Nils Fietje, Philipp Schmid, Michele Gelfand, Lars Korn, Sarah Eitze, Lisa Felgendreff, Philipp Sprengholz, Cristiana Salvi, and Robb Butler. 2020. "Ten Considerations for Effectively Managing the COVID-19 Transition." *Nature Human Behaviour* 4 (7): 677–87.

Haidt, Jonathan. 2007. "The New Synthesis in Moral Psychology." *Science* 316 (5827): 998–1002.

Haigney, Sophie. 2021. "What's New About the NFT Fad." *New York Times,* 3 May, A23.

Hale, Charles R. 2006. *Más que un Indio—More Than an Indian: Racial Ambivalence and Neoliberal Multiculturalism in Guatemala.* Santa Fe, NM: School of American Research Press.

Harvey, David. 1989. *The Condition of Postmodernity: An Enquiry into the Origins of Cultural Change.* Oxford: Blackwell.

———. 2005. *A Brief History of Neoliberalism.* New York: Oxford University Press.

Harvey, T. S. 2013. *Wellness Beyond Words: Maya Compositions of Speech and Silence in Medical Care.* Albuquerque: University of New Mexico Press.

Haskel, Jonathan, and Stian Westlake. 2017. *Capitalism without Capital: The Rise of the Intangible Economy*. Princeton, NJ: Princeton University Press.

Hayek, Friedrich. 1944. *The Road to Serfdom*. London: Routledge.

Hempstead, William H. 2006. "Mapping Hallmarks of Recognition, Guatemalan Coffees: Coffee Atlas 2006/2007." Guatemala City: Anacafé.

Hempstead, William H., and Anibal Chajon. 2016. *Anacafé: Impulsando el Desarrollo de Guatemala*. Guatemala City: Anacafé.

Hendrickson, Carol. 1995. *Weaving Identities: Construction of Dress and Self in a Highland Guatemala Town*. Austin: University of Texas Press.

Hernández Castillo, Rosalva Aída, and Ronald Nigh. 1998. "Global Processes and Local Identity among Mayan Coffee Growers in Chiapas, Mexico." *American Anthropologist* 100 (1): 136–47.

Holbraad, Martin, and Morten Axel Pedersen. 2017. *The Ontological Turn: An Anthropological Exposition*. Cambridge: Cambridge University Press.

Holland, Emil, Chris Kjeldsen, and Søren Kerndrup. 2016. "Coordinating Quality Practices in Direct Trade Coffee." *Journal of Cultural Economy* 9 (2): 186–96.

Holmes, Seth. 2013. *Fresh Fruit, Broken Bodies: Migrant Farmworkers in the United States*. Berkeley: University of California Press.

Hugøy, Isabelle, and Cecilie Vindal Ødegaard. 2021. "Becoming 'Wild' at the Intersection of Knowledges: Coffee Rust Crisis in Costa Rica." *Ethnos* 86 (2): 349–69.

Ingold, Tim. 2016. *Lines: A Brief History*. London: Routledge.

Jackson, Michael. 2011. *Life within Limits: Well-being in a World of Want*. Durham, NC: Duke University Press.

Jaffee, Daniel. 2007. *Brewing Justice: Fair Trade Coffee, Sustainability, and Survival*. Berkeley: University of California Press.

Jameson, Fredric. 1991. *Postmodernism, or the Cultural Logic of Late Capitalism*. Durham, NC: Duke University Press.

Johnson, David Conrad. 2010. "The International Coffee Agreement and the Production of Coffee in Guatemala, 1962–1989." *Latin American Perspectives* 37 (2): 34–49.

Kallio, Galina. 2020. "A Carrot Isn't a Carrot Isn't a Carrot: Tracing Value in Alternative Practices of Food Exchange." *Agriculture and Human Values*. doi: 10.1007/s10460-020-10113-w.

Karpik, Lucien. 2010. *Valuing the Unique: The Economics of Singularities*. Princeton, NJ: Princeton University Press.

Kay, John, and Mervyn King. 2020. *Radical Uncertainty: Decision-making beyond the Numbers*. New York: W. W. Norton & Company.

Keane, Webb. 2016. *Ethical Life: Its Natural and Social Histories.* Princeton, NY: Princeton University Press.

Kearney, Michael. 1996. *Reconceptualizing the Peasantry: Anthropology in Global Perspective.* Boulder, CO: Westview Press.

King, Arden. 1974. *Coban and the Verapaz: History and Cultural Process in Northern Guatemala.* New Orleans, LA: Middle American Research Institute, Tulane University.

Klitgaard, Robert E. 1991. *Adjusting to Reality: Beyond "State vs. Market" in Economic Development.* San Francisco: ICS Press.

———. 2021. *The Culture and Development Manifesto.* Oxford: Oxford University Press.

Knight, Frank H. 1921. *Risk, Uncertainty, and Profit.* New York: Houghton Mifflin.

Kockelman, Paul. 2016. *The Chicken and the Quetzal: Incommensurate Ontologies and Portable Values in Guatemala's Cloud Forest.* Durham, NC: Duke University Press.

Koehler, Jeff. 2017. *Where the Wild Coffee Grows: The Untold Story of Coffee from the Cloud Forests of Ethiopia to Your Cup.* New York: Bloomsbury.

Kohn, Eduardo. 2013. *How Forests Think: Toward an Anthropology Beyond the Human.* Berkeley: University of California Press.

Kondo, Dorinne K. 1990. *Crafting Selves: Power, Gender, and Discourses of Identity in a Japanese Workplace.* Chicago: University of Chicago Press.

Kopytoff, Igor. 1986. "Cultural Biography of Things: Commoditization as a Process." In *The Social Life of Things,* ed. Arjun Appadurai, 6–91. Cambridge: Cambridge University Press.

Krenn, Karoline, ed. 2017. *Markets and Classifications: Categorizations and Valuations as Social Processes Structuring Markets.* Vol. 42, Historische Sozialforschung.

Laidlaw, James. 2014. *The Subject of Virtue: An Anthropology of Ethics and Freedom.* New Departures in Anthropology. Cambridge: Cambridge University Press.

Lammer, Christof, and André Thiemann. n.d. "Infrastructuring Value." Unpublished manuscript.

Lamont, Michèle. 2012. "Toward a Comparative Sociology of Valuation and Evaluation." *Annual Review of Sociology* 38 (21): 201–21.

Lash, Scott, and John Urry. 1987. *The End of Organized Capitalism.* Cambridge: Polity Press.

Latour, Bruno. 1993. *We Have Never Been Modern.* Cambridge, MA: Harvard University Press.

———. 2005. *Reassembling the Social: An Introduction to Actor-Network-Theory.* Oxford: Oxford University Press.

———. 2013. *An Inquiry into Modes of Existence: An Anthropology of the Moderns.* Cambridge, MA: Harvard University Press.

Li, Tania Murray. 2007. *The Will to Improve: Governmentality, Development, and the Practice of Politics.* Durham, NC: Duke University Press.

———. 2014. *Land's End: Capitalist Relations on an Indigenous Frontier.* Durham, NC: Duke University Press.

Lingle, Ted R. 1984. *The Coffee Cupper's Handbook.* SCAA.

Lingle, Ted R., and Sunalini N. Menon. 2017. "Cupping and Grading— Discovering Character and Quality." In *The Craft and Science of Coffee,* ed. Britta Folmer, 181–203. Amsterdam: Academic Press.

Lipp, Charles. 2017. "Coffee." In *Encyclopedia of the Atlantic World, 1400–1900: Europe, Africa, and the Americas in an Age of Exploration, Trade, and Empires,* ed. David Head. Santa Barbara, CA: ABC-CLIO.

Lipstein, Ray. 2019. "The Rise of Coffee-Connoisseur Culture." *The New Yorker,* 14 March. https://www.newyorker.com/culture/culture-desk/ the-rise-of-coffee-connoisseur-culture.

Little, Walter E. 2004. *Mayas in the Marketplace: Tourism, Globalization, and Cultural Identity.* Austin: University of Texas Press.

Little, Walter E., and Timothy J. Smith, eds. 2009. *Maya in Postwar Guatemala: Harvest of Violence Revisited.* Tuscaloosa: University of Alabama Press.

Lovell, W. George. 1994. "The Century After Independence: Land and Life in Guatemala, 1821–1920." *Canadian Journal of Latin American and Caribbean Studies* 19 (37/38): 243–60.

———. 2001. *A Beauty That Hurts: Life and Death in Guatemala.* 2nd ed. Austin: University of Texas Press.

———. 2005. *Conquest and Survival in Colonial Guatemala: A Historical Geography of the Cuchumatán Highlands, 1500–1821.* Montreal: McGill Queens Press.

Lowrey, Annie. 2017. "Why the Phrase 'Late Capitalism' Is Suddenly Everywhere." *The Atlantic,* May.

Luttinger, Nina, and Gregory Dicum. 2006. *The Coffee Book: Anatomy of an Industry from Crop to the Last Drop.* New York: Bazaar Books.

Lutz, Christopher H., and W. George Lovell. 1990. "Core and Periphery in Colonial Guatemala." In *Guatemalan Indians and the State, 1542–1988,* ed. Carol A. Smith, 35–51. Austin: University of Texas Press.

Luxemburg, Rosa. 1913. *Die Akkumulation des Kapitals.* Berlin: Jugendinternationale.

Lyon, Sarah. 2007. "Fair Trade Coffee and Human Rights in Guatemala." *Journal of Consumer Policy* 30 (3): 241–61.

———. 2011. *Coffee and Community: Maya Farmers and Fair-Trade Markets*. Boulder: University Press of Colorado.

Lyon, Sarah, Sara Ailshire, and Alexandra Sehon. 2014. "Fair Trade Consumption and the Limits to Solidarity." *Human Organization* 73 (2): 141–52.

Lyon, Sarah, and Mark Moberg, eds. 2010. *Fair Trade and Social Justice: Global Ethnographies*. New York: New York University Press.

MacIntyre, Alasdair. 1984. *After Virtue: A Study in Moral Theory*. South Bend: University of Notre Dame Press.

Manz, Beatriz. 2004. *Paradise in Ashes: A Guatemalan Journey of Courage, Terror, and Hope*. Berkeley: University of California Press.

Manzo, John. 2010. "Coffee, Connoisseurship, and an Ethnomethodologically-Informed Sociology of Taste." *Human Studies* 33 (2–3): 141–55.

———. 2015 "'Third-Wave' Coffeehouses as Venues for Sociality: On Encounters between Employees and Customers." *Qualitative Report* 20 (6): 746–61.

Markman, Ellis. 2011. *The Coffeehouse: A Cultural History*. London: Weidenfeld & Nicolson.

Marks, Jonathan. 2007. "Long Shadow of Linnaeus's Human Taxonomy." *Nature* 447 (7140): 28.

Martin, Carla D., and Kathryn E. Sampeck. 2015. "The Bitter and Sweet of Chocolate in Europe." *Socio.hu* 3: 37–60.

Martinez-Torres, Maria Elena. 2006. *Organic Coffee: Sustainable Development by Mayan Farmers*. Athens: Ohio University Press.

Marx, Karl. 1963 [1852]. *The Eighteenth Brumaire of Louis Bonaparte*. New York: International Publishers.

———. 1990 [1867]. *Capital, Volume 1*. New York: Penguin.

Mauss, Marcel. 1984 [1924]. "A Sociological Assessment of Bolshevism (1924–5)." *Economy and Society* 13 (3): 331–74.

Mbembe, Achille. 2001. *On the Postcolony*. Berkeley: University of California Press.

McCloskey, Deirdre N. 2006. *Bourgeois Virtue: Ethics for an Age of Commerce*. Chicago: University of Chicago Press.

———. 2016. *Bourgeois Equality: How Ideas, Not Capital or Institutions, Enriched the World*. Chicago: University of Chicago Press.

McCreery, David. 1994. *Rural Guatemala, 1760–1940*. Stanford, CA: Stanford University Press.

———. 2003. "Coffee and Indigenous Labor in Guatemala, 1871–1980." In *The Global Coffee Economy in Africa, Asia, and Latin America, 1500–1989*, ed. Steven Topik and William Gervase Clarence-Smith, 191–208. Cambridge: Cambridge University Press.

McGee, Harold. 2020. *Nose Dive: A Field Guide to the World's Smells*. New York: Penguin.

Méndez, V. Ernesto, Christopher M. Bacon, Meryl Olson, Seth Petchers, Doribel Herrador, Cecilia Carranza, Laura Trujillo, Carlos Guadarrama-Zugasti, Antonio Cordón, and Angel Mendoza. 2010. "Effects of Fair Trade and Organic Certifications on Small-Scale Coffee Farmer Households in Central America and Mexico." *Renewable Agriculture and Food Systems* 25 (3): 236–51.

Meneley, Anne. 2014. "Discourses of Distinction in Contemporary Palestinian Extra-Virgin Olive Oil Production." *Food and Foodways* 22 (1–2): 48–64.

———. 2018. "Consumerism." *Annual Review of Anthropology* 47 (1): 117–32.

Menger, Carl. 1950 [1871]. *Principles of Economics:* Glencoe, IL: Free Press.

Mezzadra, Sandro, and Brett Neilson. 2019. *The Politics of Operations: Excavating Contemporary Capitalism*. Durham, NC: Duke University Press.

Michelet, Jules, and Roland Barthes. 1992. *Michelet*. Berkeley: University of California Press.

Mignolo, Walter. 1995. *The Darker Side of the Renaissance: Literacy, Territoriality, and Colonization*. Ann Arbor: University of Michigan Press.

———. 2011. *The Darker Side of Western Modernity: Global Futures, Decolonial Options*. Durham, NC: Duke University Press.

Miller, Daniel. 1995. "Consumption and Commodities." *Annual Review of Anthropology* 24: 141–61.

———. 1998. *A Theory of Shopping*. Cambridge: Polity Press.

———. 2008. "The Uses of Value." *Geoforum* 39 (3): 1122–32.

Mintz, Sidney Wilfred. 1985. *Sweetness and Power*. New York: Viking New York.

Mitchell, Timothy. 2005. "The Work of Economics: How a Discipline Makes Its World." *European Journal of Sociology* 46 (2): 297–320.

Miyazaki, Hirokazu. 2004. *The Method of Hope: Anthropology, Philosophy, and Fijian Knowledge*. Stanford, CA: Stanford University Press.

———. 2006. "Economy of Dreams: Hope in Global Capitalism and Its Critiques." *Cultural Anthropology* 21 (2): 147–72.

Moberg, Mark. 2014. "Certification and Neoliberal Governance: Moral Economies of Fair Trade in the Eastern Caribbean." *American Anthropologist* 116 (1): 8–22.

Moberg, Mark, and Sarah Lyon. 2010. "What's Fair? The Paradox of Seeking Justice through Markets." In *Fair Trade and Social Justice: Global Ethnographies,* ed. Sarah Lyon and Mark Moberg, 1–24. New York: New York University Press.

Montejo, Victor. 2005. *Maya Intellectual Renaissance: Identity, Representation, and Leadership.* Austin: University of Texas Press.

———. 2021. *Mayalogue: An Interactionist Theory of Indigenous Cultures.* Albany: SUNY Press.

Moore, Henrietta L. 2011. *Still Life: Hopes, Desires and Satisfactions.* Hoboken: John Wiley & Sons.

Moran-Thomas, Amy. 2019. *Traveling with Sugar: Chronicles of a Global Epidemic.* Oakland: University of California Press.

Moraña, Mabel, Enrique D. Dussel, and Carlos A. Jáuregui, eds. 2008. *Coloniality at Large: Latin America and the Postcolonial Debate.* Durham, NC: Duke University Press.

Morris, Jonathan. 2017. "We Consumers—Tastes, Rituals, and Waves." In *The Craft and Science of Coffee,* ed. Britta Folmer, 457–91. London: Academic Press.

———. 2019. *Coffee: A Global History.* London: Reaktion Books.

Motsinger, Jane H. 2018. "Virtuous Discourse in the Specialty Coffee Sector: How Social Responsibility Practices Fragment Pursuits for a Supply Chain." Master's thesis, University of New Mexico, Department of Geography & Environmental Studies.

Mouritsen, Ole G., and Klavs Styrbæk. 2017. *Mouthfeel: How Texture Makes Taste.* New York: Columbia University Press.

Muniesa, Fabian, Yuval Millo, and Michel Callon. 2007. "An Introduction to Market Devices." *Sociological Review* 55 (2): 1–12.

Murray, Douglas L., Laura T. Raynolds, and Peter L. Taylor. 2006. "The Future of Fair Trade Coffee: Dilemmas Facing Latin America's Small-Scale Producers." *Development in Practice* 16 (2): 179–92.

Náñez Falcón, Guillermo. 1970. "Erwin Paul Dieseldorff: German Entrepreneur in the Alta Verapaz of Guatemala, 1889–1937." PhD diss., Tulane University.

Nelson, Diane M. 1999. *A Finger in the Wound: Body Politics in Quincentennial Guatemala.* Durham, NC: Duke University Press.

———. 2009. *Reckoning: The Ends of War in Guatemala.* Durham, NC: Duke University Press.

———. 2015. *Who Counts? The Mathematics of Death and Life after Genocide.* Durham, NC: Duke University Press.

Netting, Robert M. 1993. *Smallholders, Householders: Farm Families and the Ecology of Intensive, Sustainable Agriculture.* Stanford, CA: Stanford University Press.

Nussbaum, Martha C. 2011. *Creating Capabilities.* Cambridge, MA: Harvard University Press.

O'Grady, Mary Anastasia. 2018. "The U.S. Funds Guatemalan Abuse: Washington Ignores Gross Human-Rights Violations Carried Out with Taxpayer Money." *Wall Street Journal,* 19 August. https://www.wsj.com/articles/the-u-s-funds-guatemalan-abuse-1534707971.

O'Neill, Kevin Lewis. 2009. *City of God: Christian Citizenship in Postwar Guatemala.* Berkeley: University of California Press.

Ocejo, Richard E. 2014. "Food and Drink." In *The cultural Intermediaries Reader,* ed. Jennifer Smith Maguire and Julian Matthews, 192–201. Thousand Oaks, CA: Sage Publications.

Ortner, Sherry B. 2016. "Dark Anthropology and Its Others: Theories Since the Eighties." *HAU: Journal of Ethnographic Theory* 6 (1): 47–73.

Paige, Jeffery M. 1997. *Coffee and Power: Revolution and the Rise of Democracy in Central America.* Cambridge, MA: Harvard University Press.

Panhuysen, S., and J. Pierrot. 2018. *Coffee Barometer 2018.* The Hague: Hivos.

Parrish, Sabine. 2020. "Competitive Coffee Making and the Crafting of the Ideal Barista." *Gastronomica* 20 (2): 79–90.

———. 2021. "'Life is Made of Courage and Coffee': An Ethnography of Specialty Coffee in Sao Paulo, Brazil." PhD diss., University of Oxford, Department of Anthropology.

Paxson, Heather. 2013. *The Life of Cheese: Crafting Food and Value in America.* California Studies in Food and Culture. Berkeley: University of California Press.

———. 2021. "Protecting Perishable Values." *Current Anthropology* 62 (S24): S333–S342.

Payeras, Mario. 1983. *Days of the Jungle: The Testimony of a Guatemalan Guerrillero, 1972–1976.* New York: Monthly Review Press.

Paz Lemus, Tatiana. n.d. "Neoliberalism in Guatemala: What Can We Learn by Focusing on the Elites?" Unpublished manuscript.

Pedersen David. 2008. "Introduction: Toward a Value Theory of Anthropology." *Anthropological Theory* 8(1): 5–8.

Pendergrast, Mark. 2010. *Uncommon Grounds: The History of Coffee and How It Transformed Our World.* New York: Basic Books.

Penny, H. Glenn. 2017. "From Migrant Knowledge to Fugitive Knowledge? German Migrants and Knowledge Production in Guatemala, 1880s–1945." *Geschichte und Gesellschaft* 43 (3): 381–412.

Polanyi, Karl. 1944. *The Great Transformation*. Boston: Beacon Press.

Ponte, Stefano. 2016. "Convention Theory in the Anglophone Agro-Food Literature: Past, Present and Future." *Journal of Rural Studies* 44: 12–23.

Ponte, Stefano, and Peter Gibbon. 2005. "Quality Standards, Conventions and the Governance of Global Value Chains." *Economy and Society* 34 (1): 1–31.

Pratt, Jeff. 2007. "Food Values: The Local and the Authentic." *Critique of Anthropology* 27 (3): 285–300.

Programa de las Naciones Unidas para el Desarrollo (PNUD). 2016. *Más allá del conflicto, luchas por el bienestar. Informe Nacional de Desarrollo Humano 2015/2016*. Guatemala City: PNUD.

Quijano, Aníbal. 2008. "Coloniality of Power, Eurocentrism, and Latin America." In *Coloniality at Large: Latin America and the Postcolonial Debate*, ed. Moraña Mabel, Dussel Enrique, and A. Jáuregui Carlos, 181–224. Durham, NC: Duke University Press.

Raxche'. 1992. "Introducción." In *Cultura maya y política de desarrollo*. Chimaltenango: COCADI.

Raynolds, Laura T., and Elizabeth A. Bennett. 2015. "Introduction to Research on Fair Trade." In *Handbook of Research on Fair Trade*. Cheltenham, UK: Edward Elgar Publishing.

Reichman, Daniel R. 2008. "Coffee as a Global Metaphor." Occasional paper no. 9, Center for Latin American and Iberian Studies, Vanderbilt University.

———. 2011. *The Broken Village: Coffee, Migration, and Globalization in Honduras*. Ithaca, NY: Cornell University Press.

———. 2013. "Entrepreneurship in a Pickle: Innovation and Arbitrage in the Sea Cucumber Trade." *Anthropological Quarterly* 86 (2): 559–88.

———. 2018. "Big Coffee in Brazil: Historical Origins and Implications for Anthropological Political Economy." *Journal of Latin American and Caribbean Anthropology* 23 (2): 241–61.

Renard, Marie-Christine. 1999. *Los Intersticios de la Globalización: Un Label 'Max Havelaar' para los Pequeños Productores de Café*. Paris: Centre français d'études mexicaines et centraméricaines.

Rice, Robert. 2003. "Coffee Production in a Time of Crisis: Social and Environmental Connections." *SAIS Review* 23 (1): 221–45.

Richards, Michael. 1985. "Cosmopolitan World View and Counterinsurgency in Guatemala." *Anthropological Quarterly* 58 (3): 90–107.

Robbins, Joel. 2007a. "Between Reproduction and Freedom: Morality, Value, and Radical Cultural Change." *Ethnos* 72 (3): 293–314.

———. 2007b. "Continuity Thinking and the Problem of Christian Culture: Belief, Time, and the Anthropology of Christianity." *Current Anthropology* 48 (1): 5–38.

———. 2012. "Cultural Values." In *A Companion to Moral Anthropology,* ed. Didier Fassin, 115–32. Hoboken, NJ: Wiley.

———. 2013. "Beyond the Suffering Subject: Toward an Anthropology of the Good." *Journal of the Royal Anthropological Institute* 19 (3): 447–62.

Rodseth, Lars. 1998. "Distributive Models of Culture: A Sapirian Alternative to Essentialism." *American Anthropologist* 100 (1): 55–69.

———. 2015. "Back to Boas, Forth to Latour." *Current Anthropology* 56 (6): 865–82.

Roseberry, William. 1996. "The Rise of Yuppie Coffees and the Reimagination of Class in the United States." *American Anthropologist* 98 (4): 762–75.

Roseberry, William, Lowell Gudmundson, and Mario Samper Kutschbach, eds. 1995. *Coffee, Society, and Power in Latin America.* Baltimore, MD: Johns Hopkins University Press.

Ruiz, Luisa Fernanda Moreno. 2011. "Coffee in Guatemala." In *Hazardous Child Labour in Latin America,* ed. G.K. Lieten, 165–89. Dordrecht: Springer Netherlands.

Ruskin, John. 1862. *Unto This Last: Four Essays on the First Principles of Political Economy.* London: Smith, Elder, and Co.

Ryan, Chris. 2020. "Elika Liftee Gets Personal for U.S. Brewers Cup-Winning Routine." *Barista,* 18 March.

Sage, Emma. 2016. "A Science Primer on the SCAA/WCR Coffee Taster's Flavor Wheel." Santa Ana, CA: SCA.

Samper, Luis F., Daniele Giovannucci, and Luciana Marques Vieira. 2017. "The Powerful Role of Intangibles in the Coffee Value Chain." Economic Research Working Paper no. 39, World Intellectual Property Organization.

Sayer, Andrew. 2000. "Moral Economy and Political Economy." *Studies in Political Economy* 61 (1): 79–103.

———. 2011. *Why Things Matter to People: Social Science, Values and Ethical Life.* Cambridge: Cambridge University Press.

Scalabrin, Simone, Lucile Toniutti, Gabriele Di Gaspero, Davide Scaglione, Gabriele Magris, Michele Vidotto, Sara Pinosio, Federica Cattonaro, Federica Magni, Irena Jurman, Mario Cerutti, Furio Suggi Liverani, Luciano Navarini, Lorenzo Del Terra, Gloria Pellegrino, Manuela Rosanna Ruosi, Nicola Vitulo, Giorgio Valle, Alberto Pallavicini, Giorgio Graziosi, Patricia E. Klein, Nolan Bentley, Seth Murray, William Solano, Amin Al Hakimi, Timothy Schilling, Christophe Montagnon, Michele Morgante, and Benoit Bertrand. 2020. "A Single Polyploidization Event at the Origin of the Tetraploid Genome of Coffea Arabica Is Responsible for the Extremely Low Genetic Variation in Wild and Cultivated Germplasm." *Scientific Reports* 10: 4642.

Schenker, Stefan, and Trish Rothgeb. 2017. "The Roast—Creating the Beans' Signature." In *The Craft and Science of Coffee*, ed. Britta Folmer, 245–71. Amsterdam: Academic Press.

Schwartz, Barry, and Kenneth E. Sharpe. 2006. "Practical Wisdom: Aristotle Meets Positive Psychology." *Journal of Happiness Studies* 7(3): 377–95.

Scott, James C. 1985. *Weapons of the Weak: Everyday Forms of Peasant Resistance*. New Haven, CT: Yale University Press.

———. 1998. *Seeing Like a State: How Certain Schemes to Improve the Human Condition Have Failed*. New Haven, CT: Yale University Press.

Sedgewick, Augustine. 2020. *Coffeeland: One Man's Dark Empire and the Making of Our Favorite Drug*. New York: Penguin Press.

Sen, Amartya. 1999. *Development as Freedom*. Cambridge, MA: Belknap Press.

———. 2002. *Rationality and Freedom*. Cambridge, MA: Belknap Press.

Sennett, Richard. 2008. *The Craftsman*. New Haven, CT: Yale University Press.

Shayne, Jon A. 2014. "Bezzle and Sardines." In *Cash on the Table: Markets, Values, and Moral Economies*, ed. Edward F. Fischer, 29–38. Santa Fe, NM: SAR Press.

Sick, Deborah. 1999. *Farmers of the Golden Bean: Costa Rican Households and the Global Coffee Economy*. DeKalb: Northern Illinois University Press.

———. 2008. "Coffee, Farming Families, and Fair Trade in Costa Rica: New Markets, Same Old Problems?" *Latin American Research Review* 43 (3): 193–208.

Simmel, Georg. 2004 [1900]. *The Philosophy of Money*. New York: Routledge.

Simon, Jean-Marie. 1988. *Guatemala: Eternal Spring, Eternal Tyranny*. New York: W. W. Norton.

Smith, Carol A. 1984. "Local History in Global Context: Social and Economic Transitions in Western Guatemala." *Comparative Studies in Society and History* 26 (22): 193–228.

———, ed. 1990. *Guatemalan Indians and the State, 1542–1988*. Ed. Carol A. Smith. Austin: University of Texas Press.

———. 1991. "Maya Nationalism." *NACLA Report on the Americas* 23 (3): 29–33.

Smith, Julia. 2009. "Shifting Coffee Markets and Producer Responses in Costa Rica and Panama." In *Economic Development, Integration, and Morality in Asia and the Americas*, ed. Donald C. Wood, 201–24. Somerville, MA: Emerald Publishing.

————. 2010. "Fair Trade and the Specialty Coffee Market." In *Fair Trade and Social Justice: Global Ethnographies,* ed. Sarah Lyon and Mark Moberg, 28–46. New York: New York University Press.

————. 2018. "Coffee Landscapes: Specialty Coffee, Terroir, and Traceability in Costa Rica." *Culture, Agriculture, Food and Environment* 40 (1): 36–44.

Smith, Timothy J. 2009. "Democracy Is Dissent: Political Confrontations and Indigenous Mobilization in Solola." In *Mayas in Post-War Guatemala: Harvest of Violence Revisited,* ed. Walter E. Little and Timothy J. Smith, 16–29. Tuscaloosa: University of Alabama Press.

Specialty Coffee Association. n.d. "A Botanists' Guide to Specialty Coffee." https://sca.coffee/research/botany?page=resources&d=a-botanists-guide-to-specialty-coffee.

Speed, Shannon. 2019. *Incarcerated Stories: Indigenous Women Migrants and Violence in the Settler-Capitalist State.* Chapel Hill: University of North Carolina Press.

Stanzione, Vincent. 2003. *Rituals of Sacrifice: Walking the Face of the Earth on the Sacred Path of the Sun.* Albuquerque: University of New Mexico Press.

Stark, David. 2009. *The Sense of Dissonance: Accounts of Worth in Economic Life.* Princeton, NJ: Princeton University Press.

Steinberg, Michael K., Matthew J. Taylor, and Michelle Moran-Taylor. 2014. "Coffee and Mayan Cultural Commodification in Guatemala." *Geographical Review* 104 (3): 361–73.

Stoll, David. 1982. *Fishers of Men or Founders of Empire? The Wycliffe Bible Translators in Latin America.* London: Zed Press.

————. 2012. *El Norte or Bust! How Migration Fever and Microcredit Produced a Financial Crash in a Latin American Town.* Lanham, MD: Rowman & Littlefield.

Stone, Deborah. 2020. *Counting: How We Use Numbers to Decide What Matters.* New York: W. W. Norton.

Storper, Michael. 2001. "Lived Effects of the Contemporary Economy: Globalization, Inequality, and Consumer Society." In *Millennial Capitalism and the Culture of Neoliberalism,* ed. John L. Comaroff, Jean Comaroff, and Robert P. Weller. Durham, NC: Duke University Press.

Storper, Michael, and Robert Salais. 1997. *Worlds of Production: The Action Frameworks of the Economy.* Cambridge, MA: Harvard University Press.

Streeck, Wolfgang. 2009. *Re-Forming Capitalism: Institutional Change in the German Political Economy.* Oxford: Oxford University Press.

————. 2016. *How Will Capitalism End? Essays on a Failing System.* London: Verso.

Suckert, Lisa. 2015. *Die Dynamik ökologischer Märkte: Eine feldanalytische Betrachtung des Marktes für Bio-Molkereiprodukte.* Original edition, Konstanz: UVK.

———. 2018a. "New Economic Sociology à La Française: Encountering the Field of the 'Economics of Conventions'—Rainer Diaz-Bone, Die 'Economie des conventions.'" Grundlagen und Entwicklungen der neuen französischen Wirtschaftssoziologie (Wiesbaden, Springer VS, 2015). *European Journal of Sociology* 58 (3): 498–505.

———. 2018b. "Unravelling Ambivalence: A Field-Theoretical Approach to Moralised Markets." *Current Sociology* 66 (5): 682–703.

Taussig, Michael T. 1986. *Shamanism, Colonialism, and the Wild Man: A Study in Terror and Healing.* Ed. American Council of Learned Societies. Chicago: University of Chicago Press.

Terrio, Susan J. 2000. *Crafting the Culture and History of French Chocolate.* Berkeley: University of California Press.

Tett, Gillian. 2015. *The Silo Effect: The Peril of Expertise and the Promise of Breaking Down Barriers.* New York: Simon & Schuster.

Theodossopoulos, Dimitrios. 2013. "Laying Claim to Authenticity: Five Anthropological Dilemmas." *Anthropological Quarterly* 86: 337–60.

Thomas, Deborah A. 2019. *Political Life in the Wake of the Plantation: Sovereignty, Witnessing, Repair.* Durham, NC: Duke University Press.

Thomas, Edouard, Sabine Puget, Dominique Valentin, and Paul Songer. 2017. "Sensory Evaluation—Profiling and Preferences." In *The Craft and Science of Coffee,* ed. Britta Folmer, 419–56. Amsterdam: Academic Press.

Thomas, Kedron. 2016. *Regulating Style: Intellectual Property Law and the Business of Fashion in Guatemala.* Berkeley: University of California Press.

Thomas, Kedron, Kevin Lewis O'Neill, and Thomas Offit. 2011. "Securing the City: An Introduction." In *Securing the City: Neoliberalism, Space, and Insecurity in Postwar Guatemala,* ed. Kevin Lewis O'Neill and Kedron Thomas, 1–21. Durham, NC: Duke University Press.

Topik, Steven. 2003. "The Integration of the World Coffee Market." In *The Global Coffee Economy in Africa, Asia, and Latin America, 1500–1989,* ed. Steven Topik and William Gervase Clarence-Smith, 21–49. Cambridge: Cambridge University Press.

———. 2009. "Coffee as a Social Drug." *Cultural Critique* (71): 81–106.

Topik, Steven, Carlos Marichal, and Zephyr L. Frank. 2006. *From Silver to Cocaine: Latin American Commodity Chains and the Building of the World Economy, 1500–2000.* American Encounters/Global Interactions. Durham, NC: Duke University Press.

Traore, Togo M., Norbert L.W. Wilson, and Deacue Fields. 2018. "What Explains Specialty Coffee Quality Scores and Prices: A Case Study from the Cup of Excellence Program." *Journal of Agricultural and Applied Economics* 50 (3): 349–68.

Trouillot, Michel-Rolph. 2003. *Global Transformations: Anthropology and the Modern World.* New York: Palgrave Macmillan.

Tsing, Anna Lowenhaupt. 2004. *Friction: An Ethnography of Global Connection.* Princeton, NJ: Princeton University Press.

———. 2015. *The Mushroom at the End of the World: On the Possibility of Life in Capitalist Ruins.* Princeton, NJ: Princeton University Press.

Tucker, Catherine M. 2010. *Coffee Culture: Local Experiences, Global Connections.* New York: Routledge.

Tzul Tzul, Gladys. 2018. *Gobierno comunal indígena y estado Guatemalteco: algunas claves críticas para comprender su tensa relación / Gladys Tzul Tzul.* Guatemala: Instituto Amaq'.

UNCTAD. 2002. *Trade and Development Report.* Geneva: United Nations.

Veblen, Thorstein. 1899. *The Theory of the Leisure Class: An Economic Study of Institutions.* New York: McMillan.

Verité. 2012. "Research on Indicators of Forced Labor in the Supply Chain of Coffee in Guatemala."

Vicol, Mark, Jeffrey Neilson, Diany Faila Sophia Hartatri, and Peter Cooper. 2018. "Upgrading for Whom? Relationship Coffee, Value Chain Interventions and Rural Development in Indonesia." *World Development* 110: 26–37.

Victor, Bart, Edward F. Fischer, Bruce Cooil, Alfredo Vergara, Abraham Mukolo, and Meridith Blevins. 2013. "Frustrated Freedom: The Effects of Agency and Wealth on Wellbeing in Rural Mozambique." *World Development* 47: 30–41.

Viveiros de Castro, Eduardo. 2014. *Cannibal Metaphysics.* Minneapolis: University of Minnesota Press/Univocal.

Wagner, Regina. 1991. *Los alemanes en Guatemala, 1828–1944.* Guatemala: Universidad Francisco Marroquín.

———. 2001. *The History of Coffee in Guatemala.* Bogotá, Coloumbia: Villegas Editores.

———. 2003. *Historia del café de Guatemala.* Guatemala: Villegas Asociados.

Wagner, Roy. 1975. *The Invention of Culture.* Englewood Cliffs, NJ: Prentice-Hall.

Wallerstein, Immanuel. 1974. *The Modern World-System I: Capitalist Agriculture and the Origins of the European World-Economy in the Sixteenth Century.* New York: Academic Press.

———. 1979. *The Capitalist World-Economy.* Cambridge: Cambridge University Press.

————. 2004. *World-Systems Analysis: An Introduction*. Durham, NC: Duke University Press.

Warren, Kay B. 2002. "Voting against Indigenous Rights in Guatemala: Lessons from the 1999 Referendum." In *Indigenous Movements, Self-Representation, and the State in Latin America*, ed. Kay B. Warren and Jean E. Jackson. Austin: University of Texas Press.

Way, J. T. 2021. *Agrotropolis: Youth, Street, and Nation in the New Urban Guatemala*. Berkeley: University of California Press.

Weber, Max. 1978. *Economy and Society: An Outline of Interpretive Sociology*. Berkeley: University of California Press. Original edition, 1914.

Weiss, Brad. 2003. *Sacred Trees, Bitter Harvests: Globalizing Coffee in Northwest Tanzania*. Portsmouth, NH: Heinemann.

————. 2016. *Real Pigs: Shifting Values in the Field of Local Pork*. Durham, NC: Duke University Press.

Weissman, Michaele. 2008. *God in a Cup: The Obsessive Quest for the Perfect Coffee*. New York: Wiley.

West, Paige. 2012. *From Modern Production to Imagined Primitive: The Social World of Coffee from Papua New Guinea*. Durham, NC: Duke University Press.

White, Stephen K. 2000. *Sustaining Affirmation: The Strengths of Weak Ontology in Political Theory*. Princeton, NJ: Princeton University Press.

Wilk, Richard R. 1996. *Economies and Cultures*. Boulder, CO: Westview Press.

————. 2001. "Consuming Morality." *Journal of Consumer Culture* 1 (2): 245–60.

————. 2006. *Home Cooking in the Global Village: Caribbean Food from Buccaneers to Ecotourists*. New York: Berg.

Wilkinson, Daniel. 2004. *Silence on the Mountain: Stories of Terror, Betrayal, and Forgetting in Guatemala*. American Encounters/Global Interactions. Durham, NC: Duke University Press.

Williams, Robert Gregory. 1994. *States and Social Evolution: Coffee and the Rise of National Governments in Central America*. Chapel Hill: University of North Carolina Press.

Wilson, Adam P., and Norbert L. W. Wilson. 2014. "The Economics of Quality in the Specialty Coffee Industry: Insights from the Cup of Excellence Auction Programs." *Agricultural Economics* 45 (S1): 91–105.

Wilson, Bradley. 2010. "Indebted to Fair Trade? Coffee and Crisis in Nicaragua." *Geoforum* 41: 84–92.

————. 2013. "Delivering the Goods: Fair Trade, Solidarity, and the Moral Economy of the Coffee Contract in Nicaragua." *Human Organization* 72 (3): 177–87.

Wilson, Bradley R., Jamison F. Conley, Trevor M. Harris, and Frank Lafone. 2012. "New Terrains of Taste: Spatial Analysis of Price Premiums for Single Origin Coffees in Central America." *Applied Geography* 35 (1–2): 499–507.

Wilson, Norbert. 2014. "When Higher Quality Does Not Translate to Higher Prices: A Case of Quality and Specialty Coffees from the Cup of Excellence Auctions." Agricultural and Applied Economics Association.

Wistoft, Karen, and Lars Qvortrup. 2019. *Teaching Taste*. Champagne, IL: Common Ground.

Woodfill, Brent K. S. 2019. *War in the Land of True Peace: The Fight for Maya Scared Places*. Norman: University of Oklahoma Press.

Woodward, Ralph Lee. 1990. "Changes in the Nineteenth-Century Guatemalan State and Its Indian Policies." In *Guatemalan Indians and the State, 1542–1988*, ed. Carol A. Smith, 52–71. Austin: University of Texas Press.

World Coffee Research. n.d. "Variety Catalog." *https://varieties.worldcoffeeresearch.org/varieties/*.

———. 2016. *Sensory Lexicon*. College Station, TX: World Coffee Research.

Yates-Doerr, Emily. 2015. *The Weight of Obesity: Hunger and Global Health in Postwar Guatemala*. Berkeley: University of California Press.

Yates-Doerr, Emily, and Rosario García-Meza. 2020. "Head Circumference." *Somatosphere*.

Zaloom, Caitlin. 2006. *Out of the Pits: Traders and Technology from Chicago to London*. Chicago: University of Chicago Press.

Zigon, Jarrett. 2008. *Morality: An Anthropological Perspective*. Oxford: Berg Publishers.

———. 2009. "Within a Range of Possibilities: Morality and Ethics in Social Life." *Ethnos* 74 (2): 251–76.

IMAGE CREDITS

Except as noted below, maps were commissioned from Mapping Specialists, Ltd. and the images are by author.

Figure 1. Elika Liftee at the 2020 United States Coffee Championships. Photo by Jennifer Hall for the United States Coffee Championships, reprinted with permission from the Specialty Coffee Association. *viii*

Figure 4. Spider Graph of Cupping Score. Graph drawn by Siyuan Wang, used with permission. *48*

Figure 7. SCA Specialty Coffee Flavor Wheel. The Coffee Taster's Flavor Wheel by the Specialty Coffee Association, World Coffee Research, and UC Davis (©2016–2021) is licensed under a Creative Commons BY-NC-ND 4.0 International License, with permission to reprint from the Specialty Coffee Association. *54*

Figure 8. Cup of Excellence Descriptor Word Cloud. Created by Siyuan Wang based on data from Traore, Wilson, and Fields (2018). *56*

Figure 9. Botanical Drawing of *Coffea arabica*. From the 1751 *Encyclopédie, ou dictionnaire raisonné des sciences, des arts et des métiers, par une société de gens de lettres* by Denis Diderot and Jean Le Rond D'Alembert. Photo courtesy of Fernando E. Vega. *62*

Figure 10. London Coffeehouse, ca. 1690–1700. Copyright: © Trustees of the British Museum, used with permission. *72*

INDEX

addictive properties of coffee, 66, 70, 87, 211
adenosine, 71
affective values, 27–28, 37, 220n19. *See also* symbolic value
Agreement on Indigenous Rights and Identity, 118
Agricultural, Commercial, Industrial, and Financial Chamber of Commerce (CACIF), 129. *See also* Anacafé (Asociación Nacional del Café of Guatemala)
Aguilar-Støen, Mariel, 183
Aguirre, Arturo, 11, 13
Aldana, Thelma, 245n53
Alliance for Coffee Excellence, 47, 178. *See also* Cup of Excellence program
Alta Verapaz, Guatemala, 99, 105, 110–111
Amsterdam, Netherlands, 64, 73–74, 81, 95, 238n27. *See also* Dutch trade networks and commodities
Anacafé (Asociación Nacional del Café of Guatemala), 123, 125, 128–131, 135–138, 169, 201–202
anti-communist campaigns, 109, 110, 113–114, 128, 183, 201

Appadurai, Arjun, 29, 65, 203
Arbenz, Jacobo, 104, 109
Arévalo, Juan José, 109
Aristotle, 28, 200
aroma wheel, 52. *See also* flavor wheel
Asociación Chajulense, 167
Asturias de Barrios, Linda, 24–25, 149
Austrian school of economics, 125, 132, 198
authenticity: as symbolic value, 4, 5, 206; Theodossopoulos on, 221n26; Third Wave coffee and, 17, 18, 20, 27, 37–38, 177
Ayau, Manuel, 132

Bacon, Christopher, 184
Badiou, Alain, 43
banana industry, 21, 108, 116
Barista Parlor, Nashville, 34, 35–36
Beckert, Jens, 218n7, 22-n18, 223n48, 225n54, 232n26, 233n36, 252n10, 256n20
beneficio, 159–160
Benson, Peter, 168
Berlant, Lauren, 23
Bernstein, Bob, 14
Berth, Christiane, 106

Besky, Sarah, 42–43
biological processes: of caffeine, 32, 66, 69–71; of taste, 46
Blue Bottle Coffee (brand), 17, 36, 45, 230n3
Boaventura, Patricia, 58
Boca Costa, Guatemala, 99, 101, 105
Bogin, Barry, 164
Bohnenkaffee, as term, 221n25
Boltanski, Luc, 29, 30, 206
Bourbon varietal, 11–12, 58, 75, 76–77, 79, 82, 96. See also *Coffea arabica*
Bourdieu, Pierre, 15, 225n55, 257n25
Brazil: coffee industry of, 85, 105, 134, 229n1, 236n12, 239n36; coffee production in, 40, 67, 75–77, 78, 82, 140, 161; Cup of Excellence program in, 41, 55; slave plantations in, 95–96; surplus coffee in, 247n7
Brewer's Cup, 1–3. See also Cup of Excellence program
brewing methods, 41–42

CACIF, 129. See also Anacafé (Asociación Nacional del Café of Guatemala)
Café de Colombia (brand), 137, 248n7
cafetaleros, as term, 96, 154
caffeine, 32, 66, 69–71, 95, 237nn20–21
Cambranes, J. C., 100
campesino movements, 93–94, 109–110
Capital (Marx), 205, 256n16
capitalism, 27, 30, 65, 158–159, 205–207, 218n8, 254n5. See also coffee market; commodification of coffee; consumerism; Fordism; trade history of coffee; values
Casaús Arzú, Marta, 91, 107
Catholicism, 146, 147, 153
Catimor cultivar, 79, 80, 82. See also *Coffea arabica*
Caturra varietal, 78, 79, 80, 81, 82, 140. See also *Coffea arabica*

Chicago school of economics, 132
child labor, 119, 151–152, 163. See also family labor; labor exploitation
chlorogenic acids, 71
chocolate, 230n4
CICIG, 94, 242n8, 247n53, 248n10
civil war (Guatemala), 21, 28, 93–94, 109–114, 120, 130, 201
classification, 63–69, 234nn3–4, 235n7
clothing, 153–154
cocaine industry, 9, 116, 183. See also narco trade
cochineal, 21, 97, *98*
Coffea arabica: Bourbon varietal, 11–12, 58, 75, 76–77, 79, 96; Catimor cultivar, 79, 80, 82; Catuai cultivar, 78, 79; Caturra varietal, 78, 79, 80, 81, 82, 140; classification of, 64, 66–69; geographic origins of, 63, 64, 67–68, 236n11; Gesha varietal, 2, 39, 79, 81; historic migration of, 73–74; Java varietal, 73, 79, 238n26; Maragogype varietal, 58, 78, 81, 82; Mocha varietal, 39, 58, 79, 81, 238n26; Mundo Novo cultivar, 78, 79; Pacamara varietal, 81, 82; Pacas varietal, 79, 82; Pache varietal, 81; Timor Hybrid cultivar, 79, 80, 82; trade history of, 74–76; Typica varietal, 68, 73, 75, 76–77
Coffea canephora (Robusta), 67, 80, 236nn11–12
Coffea eugenioides, 67, 236n11
coffee competitions. See Brewer's Cup; Cup of Excellence program
Coffee Connection, Boston, 16
Coffee Corps, SCA, 252n12
coffee culture: Cup of Excellence program in, 55–57; cupping protocols, 47–51; high-end market of, 7–8, 13–15, 32–33; marketing campaigns of, 137–139, 175, 248n7; movements of, defined, 15–17, 18, 189, 221n27; overview, 3–5, 14; taste descriptors in, 51–55. See also coffee

Founded in 1893,
UNIVERSITY OF CALIFORNIA PRESS
publishes bold, progressive books and journals
on topics in the arts, humanities, social sciences,
and natural sciences—with a focus on social
justice issues—that inspire thought and action
among readers worldwide.

The UC PRESS FOUNDATION
raises funds to uphold the press's vital role
as an independent, nonprofit publisher, and
receives philanthropic support from a wide
range of individuals and institutions—and from
committed readers like you. To learn more, visit
ucpress.edu/supportus.

www.ingramcontent.com/pod-product-compliance
Lightning Source LLC
Chambersburg PA
CBHW020830270326
41928CB00006B/477